PORT

OTHER BOOKS BY THE AUTHOR

Los Curiosos Impertinentes
(English Travellers in Spain, 1760–1855)

Blue Guides to:
Spain
Paris and Versailles
Ireland
Cyprus
Portugal
France
Austria
Switzerland

PORTUGAL

A Traveller's Guide

◆ ◆ ◆

IAN ROBERTSON

JOHN MURRAY

1145685

A catalogue record for this book is available from the British Library

ISBN 0-7195-4808-X

Typeset in 11/12 pt Garamond by Colset Pte Ltd., Singapore
Printed and bound by Biddles Limited, Guildford, Kings Lynn

Contents

Illustrations

The author and publishers wish to thank the National Army Museum for permission to reproduce Plates 11, 12 and 17; and the Portuguese National Tourist Office and Fototeca Direcçao-Geral da Comunicaçao Social for the remainder. Plate 18 is reproduced from *Wellington's Masterpiece* by Brigadier Peter Young and Lieutenant-Colonel J.P. Lawford, Allen & Unwin, 1973, now Unwin Hyman, an imprint of HarperCollins (Publishers) Ltd.

Preface

My devotion to Portugal matured slowly, as part of a general interest in the Iberian Peninsula as a whole. It was with Spain that I was first absorbed.

My wife, whose parents came from both sides of the political frontier which divides that race, had introduced me to the Basque provinces, and from them we had made numerous holiday excursions over the years.

My curiosity was stimulated further by reading the narratives of Peninsular War veterans, and the descriptions of Spain and Portugal compiled by earlier travellers from England. Several of these are referred to when reflecting my own experiences and reactions.

In the early 1960s I had been in a position to commission the writing of a concise military history of the Peninsular War: there was very little of consequence then available on the subject. The author, an extrovert American expert on firearms, who was obsessed by Wellington's infallibility as a commander, sallied out from Madrid in a hired Mercedes to explore the battlefields. It says much for the vehicle that it survived being driven like Jehu across the furrowed dusty *mesetas* of Castile and Extramadura into Portugal, and over the convoluted ranges of the Western Pyrenees. As editor, I endured months of skirmishing while unravelling the anfractuosities of his typescript, the text of which had been dictated on to cassette tape on the spot. By the time the book was published, I had acquired a fair knowledge of several facets of those sanguinary campaigns. At the time, I thought the author was too biased in favour of his hero: I am now more nearly certain that almost all the Duke's strictures concerning the equivocal behaviour of his Spanish allies, both military and civil, were only too firmly based. On the other hand, Wellington frequently complimented his Portuguese troops, who were to play an invaluable part in these battles, and he was not given to praise.

Another ten years were to pass before I first entered Portugal, and then on two brief occasions, when crossing Eiffel's bridge spanning the Minho from Tuí to Valença, and at Vilar Formoso, facing Fuentes de Oñoro, the scene of one of the more obstinately contested actions of Wellington's war. In December 1975 I made a rapid expedition from Elvas to Lagos and along the Algarve coast when I accompanied a friend nervous about some property she owned there, which it turned out was untouched by the recent 'Revolution'.

It was not until January 1980 that I set out to explore the country in any detail, and by then I had been living in Spain for a decade. Being contiguous, I had expected the two countries to have a great deal in common, but it was their dissimilarities which were progressively underlined, not least by the diminution in decibels between the vociferation and general din in any *plaza* of Badajoz and the muted murmur in that of Elvas, a mere nine miles to the west.

I reflected, too, on the candid insistence of the caretaker at the cathedral at Elvas that I should sign her Visitor's Book, so pleased was she to show the place to anyone interested: how different from the emphatic *'cerrado'* – it is closed – which had been my customary experience when attempting to enter so many buildings in Spain, particularly those under the control of clerics. Little had changed in Spain since Richard Ford, writing a century and a half earlier, had warned travellers to expect barriers, obstacles and impediments to be thrown up by such official keepers, who considered that the objects committed to their care were their own private property and source of perquisite. I remember well an occasion when I was informed condescendingly by the Cerberus at one cathedral museum that I might take photographs; but, he peremptorily added, NOT NOTES! Here, in Portugal, I felt things were very different: and I was right.

While making several extended tours of the country, it was essential for me to explore the main centres in some detail, and to concentrate on their monuments; but very often, and deliberately, I would veer off the highways – no great difficulty there – into what I chose to call 'Lusitania Deserta'. Not infrequently, I was affected involuntarily by the atmosphere of a site – its *genius loci* – the ethos of the place, engendered not so much by what there was to be seen at that moment as by the intangible weight of history which seemed to lie there like a pall. A variety of associations would take over, often impinging with more intensity and appearing to be of more intrinsic interest than the more substantial objects I had to describe.

In many cases these associations were with the Peninsular War, which as far as the British Army was concerned, had taken place largely in Portugal or close to the Spanish frontier between the summers of 1808 and 1813, although the war did not end until the

following April at Toulouse. For a selective list of books covering those campaigns in further detail, the reader is referred to the
Bibliography.

In spite of inevitable inadequacies, I have attempted in the following pages to give a new dimension to the historical background,
which may interest and stimulate the traveller in Portugal. Not
unnaturally, I have concentrated on those aspects which have interested me, while at the same time leading the reader to whatever in
my view is most worth seeing. I have described briefly its cathedrals
and churches, despite the cynical aside of Norman Douglas, who,
when referring to those of 'Old Calabria', suggested that they were
'all alike in their stony elaboration of mysticism and wrong-
headedness', and already repeatedly described 'by enthusiastic
connoisseurs who dwell lovingly upon their artistic quaintness but
forgot the grovelling herd that reared them . . .'. I had not realized
until recently that Norman Douglas had spent some time in Lisbon
in 1941, when a refugee from Italy. Although he recommended to
Rose Macaulay the fish restaurants across the estuary at Cacilhas, as
far as I know he did not otherwise describe the place.

The chapters are arranged in a form which only very roughly
follow the series of itineraries I have undertaken, although in several
instances I have chosen to conflate them; and almost all the places
described have been seen in person. Naturally, there have been a
few illusion-dispelling experiences, having myself expected too
much of some 'local lion'. I have neglected several aspects of the
country no doubt, which may merit inclusion, and failed to mention several buildings or places which do not deserve to be overlooked; but I make no claim to comprehensive coverage.

Most names – personal and topographical – have remained in
Portuguese, although I have included the usual anglicizations
Braganza (Bragança), Busaco (Buçaco), Lisbon (Lisboa), Oporto
(Porto), and Tagus (Tejo).

I have chosen to refer to Wellington by that name throughout,
although in fact he was known as Sir Arthur Wellesley until after the
Battle of Talavera (28 July 1809).

Curiosity has led me down a number of bypaths, which I personally found to be of interest, some of which the reader may chose to
follow; but well can I sympathize with Aldous Huxley, who, when
writing of uncritical guides, remarked that 'For every traveller who
has any taste of his own, the only useful guide-book will be the one
he himself has written. All others are an exasperation – they make

him travel long miles to see a mound of rubbish; they go into ecstasies over mere antiquity. . .'.

The future Lord Carnarvon, after visiting Portugal in the late 1820s, affirmed that if he could divest himself of every national partiality,

> and suppose myself an inhabitant of the other hemisphere, travelling solely for my amusement, noting men and manners, and were asked in what country society had attained its most polished form, I should say in Portugal . . . Portuguese politeness is delightful, because it is by no means purely artificial, but flows in a great measure from a natural kindness of feeling.

In this respect the country has little changed, and I have experienced likewise a great deal of disinterested help and inate hospitality; certainly more so than in several other countries, which may have a higher standard of living but are less civilized.

While it may be invidious to mention so few by name, I must acknowledge the encouragement and practical help I have received (in a variety of ways, sometimes unintentionally) from José Luis Porfírio, Maria de Céu Sá Lima, Pilar Pereira, Eugenio Lisboa, John Bury, and Bernard Bevan; from Andrew Hewson, Marion and Arthur Boyars, and from my wife Marie-Thérèse, who has accompanied me on almost all my expeditions, and has driven along all those Portuguese roads.

'Those who have never gone twenty miles from home, are apt to fancy that travelling is a very pretty thing. But let him who holds this opinion, come to travel in Portugal, and I will submit to eat thistles if he does not stagger in his notions about travelling.'

Joseph Baretti, *A Journey from London to Genoa*

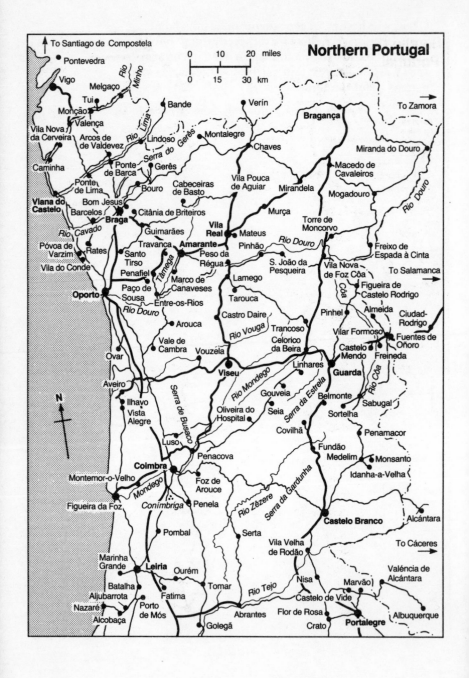

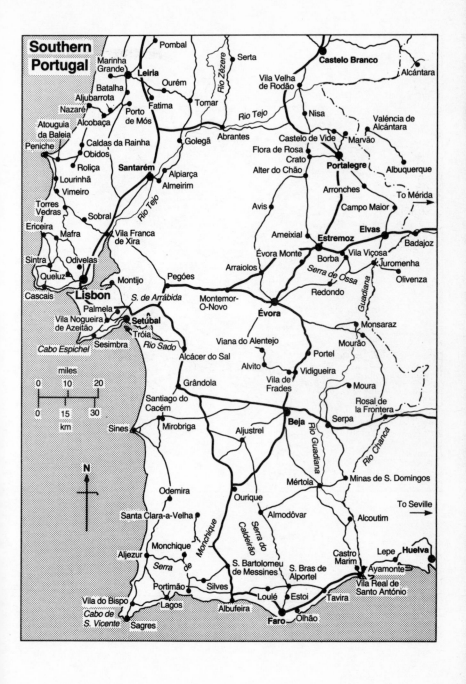

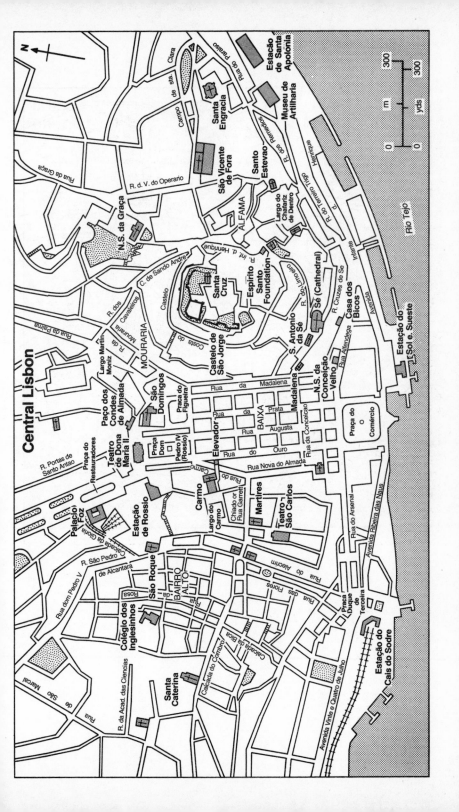

Central Lisbon

N

Estação de Santa Apolónia

Museu de Artilharia

Santa Engracia

São Vicente de Fora

R. d. V. do Operario

Santo Estevão

ALFAMA

Largo do Chafariz de Dentro

Rua da Graça

N.S. da Graça

Pr. Inf. d. Henrique

Santa Cruz

Espírito Santo Foundation

Sé (Cathedral)

Rua da Palma

C. de Sando André

R. dos Cavaleiros

Castelo

Costa do Castelo

MOURARIA

Rua do Limoeiro

R. do Terreiro Trigo

Rio Tejo

Castelo de São Jorge

S. Antonio da Sé

R. Cruzes de Sé

Casa dos Bicos

Largo Martim Moniz

R. da Mouraria

São Domingos

Praça do Figueira

Rua da Madalena

Madalena

N.S. da Conceição Velho

Estação do Sol e. Sueste

R. Portas de Santo Antao

Paço dos Condes de Almada

Teatro de Dona Maria II

Praça Dom Pedro IV (Rossio)

Praça dos Restauradores

Elevador

Rua da Prata

Rua Augusta

Rua do Ouro

BAIXA

Rua da Conceição

Praça do Comércio

Palácio Foz

Estação de Rossio

Rua Nova do Almada

Martires

Avenida

Rua Alfandega

Calçada da Gloria

Carmo

Rua do Carmo

Largo do Carmo

Chiado or Rua Garrett

Teatro São Carlos

Rua do Arsenal

R. São Pedro de Alcântara

São Roque

BAIRRO ALTO

R. da Rosa

Rua do Alecrim

Rua das Flores

Praça Duque de Terceira

Avenida Ribeira das Naus

Rua dom Pedro V

Colégio dos Inglesinhos

Calçada da Bica

Calçada do Combro

Estação do Cais do Sodre

Rua de São Marçal

R. da Acad. das Ciencias

Santa Caterina

Avenida Vinte e Quatro de Julho

0   m   300

0   yds   300

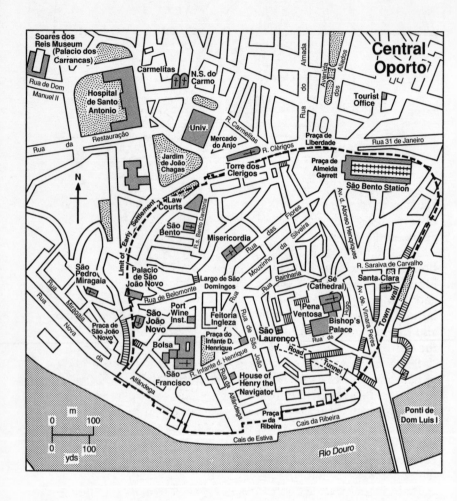

Central Oporto

Soares dos Reis Museum (Palacio dos Carrancas)

Rua de Dom Manuel II

Hospital de Santo Antonio

Restauração

Rua da

N

Carmelitas

N.S. do Carmo

Univ.

R. Carmelitas

Mercado do Anjo

R. Clérigos

Jardim de João Chagas

Torre dos Clerigos

Praça de Liberdade

Rua 31 de Janeiro

Praça de Almeida Garrett

São Bento Station

Almada

do

Avenida

dos

Aliados

Tourist Office

Law Courts

São Bento

R. São Bento Devitoria

Misericordia

Rua das Flores

Av. d. Afonso Henriques

São Pedro Miragaia

Limit of Early Settlement

Palacio de São João Novo

Largo de São Domingos

Rua Mouzinho da Silveira

Rua Bainharia

R. Saraiva de Carvalho

Santa Clara

Sé (Cathedral)

Rua Miragaia

Rua Nova da

Praça de São João Novo

Rua de Belomonte

São João Novo

Port Wine Inst.

Feitoria Ingleza

Rua de São João

Pena Ventosa

Bishop's Palace

Av. de Vimara Peres

Town wall

Bolsa

Praça do Infante D. Henrique

São Laurenço

Rua de

Road

Altândega

São Francisco

R. Infante d. Henrique

Rua da

House of Henry the Navigator

Tunnel

Altândega

Praça da Ribeira

Cais da Ribeira

Ponti de Dom Luis I

m

0   100

0   100

yds

Cais de Estiva

Rio Douro

The road to Lisbon:
Elvas – Vila Viçosa – Estremoz

Lying as it does on the main highway between Madrid and Lisbon, Elvas was the habitual halt of travellers entering Portugal from Spain, and it still is.

The frontier here is formed briefly by the river Caia, before it flows into the sluggish Guadiana just west of Badajoz, from which Elvas is approached by a gentle tree-lined ascent. Its outlying forts and Vaubanesque fortifications, which made it a notably strong bulwark against its aggressive neighbour – for it was along this road also that the country was most frequently invaded – still dominate the district.

Being so strategically sited – with a close, almost bird's eye view of Badajoz – it has always been a natural military base and bastion, in turn occupied by the Romans, the Visigoths, and from the eighth to the thirteenth century, by the Moors. Elvas had been forced to surrender to the troops of Philip II in 1580 after a token resistance; but in 1644 it held out stubbornly when invested by the Spanish, for Portugal had thrown off the Habsburg yoke, which she had borne for six decades, not long before.

By 1660 they were actually threatening their late rulers. An Englishman resident in Badajoz was reporting in July of that year that the Portuguese gave 'continuall allarmes evry daye to the very gates of this towne . . . the wether is excessive warme and all is misery. Who desires his purgatory in this world may come hither for to pass it'. A peace treaty was not signed until 1668; and that was not to last for long.

In 1705, during the confused campaigning of the War of the Spanish Succession, an Anglo-Portuguese force led by the Earl of Galway and Baron Nicolas Fagel mustered here before attempting to capture Badajoz.[1] In the fighting which followed, Galway lost an arm, and the Comte de Tessé, commanding the Spaniards, paid him a delicate compliment by sending his own surgeon across the lines to Elvas.

In the early 1760s an English-born German, Count de Lippe,[2] had been invited to reorganize the Portuguese army, and had been reasonably successful, having recruited a number of English officers to assist him in the uphill task. Among them were Brigadier-General Simon Fraser (1726–82),[3] Colonel Smith, who passed for a good engineer as well as a cavalry commander, John Forbes-Skelater (1733–1808),[4] and Charles O'Hara (c.1740–1802),[5] whose secretary, Major Charles Rainsford (1728–1809), was to become Inspector General of the Portuguese army. Lippe, who had designed the bomb-proof casemates of the fort north of the town, was honoured by having it named after him.

General Charles Dumouriez, when a captain of infantry during the earlier years of his military career, making a tour of Portugal in the mid-1760s, had reported confidentially to his masters in France that, compared with their demoralized condition previously, both the Portuguese cavalry and infantry could manœuvre well and were in a tolerable state of discipline. The former could even leap hedges and ditches in squadrons. Unaccustomed to see such advanced movements in action, the Spaniards had been quite dumbfounded. This estimate of their capacities was confirmed in 1797 by Professor Link,[6] who was of the opinion that their officers were 'not respected as they deserve in a country which has so long kept its ground by its military energy', at the same time commenting that 'the commandants of fortresses who reside at Lisbon and have at most seen their forts once in their lives, and generals who are never with their regiments, do not much contribute to this improvement'.

During the torrid summer of 1809, after the retreat of Wellington's army from Talavera, Elvas served as a general hospital, but over 4,000 soldiers were buried there that autumn.[7] It remained a base of British operations against Badajoz, until that fortress was stormed and sacked in April 1812.

A good idea of the former strength of Elvas may be gained by making the circuit of its walls, passing under the immense cylindrically buttressed Aqueduto da Amoreira, which here strides across the valley, before entering the Porta de Olivença. At the upper end of the central *praça*, flanked by the *câmara municipal* or town hall, stands the much altered early-sixteenth-century *Sé*, the former cathedral, retaining the tower of its predecessor. The *azulejos* or mural tiles in the nave and sacristy were the first I had seen of this ubiquitous Portuguese form of decoration, but equally characteristic was the elaborately carved and gilt woodwork of the rococo organ-loft, designed to fit snugly below the vault.

Nearby is the Freiras de São Domingos or Nossa Senhora da Consolação, built on the octagonal plan of a former Templar church demolished in 1580, likewise embellished with *azulejos*, and with its vaulted lantern supported by elegant ringed Tuscan columns decorated with delicate arabesques.

Continuing uphill, a *pelourinho* is passed. These stone columns are seen throughout the northern half of the country. Near the head of some survive iron supports, from which chains to manacle criminals were suspended, but although they served as a pillory or gibbet, their main significance was as an emblem of feudal and later municipal jurisdiction; and from their steps were read the edicts of town councils.

Relics of a Moorish castle within the *enceinte* are dominated by the lofty late-fifteenth-century *torre de menagem* or keep, from which alleys skirting the walls descend past several churches to regain the Porta da Olivença.

Close by is the Pousada de Santa Luzia, one of many similar establishments throughout Portugal which may be relied on to provide comfortable accommodation and good food: indeed, a Spanish wit has claimed that this particular *pousada* had the best restaurant 'in Badajoz'.

I experienced the same welcome there as did Professor Link and his party, when entering the inn at Elvas in 1797. As he wrote,

> [We] had no occasion to send out for what we wanted, or perhaps ourselves to fetch every piece of bread or glass of wine, as both food and drink are supplied in every portugueze inn, provided that the traveller is contented with portugueze fare. A dainty person might indeed find many things not quite suited to his taste; but the inconvenience of having these trifles to attend to, after a long journey, is inconceivable. We met with good and ready attendance, decent fare, and our pretty and good-natured landlady had that animation of manner, that speaking intelligence of countenance, and that well-bred politeness, which are so striking in this nation. What a difference between Badajoz and Elvas in this respect!

Most travellers would start by noting such differences almost immediately. Link went on to observe how even the dress of the common people of Portugal was better; but he was perhaps more impressed by their politeness and 'easy, gay, and friendly manners', which certainly 'prejudice a stranger more in favour of the portugueze than of the spaniards', nor was this judgement altered, in his opinion, 'so long as the traveller is only acquainted with the lower classes, though he forms an opposite judgement as soon as he begins to know the higher orders'. Only a few years later, Lord and Lady Holland likewise recorded how they were 'Very much struck . . . by the excessive dissimilitude between the Spaniards and Portuguese'; and although staunch Hispanophiles, they were the first to admit that at least as far as neatness of cultivation was concerned, that of Portugal was a great improvement.

The supplying of refreshment may have been a recent innovation, for Joseph Baretti,[8] alighting here some forty years earlier, had stated that in his experience there was no such custom as inns providing food (perhaps because the country was then only just recovering from the Great Earthquake); and few had beds, for here, with the rest of the company, he had to lie down 'on the ground . . . some on mats, some on straw-bags, some on the naked floor, all without taking off their clothes, Teresuela, Catalina, and her black-eye'd sister not excepted'.[9] And exhausted, no doubt, for most of the evening had been taken up with riotous dancing, particularly in the company of the nimble Catalina.

Baretti's description of his approach to Elvas is of additional interest as it confirms the comparative rarity of travellers at that period. On noticing a great concourse of people, he asked the reason for it:

> [I] was informed that a fair is this week kept there for horses and black-cattle. On both sides of the road there were many cloaths spread by way of tents, and the ropes which supported them, crossed the road in such a manner, that we had not a little to do to pass under them with the chaises. The merchants who had erected those temporary conveniences, expected not that any carriage would come that way, as it is but very seldom that they see a traveller going by, either towards *Madrid* or towards *Lisbon*; therefore they made no scruple to embarrass the road.

It was from Elvas on 6 January 1836 that George Borrow crossed the frontier to encounter the Gypsies of Badajoz, on the first stage of his extraordinary adventures with the Bible in Spain. He was more critical when referring to the inn recommended to him, complaining that it was inferior to a hedge alehouse in England as far as convenience and accommodation was concerned.

Among other fortresses in the vicinity is **Campo Maior**, to the north-east, also with Vaubanesque outworks, but there is little left of its citadel, destroyed in 1732 when the powder magazine was struck by lightning and 1,500 people were killed outright. The stronghold formed part of Wellington's defensive position in 1811–12, but it cannot have been a particularly pleasant spot. Commissary Schaumann of the King's German Legion, stationed there for some time, complained that 'All night we were plagued by scorpions, mosquitoes, and a piercingly cold wind', while during the day they were 'infested by snakes, blowflies, and other vermin'. Their water came from the river Caia, 'in which the whole army bathed, and cattle went to drink, and dirty clothes were washed'.

It was between here and **Arronches**, to the north-west, that an allied force, again commanded by Galway, who had his horse shot under him, was severely defeated in a brisk action in May 1709 against the Marquis de Bay's Spaniards. Unaccountably, De Bay took little advantage of the situation, merely withdrawing to summer quarters.

South-west of Elvas lies the village of **Juromenha**, with the ruins of a castle which in 1662 had capitulated to Don Juan of Austria after a short siege. It was here in 1801, during the so-called 'War of the Oranges', that the senile Duke of Lafoes, the Portuguese chief-of-staff, signed an order for the evacuation of the place, and then upbraided the unfortunate officer in command for doing so. When confronted, he excused himself by remarking that one could not remember everything!

It provides a good view east towards **Olivenza**, beyond the Guadiana, which now forms the frontier. The town – with a good Manueline church – had been Portuguese for centuries, until occupied by the Spanish during that war, but its return to Portugal was never implemented, despite the terms of the Treaty of Paris.

The main road west from Elvas traverses rolling country, passing a turning for adjacent **Borba**, a pleasant little white marble-quarrying town. One can well imagine the scene there in July 1811, when the place was full of infantry, particularly Highlanders, whose tattoos, according to Commissary Schaumann, 'carried out at night by eight pipers in old Highland costume . . . struck the inhabitants of Borba dumb with astonishment'.

Neighbouring **Vila Viçosa** is still dominated by its bastioned early-fourteenth-century castle. Although built by Dom Dinis, known as 'O Labrador' – the husbandman – who was then king, it became the original *solar* and seat of the ducal family of Braganza. In 1382 the place had been the headquarters of Edmund of Cambridge, commanding an expeditionary force sent from England to support Dom Fernando in his projected invasion of Castile, this being part of a plan to place John of Gaunt, Duke of Lancaster, on the Castilian throne. Dom Fernando had provided his allies with mounts, but the undisciplined English sent to garrison the frontier fortresses had run riot west of the Guadiana, which they pillaged in search of provisions rather than plundering in Spain, those billeted in Vila Viçosa even torturing their hosts until they revealed where they had hidden their stores of food, and murdering any who attempted to stop their voracious foraging.

Evidently these acts of outrage went far beyond the rapine and banditry which one might have expected of a fourteenth-century army, even when occupying the land of its allies, and in despair the natives retaliated by giving them poisoned bread, and casualties mounted in what was developing into a guerrilla war. Some of these troops (commanded by Sir John de Southeray, a bastard of Edward III and Alice Perres) then mutinied against Cambridge. Dom Fernando was forced to buy them off, and the fecklessly led expedition petered out soon after.

Work on the present Ducal Palace at Vila Viçosa began in 1501, and its long, monotonous classical façade was faced with Montes Claros marble a century later. It was here, in 1421, that Dom Jaime, the fourth Duke of Braganza, suspecting his wife Leonor de Guzmán (daughter of the third Duke of Medina Sidonia) of adultery with Alcoforado, her page, stabbed them both to death. The eighth duke, whose interests were in the chase and in music, here received the first overtures of the nationalist party, which in 1640 brought about his succession to the Portuguese throne – at last independent from Spain – as Dom João IV.[10]

Here, two years earlier, Catherine of Braganza was born, and also spent her youth, 'bred hugely retired' and virtually uneducated. How very different was the Court at Whitehall, where as the bride of Charles II, and soon after her arrival there in 1662, she was compelled to receive Lady Castlemaine, his mistress.

Dom Pedro III, who in 1760 married his niece Maria, stayed at Vila Viçosa occasionally, but preferred to lodge in an adjoining residence which, so Joseph Baretti was assured when visiting the place that same year, was 'elegantly fitted up' in spite of appearances. He had not been impressed by the rooms in the palace, furnished in rather a mean manner, uncharitably commenting that there were a hundred houses at Genoa incomparably better. 'The most remarkable thing I saw there', he concluded, 'are some old lamps and candlesticks in what they call the Royal Chapel, which are of pure silver and heavy enough'; but presumably not so ponderous as to be overlooked by the light-fingered French some decades later.

Dom Carlos, the penultimate king of Portugal, and his eldest son Dom Luis Filipe passed their last night at Vila Viçosa before driving to Lisbon on New Year's Day 1909, where, after landing at the Terreiro do Paço, they were both assassinated. The younger son, Dom Manuel, 'The Unfortunate', who was wounded in the arm only, was forced to abdicate in 1910.[11] To judge from the portly appearance of Dom Carlos, in his time the palatial kitchens, glittering with copper pans, formed by far the most important part of the establishment. The chapel, decorated in Pompeian style, music room, armoury, Sala de Hercules, and the imposing Sala dos Duques, with its *artesonado* or compartmented ceiling embellished with Braganza portraits, may be visited; while ranges of stables contain a spick and span collection of carriages, notably those of English manufacture, including a charabanc by Thrupp.

The walled chase known as the 'Tapada', some eleven miles in circumference, is adjacent, and it was when here that the Hon. Edward Charles Cocks, having recuperated after the Talavera campaign and rejoined his regiment then encamped there, so regretted not having his gun with him, for it pullulated with game: 'partridge, hares and red and fallow deer, wolves, etc.'.

Also then stationed at Vila Viçosa were the survivors of the 23rd Light Dragoons, which had been decimated at Talavera. Its officers, while awaiting their return to England to recruit, were getting up to any number of pranks to kill time; Commissary Schaumann records:

[All wore] the large round hat of the Portuguese peasant and carried a spiked stick, six feet long, like that of the bullock drivers. They had their heads tonsured as if they were priests. They ended their mess or their dinner every night by all getting drunk and flinging the dinner service, and finally the chairs and table,

out of the window. One morning, just as I was sitting writing, I
heard the trampling of feet in the street, and a crowd of people
collecting . . . an English bishop had arrived and was going to
pass through the town . . . [and] at that very moment the alleged
bishop really did make his appearance, riding solemnly down the
street on horseback, accompanied by all the officers . . . bearing
their helmets reverently in their hands. The bishop (a captain of
the regiment) was clad in red velvet breeches, white gaiters
trimmed with lace, a long skirted red velvet jacket, an English
flannel dressing-gown trimmed with black, a large Spanish collar
à la Van Dyck, with a clerical band, a wig, a moustache, an
old-fashioned hat with a large tassel, and gauntlet gloves. In his
left hand he carried a sceptre, on which a huge lemon was stuck,
surmounted by a cross. With his right hand he blessed the people. And thus they marched in solemn silence through Villa
Viçosa to Borba, at which place they intended to take luncheon.
The whole town was in an uproar. Everyone wanted to get a
glimpse of the English bishop. The extraordinary part of it was
that no Portuguese would believe that it was only a joke . . . I
only wished that Lord Wellington might by chance have encountered this cavalcade; how quickly it would have dispersed!

Soon after regaining the main road west, the *torre de menagem*
dominating **Estremoz** comes into view. Where, I wondered, on
entering the spacious market-place of the lower town, stood that
estalagem at which so many former travellers put up and described
so graphically? In 1760 Baretti had arrived there in the middle of a
belated masquerade in honour of the Princess of Brazil's marriage to
her ageing uncle. Having had to stretch his limbs on a straw-bag
placed over the chinks in the floor wide enough to see through, he
was awakened at the crack of dawn by the din of pipers and drum-
mers of the garrison coming to beg for drink-money.

William Beckford, when passing through Estremoz in 1787, had
sensibly taken the precaution of spreading on those draughty boards
the carpets he had just acquired at Arraiolos 'of strange grotesque
patterns and glaring colours'.

In the first bitterly cold week of January 1836 George Borrow had
entered the inn, but hardly had he settled himself in the kitchen,
where a cork tree-trunk was blazing, when an intoxicated fellow
mounted on a spirited horse dashed in from the adjoining stable to
display his prowess by wheeling about like a whirlwind among the

peasant company gathered there, causing alarm and confusion.

One wonders whether in Borrow's day the Gypsies of Estremoz follow the custom described by Luis Chaves in the 1920s. Apparently their wedding cortège, on reaching the principal gate, would halt, the bride then making off across the market-place with the groom in hot pursuit, encouraged by the guests until the girl was caught, when they broke out in applause. A dish was then thrown into the air, and its breaking into fragments on hitting the ground would be the signal that the couple were man and wife.

By the time Terence Mason Hughes, author of *An Overland Journey to Lisbon at the close of 1846*, had alighted there, things had improved to a certain extent, the Estalagem da Muralha even providing him with sheets, which to his astonishment, when his bed as if by enchantment was converted into a table next morning, passed as breakfast tablecloths!

Abutting the keep in the upper town is a former royal palace, now a luxurious *pousada* named after Isabel of Aragón (consort of Dom Dinis), who had died there in 1336. Adjacent stands the stark façade of Santa Maria do Castelo, which replaced a Gothic church built on the site of a mosque. A Gothic arcade survives from the earlier palace, rebuilt by Dom João V after being severely damaged by an explosion in 1698; but these disastrous detonations were commonplace in an age when the dangers inherent in storing gunpowder and other combustibles were little understood or heeded.

It was here early in June 1380 that Juan Fernández Andeiro, count of Ourém, after arriving from Oporto in disguise, was hidden in a tower adjoining the royal apartments while finalizing the secret negotiations between Dom Fernando and Richard II, who was to supply the projected expeditionary force under Edmund of Cambridge. On the fifteenth of the month the abortive Anglo-Portuguese alliances of 1372 and 1373 were renewed formally. But the infamous count also took advantage of his temporary propinquity to make Dona Leonor, the queen, his mistress. It soon became obvious that she was pregnant, and naturally Andeiro was assumed to be the father.[12]

In May 1663 a battle was fought at **Ameixial**, to the north-west, when the Portuguese, commanded by the Conde de Vila Flor and the Count-Duke Frederick Herman of Schomberg, decisively defeated Don Juan of Austria's Spaniards.[13] According to Colonel James Apsley,

The English foot with much pains climbed up the highest mountain which was possessed by the right wing of the enemy's army, and guarded with five pieces of cannon. The English marched on shouting as if victorious, but discharged no shot until they came within pike-thrust of the enemy, and then they poured in their shot so thick upon them that made them quit their ground and fly towards the left wing, leaving their cannon behind them, which were afterwards turned upon them much to their prejudice.

It is said that Dom Afonso VI, on hearing of the gallantry of the English contingent, which had been led by Colonel Thomas Hood, sent each company a present of snuff, which in disgust at so paltry a reward, they threw away. Charles II, partly to gratify his Portuguese bride, more generously ordered three months' pay to be distributed among them, but there appears to be some doubt whether they ever received it.

Writing two days after the battle, Schomberg reported that 'Every one is pleased here with the behaviour of the English troops', adding that he wanted to press the attack on Evora, but the Portuguese commanders 'after having done so well think of nothing but of resting themselves, instead of making use of their victory. They understand nothing about war. The soldiers are brave enough, but the chiefs carefully avoid all risks; and as to him who ought to have led us no one saw him during the battle at all'.

Another battle was fought two years later in the neighbourhood of **Montes Claros**, further east, when a Spanish force led by the Marquês de Caracena was likewise defeated by Schomberg and his English troops, in which Colonel Sheldon, who commanded them, was killed.

Evora lies to the south-west beyond the Serra de Ossa, on which rises the restored castle of **Evoramonte**. Here in 1834 Dom Miguel, the rebellious brother of Dom Pedro IV, having involved the country in several years of futile civil war, accepting military defeat, signed a Convention ostensibly abandoning all claims to the throne.

The main highway continues west across the undulating plain of the Alentejo, with woods of evergreen oak and cork extending on either side, and with the occasional view of an isolated whitewashed *monte* or farmstead. The road approaches **Arraiolos**, with its castle ruins, a town long famous for its blue and red carpets embroidered in wool on canvas or linen, of which many late-eighteenth-century examples still embellish the walls of Portuguese museums and palaces. When its manufactory was visited by Beckford, it already employed about 300 people.

A curious legend is told about the 'noiva de Arraiolos', who it is said took a fortnight to adorn herself for her wedding, at which she then appeared wrapped only in a shepherd's cloak.

Attractively sited in the vicinity is the sixteenth-century Quinta dos Lóios, formerly a convent, and doubtless that which had refused Baretti lodging, for the friar 'did not chuse to have an Heritick under his roof'. And no doubt Baretti missed seeing the remarkable *azulejos* in its church.

Another castle dominates the road at **Montemor-o-Novo**, the birthplace in 1495 of St John of God,[14] who like so many dedicated spirits in the Peninsula at that time – to mention only John of the Cross and Teresa of Avila – was of Jewish lineage. Adjacent to the castle stand the dilapidated dependencies of a convent. It was here that George Borrow caused a flutter among the nuns, who crowded to its windows to catch sight of their tall blond visitor, for he kissed his hands to them as he turned and strode away downhill.

NOTES

1. Henri de Massue (1648–1720), second Marquis de Ruvigny, had once fought under Turenne, but had been long in the English service, being created Viscount Galway and Baron Portarlington in 1692 and Earl of Galway five years later. He was given the command of English troops in Portugal in 1704.

   Baron Fagel (Nijmegen 1645–1718), had a distinguished military career in the Low Countries, to which he returned later, seeing action at Ramillies, Malplaquet and La Quesnoy.
2. Count Wilhelm von Schaumburg Lippe-Bückeburg (1724–77) – 'de Lippe' for short.
3. Son of the twelfth Baron Lovat. Another Simon Fraser (1738–1813) was a Major-General in Portugal during 1797–1800; a third, Lieutenant-General Simon Fraser (1765–1803), died in Lisbon.
4. He left for Brazil with the Court, and died governor of Rio da Janeiro.
5. Ambassador Tyrawly's legitimate son.
6. Heinrich Friedrich Link, Professor at the University of Rostock, was accompanying Count Hoffmansegg on an expedition to collect material for his *Flore Portugaise*, published in Berlin in 1809–20. Link's own *Travels in Portugal* were published in English in 1801, the same year as the German.

7. Army returns of casualties during the Peninsular War suggest that almost three times as many soldiers died from disease as from wounds. The mean strength of the British forces from January 1811 to May 1814 was about 66,750. During this period there were 35,525 deaths, of which 9,948 died in battle or of related wounds. The chief causes of death for over 25,000 men were dysentery, fevers, typhus, and hospital gangrene.

8. Giuseppe Marc'Antonio Baretti (1719–89), born in Turin and buried in Marylebone, settled in London in 1751, where he became a member of Dr Johnson's circle. The description of his journey across the Peninsula in 1760 appeared first in Italian, and his amplified version, written after a second visit to Madrid in 1768, was published in London in 1770, where it received the encomium of Johnson, who observed in a letter to Mrs Thrale, 'I know not whether the world has ever seen such travels before. Those whose lot it is to ramble can seldom write, and those who know how to write very seldom ramble'.

9. Not quite a *rebolada*, the primitive rite which, according to Rodney Gallop, was performed as late as 1863 near Elvas at the end of the olive gathering, and not in mime, when young men and girls would roll together on the ground in couples or one couple would be chosen by lot.

10. In his time he had even written a 'defence of modern music'. The important collection of music manuscripts he had assembled at Lisbon was entirely destroyed in 1755.

11. He spent the remainder of his long exile at Twickenham, dying in 1932. A great bibliophile and gifted amateur artist, he there accumulated an important collection of early Portuguese books, which were later preserved at Vila Viçosa.

12. In the event, the baby, born at Elvas, survived only four days. Late in 1383 Andeiro was assassinated in Lisbon by João of Avis. Leonor was hounded from the country, taking refuge in the convent of Santa Clara at Tordesillas in Castile, where she died in April 1386.

13. Schomberg (1615–90), who received the title of Count of Mértola for his part in the victory, had a long and varied military career, which ended with his death when commanding William of Orange's troops at the Battle of the Boyne; he was buried in St Patrick's Cathedral, Dublin. His son Meinhard, the 3rd Duke (1641–1719), became commander of the British auxiliary forces in Portugal during the War of the Spanish Succession, and was buried in Westminster Abbey.

14. Juan Ciudad Duarte, or San Juan de Dios, was the founder of the Spanish Order of the Hermanos Hospitalarios. He died at Granada in 1550, and was canonized in 1691.

Evora and its environs

Walled **Evora**, the ancient capital of the Alentejo, picturesquely sited on a low hill crowned by its stately granite cathedral, has still a Moresque appearance, with its maze of tortuous lanes flanked by dazzlingly whitewashed houses extending web-like from the Praça do Giraldo. It was here, below the low arcades of its central square, offering protection from both sun and rain, that I first saw a *pelico*, the sheepskin coat worn by the *alentejano* shepherds, with its curious square-cut tail and truncated, epaulette-like arms.

The Roman nucleus of Evora is still dominated by the imposing relics of a second-or third-century temple dedicated to Diana, which was later fortified and degraded, being at one time used as a shambles, and only in 1870 cleared of the accretion of centuries. Fourteen of its granite columns survive, all but two retaining their Corinthian capitals of Vila Viçosa marble. A curiosity is that they have only twelve flutes instead of the usual twenty-four, due doubtless to the labour of cutting the intractable stone. In September 1973 the edifice served as the rendezvous of junior officers disillusioned by the reactionary political regime, and who were to plan the bloodless revolution in Portugal the following 25 April.

The pre-Roman *oppidum* of Ebora was clearly of Celtic origin, although this has not been supported by any specific archaeological evidence. In *circa* 80 BC it may have been a headquarters of Quintus Sertorius. Julius Caesar awarded it the title of Liberalitas Julia, and the town flourished, being the residence of at least six senatorial families. In the year AD 300 a bishop of Evora was attending the influential Council of Elvira, near Granada. It was in Moorish hands between AD 715 and 1166, when during a lull in the Reconquest it was surprised and captured by a certain Geraldo Sem-Pavor, 'the Fearless', then an outlaw, who by this exploit regained the favour of the king, Afonso Henriques.

Garrisoned by the Spanish Order of Calatrava, it remained a

Christian bastion in the Alentejo until the frontiers of the Portuguese kingdom were extended to the mouth of the Guadiana, as
endorsed in 1297 by the Treaty of Alcañices. With the accession of
the House of Avis in 1385, Evora became a royal residence; the
Cortes were summoned here frequently, and by the end of the
fifteenth century its population is estimated to have grown to some
25,000 souls. Among its natives were Diego de Torralva and several
members of the De Resende and Arruda families of architects.
Juana, 'La Beltraneja', daughter of Enrique IV of Castile and Joana
of Portugal, may have enjoyed the seclusion of the convent of Santa
Clara here. She had received her nickname on account of the sup-
position that her father may have been Beltrán de la Cueva, an
unscrupulous royal favourite.

Vasco da Gama's residence before his appointment as Viceroy of
India in 1524 may have stood near the cathedral and, twelve years
later, the first branch of the Inquisition in Portugal was established
in the vicinity. In 1540 Evora became the seat of an archbishopric,
and was the residence of Henriques, the Cardinal-king, before he
assumed the throne in 1578.

Among ecclesiastics, there is little doubt that Archbishop Manuel
do Cenáculo Vilas-Boas, the son of a Lisbon blacksmith, brought
special lustre to Evora during his incumbency, otherwise not a
particularly enlightened period. Robert Southey, who met him in
1801, described him as 'a little, cheerful, large-eyed man'. At that
time he was Bishop of Beja, where apparently he was the only person
who ever bought a book; and there he had liberally provided the
young poet with cheese and 'an incomparable wine' on his fatiguing
journey south to the Algarve.

Although heaps of manuscripts were destroyed, most of his
library survived the depredations of the French in July 1808, when
General Loison, having first massacred the garrison, brutally sacked
the place. Having given the archbishop his word 'of honour' that his
palace would be respected, he broke into Vila-Boas' cabinet of
antiquities and 'plundered the collection of all the gold and silver
medals, of which he had a very considerable series, leaving the
copper and bronze untouched'; and – so Lord Holland was assured
by a priest, when in the following July he enjoyed the hospitality of
the archbishop's palace, with its 'handsome, lofty, well-furnished
rooms' – whilst the archbishop was sleeping, Loison himself stole
his episcopal ring from a table and pocketed it.

Even George Borrow, not usually so impressed by the opulence of the Romish Church and its dignitaries, was enthusiastic about the 'superb library' and 'collection of pictures by Portuguese artists, chiefly portraits' which he saw there. By then, in December 1835, the palace was in use as the Governor's residence: not that there were many to govern, for the population had dwindled to a mere 5,000 according to Borrow's computation, largely due to the generally confused state of the country during the immediate aftermath of the civil war between the supporters of Dom Pedro and his brother Dom Miguel.

The palace is now the museum, containing one of the smaller but more important collections in the country, including a charming bas-relief of the lower half of a diaphanously draped Vestal Virgin or Bacchante, and the tomb of Alvaro da Costa, carved by Nicolau Chanterène, who was working in Evora during the 1530s. Remarkable among the paintings is a series depicting the life of the Virgin by the Flemish Master of the retable of Evora Cathedral, and a Nativity by Frei Carlos, not forgetting an anonymous portrait said to be of Catherine of Braganza in her youth.

The cathedral, with its deeply recessed porch, probably erected on the site of a mosque, was virtually completed by the mid-thirteenth century. Parts of it – notably in the cloister – are the work of *Mudéjar* or Christianized Moorish masons. The incongruous *capela-mór* or chancel was reconstructed by Ludovice, the architect of Mafra. Among cult objects in the treasury is an unusual figure-triptych of the Virgin. Of interest too is the central *zimbório*, an octagonal lantern with scale-like tiles of Salmantine type, and subsidiary turrets, best viewed from the flat roof. This spot also provides a tawny panorama, with the Serra da Ossa on the horizon to the north-east and the Monfurado to the north-west, dense with cork woods.

Adjacent to the Roman temple is the former monastery Dos Lóios, now a *pousada*. Its Gothic cloister is surmounted by a Renaissance gallery, where beneath the crowning ogee of the Luso-Moorish doorway of the chapter-house is a carving of a stockade perhaps representing Azammur, on the north coast of Africa, taken by the Portuguese in 1513, when the first Earl of Tentugal was wounded; tombs of that family lie in the adjoining church.

A lane behind the cathedral apse leads to the buildings of the university, founded by the Jesuits in 1559, and which survived two centuries before its suppression by Pombal, the enlightened although authoritarian chief minister of Dom José. Its arcaded courtyard, the *azulejo*-lined Sala dos Actos, and the refectory vaulted from a central row of pillars, are notable.

More of an architectural curiosity, and attributed to Diogo de Torralva, is the ungainly if striking Mannerist façade of Nossa Senhora da Graça, embellished by two huge 'rosettes' and crowned by colossal figures appearing to support globe-like grenades.

A vaulted building, formerly a royal grain store, which stands opposite the north side of the church of São Francisco, was probably the hostelry at which George Borrow put up. And it was perhaps with a shopkeeper in the neighbouring market-place that he deposited a load of Testaments. He then made his way to a fountain beyond the pinnacled hermitage of São Brás, not far south of the bastioned walls, where each day he would spend two hours, entering into conversation 'upon matters relating to their eternal welfare' with the wide-eyed muleteers, water-carriers and local gaffers who would regularly congregate there. It would appear that 'none of them had seen the Bible, and not more than half a dozen had the slightest knowledge of what the Holy Book consisted'.

Borrow had no compunction in emphasizing repeatedly to this peasant audience that 'the Pope, whom they revered, was an arch deceiver, and the head minister of Satan here on earth, and that the monks and friars, whose absence they so deplored, and to whom they had been accustomed to confess themselves, were his subordinate agents'. In spite of such inflammatory disclosures, and because of the 'utter fearlessness' which he displayed, he experienced no insult or ill-treatment. Well may one wonder what these rustics thought of the strange foreigner in their midst. Borrow had fervent hopes that the words he uttered had sunk deep into the hearts of his listeners, for he observed 'many of them depart musing and pensive'; and – dare one add – perhaps baffled?

Rose Macaulay has suggested that one explanation, 'which did not, apparently, occur to him is that very little of what he said was understood. Even his gift of tongues cannot have enabled him, after a few days in Portugal, to talk Portuguese as the Portuguese talk it; he probably pronounced it rather as if it were Spanish'.

Aisleless São Francisco contains a gruesome charnel-house, which tender-hearted young Southey found 'really shocking'. What struck me more when I entered the place was the number of photographs of young soldiers that had been left on an adjacent altar to ensure them divine protection: photos had taken the place of *ex-votos*!

Most of the other churches of Evora are of comparatively minor importance, but the indefatigable ecclesiologist may spend some time in the continuing exploration of the city, having first enquired at the tourist office as to the whereabouts of their respective keys and guardians.

Evora is a pleasant base from which to radiate into this part of the Alentejo. Within three miles or so there are several things worth seeing, among them the cloister of the convento of **Nossa Senhora d'Espinheiro**, at which Frei Carlos, painter of the Nativity in the museum, professed in 1517, and with the tomb of Garcia de Resende in its chapel. The elaborate Manueline *porta-pax* originally preserved here is now one of the treasures of the Museu Nacional de Arte Antiga in Lisbon.

On the road to Arraiolos, first skirting Evora's aqueduct, the 'Agua de Prata', succeeding the Roman original, is the **Cartuxa**, one of two Carthusian houses in Portugal. Its imposing classical façade is attributed to Filippo Terzi, an Italian military engineer responsible for several buildings of importance in Portugal during the late sixteenth century.

Not far beyond is **São Bento de Castris**, a Benedictine foundation of some interest, its cloister, like that of the cathedral, displaying *Mudéjar* influence.

Further afield is the **Quinta de Valverde** or **Mitra**, a former retreat of the archbishops, where the diminutive church of Bom Jesus, probably by Diogo de Torralva, is a curious architectural conceit, in plan consisting of five domed octagons separated by four squares, the central dome supported by free-standing marble columns, while others abut the walls.

To the south, on the northern slope of a range of low hills, stands the castle of **Viana do Alentejo**, within the *enceinte* of which is a substantially buttressed and crenelated church embellished by a wealth of conical pinnacles, and a Manueline portal. To the east is the grandiose pilgrimage church of Nossa Senhora de Aires, its interior plastered with *ex-votos*.

Beyond **Alvito**, its half-Moorish, late-fifteenth-century castle retaining the moulded brick horseshoe arches typical of the district, a Roman bridge spans the Odivelas. The road then winds over the hills towards **Vila de Frades**, passing a turning for **São Cucufate**.

Here are the idyllically sited relics of a Roman villa converted into a monastery, which it remained until the sixteenth century. This may have helped to preserve the mural decoration still to be seen in some of its brick-vaulted rooms. When I first saw it, a dozen years ago, the place stood silent and deserted under a baking sun, only a darting lizard distracting me from the enchantment.

Neighbouring **Vidigueira**, on the main road between Evora and Beja, was possibly the home of Baruch Spinoza's family prior to the expulsion of its *Marrano* community during the early years of the sixteenth century, when numerous Portuguese Jews, including the Espinozas, emigrated to Amsterdam. Vasco da Gama's remains long rested in the Carmelite church here before their translation to Belém and more recently to Santa Engrácia in Lisbon.

Portel retains a Braganza castle, but a better-preserved example may be seen at **Amieira**, to the east.

Some distance south-east of Evora, beyond the Guadiana, lies **Mourão**, a frontier village of some character. On a ridge to its north rises picturesque **Monsaraz**, commanding wide views and preserving medieval fortifications and later Vaubanesque outworks. After its reconquest by Geraldo Sem-Pavor in 1167 it became a stronghold of the Templars, before passing into the hands of the Order of Christ. The place was probably sacked in 1381 by the unpaid archers of Edmund of Cambridge.

3

Setúbal – the Serra da
Arrábida – Palmela

Beyond Montemor-o-Novo the main highway leads across the lonely, undulating plain of the Alentejo, traversing occasional ever-green oak and cork woods to **Vendas Novas**. Here, in one of the recurrent fits of extravagance which contributed to the financial ruin of his country, Dom João V ordered the erection of a palace merely to accommodate the bridal cortège of the fourteen-year-old Mariana Victoria, a daughter of Philip V of Spain and the future wife of Dom José. (The birth of Dom José's brother Pedro sixteen years earlier, in 1712, had been an excuse for the king to indulge himself by building the magnificent but ruinously costly monastery at Mafra.)

The soil becomes more sandy as the desolate crossroads or *cruzamento de* **Pegões** are approached, where Joseph Baretti met with no living thing 'except a small flight of birds, half a dozen sheep, with a goat, and two men following three wretched asses heavily loaded', the leaden hours animated by the 'incessant mournful singing of the Calesseiros, accompanied by the incessant tinkling of the mules' bells, together with the incessant sun hotly reverberating from the incessant sand through an incessant solitude'. On dismounting at an *estalagem*, he was then pestered persistently for pin money by women, to whom, he assured himself, if he had given one eye, would have asked for the other; but such were the least aggravations of travel.

In those days the old track led due west from here to **Aldeia Gallega**, now **Montijo**, from which ferries plied across the wide estuary of the Tagus to deposit travellers on the Terreiro do Paço at Lisbon. This service was suspended as recently as 1951, when the Maréchal Carmona bridge was thrown across the river upstream at Vila Franca de Xira; and then, only fifteen years later, this overland route was largely superseded by the alternative and more impressive

19

approach to the capital provided by the Ponte 25 de Abril, spanning the strait immediately south of the capital.

The saline estuary of the Marateca, flowing into the Sado, with its salt-pans, is skirted on approaching Setúbal, overlooked to the north by the castle-crowned hill of Palmela. While no longer the 'terrestial Paradise' described by Hans Andersen, the busy port, long reputed for its rice, oranges, sardines, and muscatel grapes, still retains its characteristic *enceinte*.

Setúbal takes its name from the Roman *oppidum* of Caetobriga, once assumed to have been at **Tróia**, on the long spit of sand extending north from the far shore, where, since the 1850s, more obvious relics of the past had been brought to the surface. It is likely that this thickly silted site, possibly of Phoenician foundation, was overwhelmed by a tidal wave in the fifth century; but what was described fifty years ago as 'a wilderness of sand, gay with flowers in Spring', has been overwhelmed again, this time by what is promoted as a 'Tourist Complex'.

Phoenician and Carthaginian ceramics have since come to light in Setúbal itself, among them amphorae containing hoards of fourth-century coins, while more tanks for salting fish have been found there, to complement those at Tróia.

The present port was established in the twelfth century. It was here in 1471 that Dom João II married Leonor de Lencastre [*sic*], and 'Saint Ubes', as it was called familiarly by English sailors, was favoured frequently by his presence. Little remains of its medieval walls, which were later strengthened. To the west rises the Castelo de São Filipe (now a *pousada*), ascribed to Filippo Terzi, and constructed on the orders of Philip I to cow the Portuguese, and to deter English attempts to land in the vicinity, as they were likely to do during that period of enmity.

The wide avenue skirting the quay is named after Luisa Ferreira – better known as Todi – a diva celebrated throughout Europe in the late eighteenth century, who was a native. Another was Manuel Maria de Bocage, described by William Beckford as a 'pale, limber, odd-looking young man', whose poetical compositions 'thrilled and agitated' him. In the Praça de Bocage stands São Julião, with a Manueline portal, while in the main avenue are two museums, one devoted to ethnography, the other to the fishing industry, where the guardian will set its scale models of dredgers a-whirring if given the slightest encouragement.

The main monument in Setúbal is the Igreja de Jesus, an imposing hall-church begun by Diogo Boitac in 1494, its vault sustained by thick cable-like breccia columns which, with the rope-like ribs in the apse, are among the more characteristic features of the Manueline style. Among the better paintings there are an Annunciation and Calvary by the so-called Master of Setúbal.

The coast road ascends the limestone ridge forming the Serra da Arrábida, on the steep seaward scarp of which are perched the dependencies and scattered hermitages of the **Convent of Arrábida**. Belvederes command views both of the yellow strand of the Trója peninsula extending towards the distant Cabo de Sines, and north towards Lisbon and the cloud-capped Serra de Sintra.

Continuing west, the road winds above the fishing-port of **Sesimbra**, defended by a castle of Moorish origin and a seventeenth-century fort, to approach Cabo Espichel, the Roman Promontorium Barbaricum. At the far end of the peninsula, high above the heaving Atlantic, stands the long derelict church of **Nossa Senhora do Cabo**, dating from 1701, its windswept forecourt flanked by dilapidated ranges of pilgrimage accommodation.

At **Vila Noguera de Azeitão**, on the north slope of the Serra da Arrábida, is a former palace of the Távora family, its escutcheon erased by Pombal after their alleged complicity with the Aveiros in a plot to assassinate Dom José in 1758. Several members of the Aveiro household, including the eighth duke, were either executed or broken on the wheel and their ashes scattered over the Tagus. Teresa, the younger Marchioness of Távora, had been the king's mistress: but that is another labyrinthine story.

Close by is the Quinta das Torres and, behind its thick hedge, the **Quinta da Bacalhôa**, an enchanting small palace built in 1480 for the Infanta Brites. Sacheverell Sitwell suggests that Andrea Sansovino, who had spent six years in Portugal at this time, might well have been the architect. It was later acquired by the son of Afonso de Albuquerque, the great governor of Portuguese India. Gardens were laid out and the triple-towered pavilion added, which contains the earliest dated tile picture in Portugal, of 1565, depicting chaste Susanna and the Elders. The *quinta* was much neglected until the mid-1930s, when Mrs Herbert Scoville from Connecticut brought some order to the place, restoring the water-tank and melon-domed towers and reviving its topiary hedges and orchard.

The fortress of **Palmela** now houses a palatial *pousada*. It had been largely abandoned since the earthquake of 1755, when one church here, built on the site of a mosque, was entirely destroyed; the other contains the tomb of Jorge de Lencastre, a son of Dom João II. He died in 1551, the last Grand Master of the Order of São Tiago, which had its headquarters here from 1288.

The hilltop view was described by the impressionable young Southey as the most beautiful he had ever seen: today, he might well have had reservations.

Pinewoods cover much of the area to the north, known as the Outra Banda – the 'other side' of the Tagus, at least from Lisbon. The river is spanned here by the Ponte 25 de Abril, renamed to commemorate the revolution of 1974. This, the longest suspension bridge in Europe, was inaugurated in 1966 as the 'Salazar Bridge' to flatter that dictator, under whose regime, only a few years earlier, the south bank had been blighted by the erection of a grotesquely disproportionate image of Christ.

Until the construction of the bridge, travellers had no alternative but to take a ferry across the estuary. Until a century ago passengers arriving by sea from exotic foreign parts had to spend several days in a nearby *lazareto* or quarantine station.

To the west lies **Trafaria**, formerly a fishing village of rush-roofed huts, which had been burnt to the ground in January 1777 on Pombal's orders for harbouring those avoiding rapacious press-gangs. This draconian measure was one of several held against him when, only a month later, the dictator fell from power. Not surprisingly, in later decades, officers of the law, when having to visit the spot in search of a delinquent, preferred to be accompanied by a military detachment.

The fastidious will avoid the neighbouring Costa da Caparica, the pullulating playground of the Lisbon populace.

To the east of the bridge extend industrial **Almada** and contiguous **Casilhas**. The former villages were razed by the Great Earthquake of 1755. It was on this southern shore of the estuary, only five years after the catastrophe, that Joseph Baretti, having 'enjoyed the prospects' to his satisfaction, visited an English hospital set up here and run by an elderly physician 'rendered ill bred by jealousy, as he had the weakness at seventy to marry a pretty Portuguese girl of eighteen'. Close by were the cellars of Mr O'Neal, an Irish wine-merchant, more civil and hospitable, whose house was defended from the encroachment of the Tagus by a mole of large flat stones. Two negroes were 'playing gambols' in the water here and, as Baretti confesses, had he not seen men of that colour before, of which there were plenty in Lisbon, he would have mistaken them easily for 'some particular species of fish', so lithely limbed were they.

4

Lisbon before the Great Earthquake

Few would dispute that the most impressive view of Lisbon is that from the transpontine Outra Banda, or when crossing the Ponte 25 de Abril as slowly as possible, for vehicles are prohibited from actually stopping. The panorama alone – to paraphrase in part Joseph Baretti – gives 'much satisfaction to an inquisitive pair of eyes', making one impatient 'to range about such a wide scene of curiosity as this metropolis', his first sight of which, from the level of a heaving deck, he compared with pride to that of water-lapped Genoa.

Others, sailing from the Atlantic into the wide estuary of the Tagus past the glistening Torre de Belém and the conspicuous bulk of the Jerónimos' convent, would claim that the prospect was only surpassed by Naples or Constantinople. It was certainly all very grand and picturesque, with the older town rising steeply from its animated quays, and with the Castelo da São Jorge coming into view on a distant height as the water-lapped Terreiro do Paço was approached.

How many fleets had ridden at anchor here since, over a thousand years before Christ, the Phoenicians, edging cautiously along the Iberian coast from their trading stations at Cadiz and after skirting the Tartessian shore west of Huelva near the copper mines of the Río Tinto, had entered the estuary?

A permanent settlement had been made on the hill of São Jorge, known as Olisipo, which convinced some earlier chroniclers that Lisbon most certainly had been founded by Ulysses: others attributed it to Elishah, a grandson of Abraham, and dated it to 3259 BC precisely, for they were marvellously exact at establishing the year of such remote events. (And even now you will notice in Portugal that very specific dates are placed on recent buildings to commemorate their inauguration, which doubtless will assist archaeologists and architectural historians in the distant future.)

In 205 BC, after the end of the Second Punic War, the hill was occupied by the Romans, and their hold on the place was strengthened by Decimus Brutus in 137 BC. Raised to the rank of *municipium* by Julius Caesar, it was invested with the title Felicitas Julia Olisipo, and under the Empire became, with Emerita Augusta (Mérida, in what is now Spanish Extremadura) the most important city in Lusitania. In AD 409 it fell to the invading Alans, who were in turn superseded by the Suevi and, half a century later, by the Visigoths.

Little survives of the Roman occupation, although after the convulsion of 1755 relics of a theatre were discovered, its *cavea* carved into the western slope of the hill; and part of a *cryptoporticus* remains below the Rua da Plata.

Together with the rest of Lusitania, Lisbon was overrun by the Moors in AD 714, who after landing on the coast of western Andalucia three years earlier, had by then a tenuous control of a large part of the Iberian Peninsula. Four centuries were to elapse before any serious attempt was made to recapture it, when a fleet of Anglo-Normans, including contingents from Hastings and Southampton *en route* to join the Second Crusade, made an unsuccessful descent on the place, having to content themselves with sacking the suburbs before re-embarking. It was not until 1147 that the city surrendered to Afonso Henriques, Count of Portugal, intent on making the line of the Tagus his temporary frontier before extending his dominion further south.[1]

The Court was transferred here from Coimbra eighty years later, and the following century and a half brought Lisbon increasing prosperity, causing it to be raided by Enrique of Castile in 1373, when the Rua Nova and the *Judiaria* or ghetto were set alight. It was after this incursion that Dom Fernando erected new walls, said to possess no less than seventy-seven towers and sixteen gates on its landward side alone, while the fortifications flanking the Tagus contained another twenty-two gates, allowing for the usual medieval exaggeration.

Its Sephardic community, although suffering an isolated antisemitic attack from the more zealous citizens in 1449, increased dramatically in numbers after 1492, when some 60,000 *Conversos* banished from Spain were allowed temporary residence in Portugal. Dom Manuel, on coming to the throne three years later, acquiesced to giving them asylum, at least until his marriage in 1497 to Isabel, daughter of the bigoted Catholic Kings of Spain, when it was decreed that the children of Jews would be either baptized, forcibly if necessary, or deported if they refused; there would be no discussion.

Derogatorily named *Marranos*,[2] these 'New Christians' were the object of a savage pogrom in 1506, once it was realized that very often they had converted only ostensibly. That this community had in so many ways enriched the country was expediently ignored by the more fanatical members of the Church, and later by the myrmidons of the Inquisition, introduced into Portugal in the 1530s. It was bad enough that it was a rabbi who had first set up a printing-press in the capital in 1489, but inexcusable that the first eleven Portuguese incunables should have been in Hebrew, of all tongues.

During the next two centuries the Holy Office, in attempting to extirpate heresy in Portugal, investigated almost 25,000 citizens, notably those of the growing middle classes who had intermarried with 'New Christians'; but although large numbers incurred a variety of punishments, less than 1,500 were actually condemned to death.

Enormous material wealth and incredible cargoes of curious and exotic commodities were converging on Lisbon in the wake of Vasco da Gama's discovery of a sea route to the Indies in the penultimate years of the fifteenth century and by subsequent trading with the Orient. In 1500 Pedro Alvares Cabral had sighted the coast of Brazil, although its resources remained untapped for several decades. And in spite of experiencing frequent virulent visitations of the plague and other epidemics concommitant with trading, the port continued to flourish: by the mid-sixteenth century its population had risen to 100,000.

Quixotically obsessed with the idea of extending his dominion into Morocco, in 1578 Dom Sebastião, having concentrated his forces in the Algarve, had set sail that August – not exactly the month for campaigning under an African sun – and together with half his army and the flower of the Portuguese nobility, had met his death in the subsequent battle of Alcácer-Quibir, leaving the throne vacant. Those who had not been slaughtered were held to ransom.

The nation was thoroughly demoralized. Few could take on board the fact that a disaster of such proportions had occurred: indeed, for several decades there was a popular Messianic belief that Dom Sebastião, 'the Regretted', was still alive and would surely return one day, an assumption taken advantage of by several 'false Sebastians'.

Philip II of Spain (whose mother had been Isabel of Portugal, a daughter of Dom Manuel), and who had been the uncle of Dom

Sebastião, likewise laid claim to the kingdom, and in June 1580 stepped into the breach by sending his troops across the frontier. Although thus forcibly annexed, Portugal was naturally 'promised' a certain autonomy.

Some months later Philip himself took up residence in Lisbon, where he was to remain until February 1583. It has been argued that if he had paid heed to his advisors and chosen Lisbon as his capital instead of Madrid – which had little in its favour apart from being centrally sited in the Peninsula – the future history of his Hispano-Portuguese empire might have been very different.

Meanwhile, the estuary of the Tagus saw the protracted assembly by the Marquis of Santa Cruz of an *armada* of sufficient size to ensure the success of Philip's projected 'Enterprize of England', which would crush entirely the inadmissible pretensions of Queen Elizabeth and her heretical henchman. There were interminable delays, caused partly by storm damage to the fleet during the summer of 1587, when it set sail to frustrate Drake's interception near the Azores of the treasure fleet from the Indies, and also by the death of Santa Cruz. It was not until the following May that the huge fleet, now commanded by the Duke of Medina Sidonia, and so soon to be humiliated, weighed anchor and sailed out into the Lisbon Roads.

A year later, in retaliation, Drake and Norris made an abortive attempt to sack Lisbon, but this and other English attacks on mainland Portugal were of little consequence compared with the adverse economic effects Philip's war had on the country, for in his endeavours to damage English trade, he had ruined that of Portugal. Lisbon suffered a further economic blow with the growing rebellion in the Spanish Netherlands. In 1594 fifty Dutch vessels were seized in the Tagus, and all trade with those provinces was prohibited. The shattered state of Spain's finances was no doubt a contributory factor to the gradual infringement of any remaining Portuguese liberties.

During this long period of hostility between England and Spain, particularly after the 'Flight of the Earls' from Ireland in 1607, numerous dispossessed Irish Catholics exiled themselves to Portugal, as had already, in 1594, the Bridgettine nuns of Syon together with Father Joseph Foster, their confessor. In the previous year an Irish College had been established in Lisbon. Among those resident in the capital were Philip O'Sullivan Beare, whose *History of Ireland* was published there in 1621; while in 1628 Simon Fallon of Galway was composing his treatise on mathematics and astronomy in the agreeable company of his fellow countrymen in Lisbon.

But the English establishment there did not always take kindly to other than their co-religionists, and were only too ready to listen to any scandal confected against a nunnery priest such as Father Foster, who found himself abused in a slight volume printed in London in 1622 entitled *The Anatomie of the English Nunnerie at Lisbon Dissected and laid open by one that was sometimes a younger brother of the Convent*, a scurrilous and unmerited attack by a certain Thomas Robinson, who bore them a grudge. The Bridgettines, who were to remain in Lisbon until 1861, are referred to later.

In 1628 the Colégio dos Inglesinhos was founded in Lisbon for the education of seminarists during those penal times, followed in 1634 by the Irish Dominican community of Corpo Santo, the Rector of which was a Father Daniel O'Daly from County Kerry; and five years later it was the turn of the Dominican nunnery of Bom Sucesso to be established. (In 1640, with the Restoration, the new queen was to choose O'Daly as her confessor.)

It was not until 1619 that Philip II – Spanish Philip III – condescended to visit Lisbon, when he was fêted lavishly by the Portuguese in an attempt to protect privileges and gain concessions, but under his successor the ground swell of revolt intensified as the country was increasingly exploited by a virtually bankrupt Spain. An English Franciscan, who had visited the Peninsula in 1633, wrote privately that 'The Portuguese prefer the English to any other nation, and they have more hatred for the Castilians than they have for the Devil', which was perhaps a somewhat partisan reflection of national feeling at the time.

When in 1640 Philip IV's chief minister, the Count-Duke of Olivares, demanded exceptional taxes to pay the expenses of his war against the rebellious Catalans, a number of Portuguese nobles, knowing the temper of the populous, prevailed on the pretensions of the eighth duke of Braganza (whose ambitious wife, Luisa de Guzmán, happened to be a grand-daughter of the seventh duke of Medina-Sidonia) to join in their conspiracy. On 15 December of that year, a platform having been erected in the Terreiro do Paço for the solemn occasion, the Portuguese proclaimed their independence and the duke was crowned Dom João IV of Portugal: their 'sixty years' captivity' was over.

To consolidate her precarious independence, Portugal set out to strengthen her former frontier fortresses, some of which were recaptured the following June by Spanish troops, who made several other incursions during this unsettled period, notably in 1662, when they pushed as far west as Borba; but in the following year, although they entered Evora, which caused rioting in Lisbon, the invaders were repelled at Ameixial. Sporadic military activity on the border continued until the Spanish were worsted at Montes Claros in 1665, but another three years were to pass before Spain reluctantly recognized the Portuguese Restoration.

Meanwhile, Portugal had sought the support of Spain's rivals: France, Holland, and particularly England, with whom she had signed a commercial treaty in 1642. But during the English Civil War relations between the two countries had become strained. Late in November 1649 eleven men-of-war, under the command of Prince Rupert and Prince Maurice, dropped anchor at Lisbon, which, cavalierly, they proceeded to make a base of naval operations against the Commonwealth. In the following spring, Admiral Blake, sent to seek them out, even contemplated forcing the entrance to the Tagus in view of Dom João's refusal to expel the Royalists. Unsuccessful in blockading the estuary, he eventually set sail in October; but Prince Rupert's squadron, escaping soon after, were sighted by Blake off Cartagena two months later, and scattered.

Further commercial agreements with England were being proposed, and in 1654 the important Commonwealth Treaty was signed, which not only confirmed many former concessions, but granted additional privileges to English merchants in Lisbon. In January 1657 Thomas Maynard, a rigid Puritan, and an energetic, opinionated and argumentative character, landed there in the capacity of Consul. He was a skilful negotiator and drove a hard bargain. Always deeply suspicious of the English Catholic community, he reported that Richard Russell, 'a mass priest, and a member of the seminary', of all people, was on his way back from London, where apparently he had been acting as the Portuguese ambassador's secretary during the protracted negotiations then in progress, which were to culminate in the marriage of the Infanta Catherine to Charles II in 1662.

Indeed, Russell had assisted at the nuptial ceremony in London before his return to Lisbon as one of the future queen's English preceptors and chaplains. (For his part in this matrimonial mission, Russell was rewarded by the Braganzas with the bishopric of the Cape Verde Islands, but – perhaps after seeing him crestfallen – with the promise that he would have the first see that should fall vacant in Portugal. In the event, this was to be Portalegre, from which he was translated to Viseu in 1682, where he was to spend the last decade of his life.)

Consul Maynard was largely responsible for the setting up of the English Factory in Lisbon, where he was to remain until 1689. English merchants had been long established there – Thomas Daniel had been importing cloth from Bristol as early as 1378 – but they were now able to operate as a formal corporate body. This association, which came to be known as the Feitoria Inglesa, and has been described as 'a kind of Chamber of Commerce-cum-Consulate . . . a Meeting house where the principal Merchants and Factors foregathered to discuss matters of trade, politics, and local interests of the British community', was to survive for the next century and a half.

The Consul did not always see eye to eye with the chaplain. Maynard was certainly at odds with the Revd Zachary Cradock, chaplain in 1657, which, as he was part of the Consular household and lived under the same roof, naturally led to further friction. Yet when Cradock returned to England late in 1659, Maynard had emphasized that in spite of such tribulations, a replacement was essential, for without a chaplain the young men of the community 'will take too much liberty and growe more Extravagant in their vices if they be not restrained'.

Cradock was replaced by the Revd Thomas Marsden, who in the summer of 1661 came out in the retinue of Sir Richard Fanshawe, the Envoy Extraordinary. He was more tractable; indeed, his departure four years later was regretted by several merchants, who certified that Marsden had been 'assiduous and laborious in his studies, constant and orthodox in his preachings, pious and exemplary in his life'. Yet, according to Sir Robert Southwell, it would appear that his influence did little to moderate some of the 'factious unquiet spirits' among them: those who 'delight in debauching all the young men to make up a party', and who for the most part, 'having been bred up in the Licentious Principles of the late bad Times have not as yet mended their manners nor their operations'.

In March 1662 Edward Montagu, first Earl of Sandwich, entered the Tagus with an English fleet to escort young Catherine of Braganza to England.

Fanshawe's interest in Portugal was not merely diplomatic, for as early as 1655 his translation of Camoens' *Os Lusíades* had been published in London. Lady Ann, his wife, accompanied Fanshawe when in September 1662 he returned to Lisbon as Ambassador, and described Lisbon in her *Memoirs*[3] as having with its river the 'good-

liest situation' that she ever saw, even if the old town was decayed.
They were making new walls of stone

> which will contain six times their city. Their churches and chapels
> are the best built, the finest adorned, and the cleanliest kept of
> any churches in the world. The people delight much in quintas,
> which are a sort of country houses, of which there are abundance
> within a few leagues of the city, and those that belong to the
> nobility very fine, both houses and gardens. The nation is gener-
> ally very civil and obliging . . .

And yet it must have been with a certain sense of relief that
Fanshawe escaped from the officious Mr Maynard and set sail for
England in August 1663, prior to taking up the post of Ambassador
to Madrid. Southwell, his successor, found the Consul equally abra-
sive although admittedly 'very fit and equal to the employment he
bears'.

In 1683 Maynard had an additional problem to deal with, this
time in Oporto, for the Revd Samuel Barton, the chaplain to the Factory there, had been summarily dismissed, due doubtless to the
machinations of Edward Murcot, the vice-Consul, who, with several
Oporto merchants, had recently apostatized to Rome; and most certainly with the collusion of the Inglesinhos . . .

Then, only three years later, the Revd Michael Geddes,[4] Chaplain
in Lisbon since 1678, was forbidden by the Inquisition to hold services in any other place than the Ambassador's residence, which
caused Maynard to complain to the Inquisitor General in person,
and with righteous indignation: and so the warring continued.
(Maynard had not forgotten his treatment by the Catholic authorities during the Throckmorton affair in 1660, another long drawn out
campaign against the ecclesiastical establishment, too tedious to
detail.)

Meanwhile, by 1667, after two years of unconsummated marriage
to Dom Afonso VI, the wilful Maria-Francesca of Savoy had had
more than enough, and made a strategic retreat to the convent of
Esperança. It was without much difficulty that a palace revolution
was hatched, whereby the third Conde de Castelo-Melhor, the
king's *escrivão da puridade* or secret secretary, the *de facto* Prime
Minister, was banished, and the degenerate king himself was
forcibly deposed and kept in close confinement. At first this was
in the Azores, but his brother Dom Pedro, now Prince-Regent,

wishing to keep him under closer surveillance, later had him transferred to Sintra, where he died, deranged, in 1783.

Sir Robert Southwell goes into intimate detail in several letters to
Lord Arlington concerning the delicate matter of Dom Afonso's presumed impotence, reporting that when in conversation with the
queen at the gate of her convent – where she 'lives very gay and
chearful' – she had confided to him

> the unspeakable crosses and discomforts she had with the King,
> and sometimes to that degree of outrage that he once put his hand
> on a knife to do her a mischief, as they lay in bed, though (said he)
> finding that I answered him resolutely, he excused the matter
> with saying, he meant to draw it against himself: That he came
> not to her bed sometimes in two months together . . .

Writing a week later, Southwell disclosed that the queens's 'total
disappointment in her bed' was the consequence of

> an accident, which befel the King in his childhood, of being
> blasted, and ever since paralytical on his whole right side, did
> not only crack and shatter his understanding, but made him impo-
> tent as to the use of a virgin at least.

He confirmed that the

> Canons of the Cathedral have already named three Judges for
> deciding the Queen's complaint about the nullity of her mar-
> riage, who are the old Bishop of *Targa* [? Braga], the Bishop elect
> of *Elvas*, and the Vicar General: The first and last persons, suffi-
> ciently inclinable to slubber over the business, as she would have
> it; but the second a learned rigorous man without mercy, whom
> the Queen apprehends will pursue the rule of search and inspec-
> tion; against which she is very averse, and already pleads the pre-
> rogative of her quality to excuse her from the common method of
> proceeding.

The ambitious queen had little difficulty in having the marriage
annulled, and forthwith obtained a dispensation to marry Pedro,
her brother-in-law, who although more personable, was hardly an
improvement.

Three years after her death, Dom Pedro remarried; his bride,

Maria-Sofia-Isabel of Neuberg, was escorted to Lisbon by a squadron of English men-of-war.

Among those who found the new queen sympathetic was the Revd John Colbatch, Chaplain to the Factory from 1693 to 1700.[5] Perhaps he found her 'exceedingly Fair' largely because, unlike 'Portuguese Women of all ranks', she did not discolour her face 'with Red Paint', which rendered them, as far as he was concerned, 'a very disagreeable Spectacle in the Eyes of Strangers'. Colbatch was a man of principle, and he did not flinch from condemning royal morals, for however temperate the king might have been as far as his diet and drinking habits were concerned,[6] the same could hardly be said for

> certain forbidden Pleasures, that are too much allow'd of in Portugal: in which . . . he hath indulg'd himself very much: And they say, he has not been wholly free from the Inconveniences consequent to such a Practice. I never heard, that he hath any declared Favourite of the Sex, unless it were one French-Woman [Mme Laverger]; who had that Title, for some time, at least, among the People: But those he hath this commerce with, are said to be of the lowest Rank (the French-Woman excepted), and very many, and not all of the same Colour. He hath not as yet, acknowledg'd any unlawful issue, save one Daughter, whose Mother was a mean Person.

Colbatch refers to the mother as having been 'imploy'd about the Palace, to sweep the lower Rooms', and the unfortunate child as being married off in 1695 to the eldest son of the Duke of Cadaval, 'to the great Dissatisfaction of the Nobility'. He also describes at length the sordid life of the Braganza Court during the confused reign of Dom Afonso, who had died ten years before Colbatch took up the chaplaincy, and it is thus at second hand. The tastes of the two brothers were very similar, for Colbatch had been assured that the elder was also

> guilty of many Extravagancies on account of lewd Women, as in truth, his vicious Inclinations to them were apparently the cause of most of those Disorders they lay to his Charge. He took great pleasure in walking the Streets a Nights in Company of his Braves, to haunt the Houses of lewd Women, and sometimes he would order the Prostitutes to be brought to him to the Palace; he is reported likewise to have committed several Outrages upon those

he met with in his Night-Walks; nor did he wholly abstain from those Pranks in Day-time.

By the time Colbatch was writing, perhaps because the king was influenced for the better by his new wife, a man might

> pass through the City at any time of Night, without meeting with the least Affront or Disturbance . . . except it be on such Nights, when People of all Sorts and Sexes, are let loose to visit the Churches; but those are Times of Indulgence, and they take a Liberty then to commit all manner of Wickedness.

This merely added to the burden of the sorely tried chaplain, for he found the laxity of life among the members of the Factory, and their families in general, equally intolerable: they were 'such a horrid crew' that he fancied himself in Hell while he was among them. And the scandalous relations of John Methuen with Sarah Earle, the Consul-General's young wife, was a constant source of embarrassment.

Methuen had arrived in Lisbon in the spring of 1692 as Minister at the Legation, where he was succeeded by his son Paul five years later; and between them they were responsible for negotiating the important commercial treaties of 1703.

In 1702 Portugal was drawn into the War of the Spanish Succession, which was in fact a series of campaigns taking place in several parts of Europe, dragging on for a decade. The Archduke Charles, the Habsburg claimant, disembarked at Lisbon in March 1704, and remained in Portugal until July of the following year, when he sailed for Barcelona in a fleet with the Earl of Peterborough and Sir Cloudesley Shovell. Other British squadrons under the command of Sir George Rooke and Sir John Leake had likewise made good use of the Tagus estuary on more than one occasion.

Although sporadic fighting did occur on both sides of the frontier with Spain, comparatively little took place on Portuguese soil after the accession of Dom João V.[7] It was during his long reign that Lisbon achieved its greatest material magnificence, with the discovery, exploitation and influx of Brazilian gold and diamonds; although few would dispute that too much of this wealth was lavished on the meretricious embellishment of the city's numerous churches. This had the desired effect of endowing the capital with the hollow dignity of a patriarchate within a decade of Dom João's accession.

Regardless of expense, the king also put in hand the construction of the immense convent of Mafra. Portuguese cardinals attending the conclave in Rome in 1721 were in a position to take with them no less than two crates of gold bars and over fifty dozen of gold and silver plate! Little thought was given to other than the souls of the lower orders, particularly in Lisbon, where they continued to languish in poverty. Nor had the Church any intention of relinquishing one iota of its dominance over the sovereign, who showed his submission to its authority in several curious ways. Nor were its decisions seriously challenged, even as late as 1739, when the dramatist António José da Silva was strangled and burnt at an *auto-da-fé* in Lisbon, merely being unfortunate enough to have been born of Portuguese Jewish parents in Rio da Janeiro.

Apart from other enthusiasms, Dom João was passionately addicted to music, church music in particular. For several years after 1721 Domenico Scarlatti attended the Court as music master to the Infanta Maria Barbara, Dom João's eldest child, later to marry Fernando, the heir to the Spanish throne. In 1729 Scarlatti was invited to follow her to Madrid, where he was appointed palace harpsichordist, a position he held until his death almost thirty years later: a gain for Spain, but a loss for Portugal.

Among the more flamboyant characters sent out as Envoy from England was James O'Hara, second Baron Tyrawly, who remained at Lisbon from 1728 to 1741.[8] A peppery soldier by profession, and described by Horace Walpole as being 'imperiously blunt, haughty and contemptuous, with an undaunted portion of spirit', he replaced General James Dormer, who had been recalled to London in disgrace. Dormer had become insanely jealous of Thomas Burnet, who was then Consul, more welcome at Court than himself. Taking umbrage when Burnet let it be known that he intended to give a party to celebrate the coronation of George II, Dormer had gone so far as to order his servants to beat up the Consul, who was dragged from his coach and wounded in the affray.

At a later date Tyrawly was complaining to London of the expense involved in maintaining a chapel for the British Protestants – 'such a bigoted mob' – for whom he had to provide a room at the embassy large enough to accommodate 700 people, in which weekly services might be held. The Factory at that time had possibly 100 full members. Including their families and temporary residents, as well as his own household, this figure is most probably accurate. It was essential that the community should have such a place of worship, for otherwise some might have been ensnared by those Irish friars that infested Lisbon, 'the vilest set of fellows who ever breathed'.

The irascible envoy was easily irritated, and once when excusing himself to the Duke of Newcastle in London, remarked that 'between the Portuguese and our fellow-subjects here, I have had so many occasions to try my patience that I have, I hope, picked up an inexhaustible fund'.

One of his non-diplomatic duties was to provide advice on the rare plants which were becoming known in Portugal, and which might be cultivated in King George II's own kitchen-garden. In a dispatch of June 1733 he writes:

> I don't know that I have any other vegetables worth sending you except tomatoes, which is a large round fruit, as big as a small orange (of which I believe you have none in England). It is not to be eaten by itself, yet comes within your rule of having nothing but belly timber.

During several months of 1735 Sir John Norris's fleet was based in Lisbon, where his vessels were being careened under the supervision of William Warden, who then held the important post of dock-master and naval architect to Dom João. Unfortunately Tyrawly and Norris were at loggerheads, and frequently the Envoy had reason to complain of the high-handed attitude of British naval captains and their indiscretions, particularly when indulging in the export of contraband gold, which was likely to exacerbate further what was already a delicate political situation.

In that same year Charles Mordaunt, the third Earl of Peterborough, who had fought so gallantly in several campaigns during the War of the Succession, sailed to Lisbon seeking to recover his health (he had been operated on for stone not long before), but he survived there a week only.

Sir Benjamin Keene,[9] when proceeding to England from Spain in 1739, had set sail from Lisbon, and was evidently attracted by the place. He returned there as Minister Plenipotentiary in September 1746, where he remained until early in 1749, being succeeded by Abraham Castres. Keene seems to have rather enjoyed the company of what he called the 'jolly free factory', but then he was more convivial – and more chaste – than his predecessor, even if Tyrawly did mellow later.

Although at first critical of Dom João, Tyrawly had come to admire him, and the feeling must have been mutual, perhaps

because they had susceptibilities in common. In recognition of his
plenipotentiary services, João presented him on his departure for
England with fourteen bars of gold. Tyrawly apparently embarked
accompanied by three 'wives', one a Portuguese, Dona Anna, 'with
long black hair down to the bottom of her back', and no less than
fourteen illegitimate children.[10] No wonder Horace Walpole considered him 'singularly licentious, even for the courts of Russia and
Portugal'.

Tyrawly may have had his weaknesses, but he was certainly no
fool. He had many years of experience of Portuguese affairs, and was
intimately acquainted with the foibles of members of the Factory,
several of whom he considered had treated him with 'disrespect and
rudeness'. For his part, he had no compunction in pronouncing the
majority of them 'a parcel of the greatest Jackasses I ever met with,
Fops, Beaux, Drunkards, Gamesters, and prodigiously ignorant,
even of their own business'.

In another of his memoranda Tyrawly censured their relations
with the Customs authorities. When discussing mutual problems
with the Provedor d'Alfândega, the latter had remarked that the
members of the Factory

> were a set of Casquilos (Petits Maîtres) that attended more to their
> Quintas, Balls, Masquerades & Gaming than to their business;
> that scarce one of them would give himself the trouble of going to
> the Custom House to dispatch their own goods, but left it to their
> Caixeiros (Book-keepers) who were all Portuguese Trapasseiros
> (Pettyfoggers) and the greatest Rogues in the Country, and that
> there was neither Regularity or Fair dealing scarcely to be met with
> in our Factory. I did ask some of them (Merchants) why they did
> not goe to the Custom House to clear out their goods themselves
> as I had known all their Predecessors in the Trade constantly doe. I
> was answered that it was so dirty and mobbish a place that no
> Gentleman could set his foot into it.

At Newcastle's request Tyrawly returned to Lisbon in April 1752
with Abraham Castres to look into what had been exaggerated complaints on the part of 'a great body of His Majesty's subjects, rich,
opulent, and every day improving their fortunes and enlarging their
dealings'. David King, a member of the Factory committee, was
referred to in a querulous letter by William Mawman addressed to
Tyrawly, stating that 'whilst ye Sherlys, Burrells, King & Hake are of

ye number I expect no good from ye Committee'. Mawman wisely added a postscript: 'I beg your Lordship to keep this letter to yourself, being unwilling to bring on my head this nest of Waspes'. No doubt it was William Shirley, the dramatist turned merchant, to whom he was referring, the same who had been involved in a dispute with Consul George Crowe. Poor Crowe, who was then recalled to London, died of apoplexy before leaving Lisbon.

At about this time Lisbon was getting a reputation for its fine climate, but few of the valetudinarians hoping for a fresh lease of life there were very fortunate. Sir Thomas Browne's warning: 'He that is tabidly inclined, were unwise to pass his days in Portugal', was disregarded. Philip Doddridge, the guest in 1751 of the aforementioned David King, died only a fortnight after his arrival. Nor did Henry Fielding, the ailing author of *Tom Jones*, having disembarked there in August 1754, last much longer, leaving his *Journal of a Voyage to Lisbon* uncompleted.

During April of that year the vessel in which the Revd George Whitefield was sailing to America, put in there with a cargo, happily allowing him to spend some days methodically in search of examples of 'superstitious pageantry', which he described in several letters home. These were later published in a tract entitled *A brief account of some Lent and other Extraordinary Processions and Ecclesiastical Entertainments seen last year at Lisbon*.

NOTES

1. As described in *De Expugnatione Lyxbonensi: The Conquest of Lisbon* (New York, 1936), edited and translated by Charles Wendell David. Its authorship is discussed by Harold Livermore in Vol. 6 of *Portuguese Studies*, published by the Modern Humanities Research Association and edited by the Department of Portuguese, King's College, London.
2. This was an early medieval Spanish word for swine, probably used ironically with reference to their aversion to pork.
3. First issued in 1829–30, but the edition of 1907 is more scholarly. Lady Fanshawe's *Memoirs* were reprinted, together with those of Anne, Lady Halkett, in 1979. In 1681 Charles, fourth Viscount Fanshawe, a cousin of Richard's, had the difficult task of extracting from Portugal the balance of Queen Catherine's promised dowry.
4. Geddes (?1650–1713) was the author of several volumes of *Miscellaneous Tracts*, including *A View of the Inquisition in Portugal*, later published in London.

5. John Colbatch (1664–1748) later in his life fell foul of the formidable Dr Richard Bentley of Trinity College, Cambridge.

6. Alcohol was anathema to Dom Pedro, and anyone he suspected of drinking wine would be banished from Court. In general, the Portuguese were abstemious in this respect, and abhorred drunkenness; and to call a man an 'English sot' was one of the worst insults they might hurl in anger. However, the king paid dearly for his other excesses, probably having contracted a venereal infection as early as 1670. His palate was so damaged towards the end of his life that he required an interpreter when speaking to strangers, and even those with whom he was on familiar terms found it difficult to understand him. In January 1705 he had a stroke, although he survived for another twelve months.

7. I do not intend to get drawn into writing a narrative of the war. Many aspects of the complex subject have been well covered by Henry Kamen, David Francis and J.A.C. Hugill (see Bibliography).

8. James Tyrawly, or Tyrawley (1690–1773), succeeded his father Sir Charles O'Hara, first Baron Tyrawly (?1640–1724), who had also fought with distinction during the War of the Succession, being at one time Galway's second-in-command in Spain. From 1743 to 1745 he was Ambassador to Russia. In 1752–6 he was governor of Minorca, and in 1756–7 of Gibraltar. Charles, his son (?1740–1802), also saw service in Portugal, and later in America, being captured at Yorktown in 1781, and again, by the French at Toulon in 1793. From 1795 until his death he was also governor of Gibraltar.

9. Born in 1697, Keene was Ambassador at Madrid in 1727 to 1739 and again from 1748 until his death in 1757.

Castres had been Consul-General at Lisbon since 1742. He too died in 1757, and was in turn succeeded as Envoy by Edward Hay. There are numerous references to members of the Factory in Keene's letters written from Madrid to Castres during this period (see Bibliography).

10. One of these children, by a Miss Seal, was later to become acquainted with David Garrick and, as George Anne Bellamy, in 1750 played Juliet to Garrick's Romeo in rivalry with Barry and Mrs Cibber. It is a coincidence that in the 1730s young Garrick was also in Lisbon, working for his uncle David Clough, a wine exporter.

5

Lisbon after 1755

On the morning of 1 November 1755, Lisbon was shaken to its foundations by an unprecedented earthquake, followed by a series of tremors, a ravaging fire and a tidal wave which submerged the quays and overwhelmed the shipping. Joseph Baretti, in describing the devastated part of Lisbon almost five years later, which even then left 'a dreadful indelible image' on his mind, stated that nothing was to be seen 'but vast heaps of rubbish, out of which arise in numberless places the miserable remains of shattered walls and broken pillars'.

The catastrophic state in which its citizens found themselves was alleviated by the presence of mind of the Marquês de Pombal,[1] the only able minister, who ordered several vigorous measures to be taken without any delay. Certainly his name – dovecot in English – belied him. He insisted that there must be no further talk of Dom José decamping to Rio da Janeiro, which had been mooted. Any such move would have a disastrous effect on morale: the king and his Court would remain under canvas in their palace garden at Belém.

The tottering ruins of any houses left standing in the lower town were razed. Military patrols were posted in and around the capital in an attempt to prevent looting. Not much was saved from the wreckage: the losses were incalculable. Fine libraries, including Dom João IV's invaluable collection of music, had been consumed in the conflagration, together with irreplaceable works of art. Wardrobes were scattered; indeed, many survived only in the clothes they were wearing; some less, for they had not yet dressed for Mass on that All Saints' Day.

The British Parliament, on hearing of the disaster, immediately voted £50,000 as an earnest of their solicitude, and sent out quantities of food, supplies and equipment, including pick-axes, crowbars, spades, etcetera; but bad weather held up the convoy.

It has been estimated that of the entire population of 270,000, some five per cent perished. Of the British subjects in Lisbon, there were some seventy-eight dead, including forty-nine women (those of note being the wife of Christopher Hake senior and Mrs Perochon), and about sixty missing 'of the poorer sort', largely Catholics, who were at that time still excluded from membership of the Factory, and were referred to as 'so obscure as not to be known to any but the Irish friars'. It is difficult to establish exactly how large the British community was at the time: it may well have been over 2,000, but the number of religious and other Catholics who had settled there to avoid the recusancy laws is uncertain. Another list comprises 155 men with business interests, thirteen widows associated with commercial houses, fifteen persons unconnected but nevertheless 'worthy of every consideration'; 165 who were in some way connected with shops, eating-houses, inns, etc., and, in addition, there were carpenters, tailors, cobblers, barbers, writing teachers, seamen and accountants, not forgetting a mustard-maker.

While awaiting their passage to England, the homeless took shelter in the garden of Abraham Castres' residence of 'Santa Martha', which stood in the district of Buenos Ayres. Castres, then in charge at the embassy, and who had escaped by jumping from a second floor window, together with the Honourable Edward Hay, the Consul, did everything in their power to assist the community, as did Mr Williamson the Chaplain, and Doctor Cantley. It took some time to assess the magnitude of the destruction. Many who survived were in a sorry state of shock and confusion, and plans were made to repatriate some 300 who were entirely destitute.

'Our poor Factory, from a very opulent one, is totally ruined, at least for the major part', had been Castres' verdict. However, although much property was lost, at least some was saved. Far more serious losses were caused by the Factory's inability to collect debts from the Portuguese traders, who all pleaded ruin. Tyrawly, reporting in a long memorandum to the British Government after the calamity, stated that he believed 'the affairs of Portugal were seldom thought of but when some Point very grievious to the Merchants Engaged our attention to it'. He continued that, from his knowledge and experience of the country, and particularly during his recent visit to it, he 'was thoroughly persuaded that our trade there was running headlong to its ruin, notwithstanding its prosperous outward appearance'. He had found the Factory totally changed

from the respectable, regular & frugal Merchants I had seen there when I was employed before in that Country, and the business in the hands of men of very different character. Our Merchants were become Universal Traders more than English Factors, and many houses there dealt More or at least as Much in French Goods, Hamburg Linnen, Sicilian Corn, or other commodities from different countries than in the Produce of their own.

In March 1762 Tyrawly disembarked at Lisbon once again, this time, in spite of his seventy years, having been asked to command Portuguese troops massing on the frontier in expectation of another Spanish invasion, for Portugal was being drawn into the Seven Years' War between Spain and France, and England. But it was not long before he was succeeded by Count Wilhelm von Schaumburg-Lippe.[2] Among other officers at the front were Prince Charles of Mecklenberg-Strelitz, the Earl of Loudon, John Burgoyne (dramatist and general), and Tyrawly's son Charles O'Hara. John Hunter, later to become a celebrated surgeon, was superintending hospitals at Lisbon, Santarém, and Coimbra. By November a truce had been declared.

Richard Twiss (1747–1821),[3] visiting Lisbon in 1772, was surprised to find that the streets were still 'in many places stopped up by the ruins', which recalled the similar condition – 'caused by war and fire' – in which he had seen the city of Dresden. Yet members of the Factory appeared to have recovered their fortunes to a large extent. An Assembly was held twice a week during the winter, to dance and play at cards, where Mrs May performed on the harpsichord with 'delicacy and taste'. Twiss noted with approval that 'any British stranger who does not intend to reside six months in Lisbon is admitted gratis to these assemblies', held in two long rooms (and since his departure a very large room had been built for the purpose, so he heard). Their attentiveness to visitors is corroborated by Richard Croker, who when passing through Lisbon a few years later, remarked that the expatriate community lived 'in a very sociable and pleasant manner', and were 'particularly civil and hospitable'.

Twiss appears to have spent much of his time merely sauntering around the city. The apparent lack of any town plan did not seem to worry him as it did Baretti, who was surprised – 'considering its extent', and being 'the great resort of strangers' – that no one had thought of making one, but then Pombal's project for the rebuilding of the lower town or Bairro Baixa was only just being put into effect. On one of his excursions, Twiss was astonished to see two men

seated on the pavement, each of them with a large baboon on his
shoulders dextrously searching their hair for vermin. Apparently
these apes were the property of a man who gained his livelihood by
thus employing them, and it was quite common to see people 'sitting in the sun, with their heads in each other's laps alternately,
having their "retinue abridged" '. The lower orders, especially the
women, were lousy, having enormous quantities of hair. But lice
were no respecters of persons; another traveller 'saw the sister of the
bishop and of the governor of Oporto, a charming young widow of
an ancient noble family, in an afternoon, before her door, laying
her head in the lap of her waiting women to be loused . . .'.

Wandering around at night alone was still hazardous, the streets
being unlit; only a few days after Twiss had arrived, an imprudent
Italian had been murdered and robbed among the ruins. Assassination continued to be commonplace, according to Professor Link,
whose description of Lisbon at the close of the century is accurate, if not very flattering. What first struck the foreigner on
entering the capital was the filth lying everywhere in noisome heaps,
which

> in the narrow streets where the rain does not wash it away, require
> great skill in walking, to avoid sinking into them. In one of the
> most frequented streets on the river leading to the Ribera nova,
> there is only a narrow path winding near the houses . . . while the
> carts pass as near to the houses as possible, that the horses may not
> go in the deepest part of the mud; and thus all the dirt and filth
> is blindly splashed upon the passengers, in the worst manner
> conceivable.
>
> As to the night, the city was formerly lighted, but now this
> practice has ceased; and, as window-shutters are shut early, there
> is no light to diminish the darkness of these dirty, narrow, ill-
> paved streets. A host of dogs without masters, and living on the
> public, wander about like hungry wolves; and, still worse than
> these, an army of banditti . . .'.[4]

In many parts of Lisbon the streets were so steep that it was quite a
labour to ascend them, while during the heavy rains 'the water
rushes down . . . with such violence that they are often impassable
. . . Instances have occurred of men and horses being carried away
by the torrent and almost precipitated into the river'.

Among other English travellers visiting or resident in Lisbon during the 1770s, several of whom left accounts of their time there, were Major William Dalrymple, Nathaniel Wraxall, William Julius Mickle (whose translation of Camoens' *The Lusiad* was published in 1776), Major James Ferrier, who, under the pseudonym of Arthur Costigan, was the author of *Sketches of Society and Manners in Portugal*, and Richard Cumberland, the dramatist, then engaged in abortive diplomatic negotiations with Spain.

William Hickey, living in Lisbon in 1782, refers in his diaries to the Irish artist Thomas Hickey – not related to him – who had arrived in distressed circumstances, the ship in which he had been sailing to India having been captured by an enemy vessel. On his release he made his way there, where providentially he received numerous commissions to paint the portraits of the Portuguese nobility and members of the British community; indeed this kept him so well occupied that it was not until 1784 that he decided to embark again for Calcutta, his original destination.

In 1787 William Beckford, England's notorious 'wealthiest son', reached Lisbon, where he was befriended by the Marquês de Marialva, but *not* received by the Honourable Robert Walpole, Envoy there since 1772, and Horace Walpole's cousin. Both Walpole's wives had been daughters of Factory merchants, and many of these duly ostracized Beckford. Venting his spleen on the Envoy, Beckford damned him as a 'blundering puppy' from whom he had received 'abominable usage'. Beckford could well afford to ignore the lot of them, although he still hankered to be presented formally at Court, which he never was on any of the three occasions he visited Lisbon.[5] Meanwhile, he made his self-imposed exile more tolerable by renting a *quinta*.

Less affluent English visitors would put up at either Reeves Hotel in the Rua do Prior, or at Mrs Williams' or Mrs Duer's house. It was probably the latter which was described by Twiss as an 'English inn, kept by one De War, on the hill of Buenos Ayres, where there is an ordinary every day, frequented by Englishmen, who reside in Lisbon for their health, and by members of the factory'. Baretti, in 1760, stayed at a kind of inn kept by a Mr Kelly, an elderly Irishman, in a house rebuilt since the earthquake, standing on the summit of the same hill, and this may have been acquired by De War. In 1786 Walpole refers to a tavern-keeper named Dwyer – presumably the same person or a member of the same family – who had gone to London 'to seduce from England cotton manufacturers for this country'.

During the next few years Lisbon was visited by such disparate travellers as Mary Woolstonecraft, only briefly there in the autumn of 1785, having sailed out to nurse a female friend who died before she arrived; and by Lady Craven, openly accompanying the Margrave of Anspach, which must have deeply shocked the smug British community. In 1792 Dr Francis Willis, having treated George III, was summoned to Portugal to attend the melancholy Dona Maria I, whose mental condition had continued to deteriorate. In fact, by then the queen was incurably insane, although she did not die until 1816.[6]

Robert Southey spent five months of 1796 in Lisbon, where his uncle the Revd Herbert Hill was chaplain.[7] The priggish young poet proceeded to carp at the expatriate congregation, condemning them as 'the most indefatigable dancers and the most inveterate casino-players in Europe' – not that he had yet been elsewhere on the Continent, apart from crossing Spain.

In that December Sir John Jervis's squadron entered the Tagus, only a few weeks later sailing out to defeat a Spanish fleet off Cape St Vincent.

On his second visit, in 1801, Southey, accompanied by his wife Edith, sailed direct from Falmouth to Lisbon.[8] Together with Samuel Waterhouse, he made the excursion to Coimbra and Tomar, and later the rougher cross-country expedition to the Algarve; but much of his time was spent writing. Although he had the run of his uncle's library, Southey was also eagerly buying books from Jorge Bertrand's shop – Bertrand, in his opinion, being 'the only civil and reasonable man in the trade'. He was less critical now of the British community, having struck up a friendship with John Bell, a senior member of the Factory; and it was on the Factory's behalf he vented his disapproval of John Hookham Frere, who had succeeded Robert Walpole as Envoy. Frere was acting foolishly in his opinion, for with Charles Arbuthnot, the Consul, he was 'establishing a little aristocracy with the quality-strangers, emigrants, and corps diplomatic', and thus slighting the English merchants.

From 1802 the Secretary to the Legation was Byron's 'Hibernian Strangford', the 6th Viscount, and author of insipid but popular translations of Camoens.[9] John Adamson, whose study of Camoens was not published until 1820, was living in Lisbon from 1803 to 1807. Among others were Francesco Bartolozzi, director of the National Academy from 1802 until his death in 1815; while during the first three months of 1805 Lord and Lady Holland were resident there, while the latter was recovering from an illness.

In that October the news of Nelson's victory at Trafalgar was celebrated on the Tagus by British ships firing salvos all night.

French troops crossed into Spain exactly two years later; and another six were to pass before the Allies thrust them out again. Several of the battles of this long drawn out and sanguinary 'Peninsular War' were fought on Portuguese soil, and have been described in their place.

Lisbon itself was occupied by General Junot's troops from December 1807 until some nine months later, when they were repatriated in accordance with the terms of the Convention of Cintra. These terms had caused such an uproar that its signatories, including Wellington, had been recalled to London to face inter-rogation by the Board of Enquiry convened under the presidency of Sir David Dundas, which sat from mid-November until just before Christmas.

Meanwhile, Sir John Moore had been appointed Commander-in-Chief of British forces in Portugal. By mid-October those regiments encamped in the vicinity of Lisbon were on the move north-east to act in concert with allied forces in Spain. It had not been so easy to get them moving, as increasing numbers had reported sick. But neither was Moore easily fooled, and in a General Order gave his opinion that it was 'owing to their own intemperance that so many . . . are rendered incapable of marching against the Enemy'; having stated this, he felt confident that he need say no more to ensure their sobriety. He was less successful when attempting to dissuade the soldiers' wives from joining what was expected to be a long and hazardous march. Many of them had infants in arms and more at heel, and some were far advanced in pregnancy.

Anstruther, at Almeida, had written to warn him: 'There is hardly a road in Portugal in which there are not some very bad steps; these are generally in or near villages, of which the streets are almost universally narrow, rocky, and full of short turns impracticable for carriages of any sort . . .'. This proved only too true, and within days of setting off from Lisbon Moore was protesting to Lord William Bentick about the lamentable situation in which he had been placed:

information respecting roads should have been got, and arrange-ments for supplies should have been made, before the troops began to march. But when I got the command, nothing of the sort had been done. They talked of going into Spain as going into Hyde Park . . .

Within three months of the news of Moore's death at La Coruña reaching London, Wellington had set sail for Lisbon, where Sir John Caradoc (or Cradock; first Baron Howden) had meanwhile concentrated most of the troops at his disposal.

Within thirty-six hours of disembarking (on 22 April), Wellington was in the saddle, leading north the army which was to evict Soult from Oporto.

In that January the Hollands were again briefly in Lisbon. Not surprisingly, Lady Holland found the town 'full as dirty as formerly. The houses bear evident marks of decay from being shut up, neglected, and uninhabited'. And partly because the defensive forts on the Tagus were being dismantled, there was also 'Great alarm among the merchants, many of whom are already dispatching their property on board of ships'; while it was suspected that any number of French spies were skulking about 'under the disguise of friars and priests'.

The Hollands, returning from Spain via Evora and Setúbal, crossed the estuary to Belém on 13 July, sailing for home on the 17th. Their paths almost crossed that of Lord Byron and John Hobhouse, *en route* to Greece, who on 12 July were already on their excursion to Sintra and Mafra. During his brief stay in the capital, which did not appeal to him, Byron also chose to swim the width of the Tagus before departing for the frontier (on the 21st, according to Hobhouse).

Less than a fortnight earlier, after concentrating his forces at Abrantes, Wellington had marched into Spain, where on 28 July took place the battle of Talavera.

In October 1810, having checked Masséna at Busaco, Wellington retired with his Anglo-Portuguese forces behind the previously constructed defensive Lines of Torres Vedras. Thus protected, Lisbon never experienced the physical destruction that so many other towns in Portugal were to suffer from the French, nor was it ever again so close to the front, although, until the closing stages of the war, it continued to be used as the main port of supply, and the base of army contractors.

It was also the occasional retreat of officers on leave, who might there indulge in the most dissolute distractions; and also of convalescents. Any who stayed too long or showed insufficient eagerness to return to their regiments were nicknamed 'Belemites', for the main cavalry depot and several other barracks were situated in the suburb of Belém, apart from Barnes's hotel and La Tour's. Writing from Belém in September 1811, Captain William Bragge was surprised to see Portuguese men and women bathing together, and remarked that 'watching them is considered a high compliment'. Nevertheless, one should keep one's eyes open: he had been cautioned 'against leaving a Single Article without a Guard as the Natives of the Country make no Bones of marching out of a Stable with Arms, Accoutrements or any Thing else belonging to the English . . .'.

Elaborate instructions had been laid down regarding the proper behaviour of both officers and men when in Lisbon, where General Peacocke was Commandant. According to Commissary Schaumann, as he was 'incapable of taking command in the field, [he] had been specially sent here by Lord Wellington, who knew his eccentric and harsh character, in order, by means of every kind of interference, to make the life of English officers in Lisbon as difficult and unhappy as possible'. Wellington, who remained at the front, was intolerant of officers requesting leave to visit the capital; and it is recorded that he once remarked that if so-and-so wanted to go to Lisbon, 'I have told him that he may stay there forty-eight hours, which is as long as any reasonable man can wish to stay in bed with the same woman'. Two of his generals were killed by falling from balconies in Lisbon, but there was some doubt as to whether it was cowardice or some other disgrace, or merely inebriation, which caused them to end their lives in this way.[10]

There was 'a very excellent coffee-room in the Largo de São Paulo' (probably at Lahmeyer's Hotel), while the most fashionable gambling-house was kept by a dignitary of the Church. Or one might attend the São Carlos opera-house, where there were 'a number of pretty ballet dancers in amazingly short skirts, all of whom were kept by various notabilities in the city', according to Schaumann, who confided that 'As soon as the ballet was over we would visit certain houses, of which there were plenty in those days, where girls both young and pretty were to be found'.

It was to take many years for Portugal to recover from the ravages of war. The subsequent history of Lisbon was punctuated by several disturbances, some more violent than others, such as the vigorously suppressed Liberal conspiracy of March 1817, led by General Gomes

Freire, who was executed for his involvement. This did not enhance
the waning popularity of Marshal Beresford, who nevertheless
remained Commander-in-chief of the Portuguese army he had so
successfully trained.[11]

In that same year Lisbon was visited by Henry Matthews, whose
Diary of an Invalid was published in 1820. But while some
valetudinarians may have found their health improved by a residence there, certainly any reader of the Revd Kinsey's unreliable
impressions would have given it a wide berth, for he suggested that
among the principal disorders of the physical constitution for which
Lisbon might be held responsible, were 'apoplexy, paralysis,
derangement of the digestive system, malignant catarrhal affec-
tions, liver complaints, acute rheumatism, colds, and constipaçoes,
or inflammations in the bowels'.

When in March 1821 Lisbon was illuminated to celebrate the
passage of a draft political constitution, the Papal Nuncio's window
there was stoned and shattered, merely for remaining unlit.
Although Constitutionalism had come to stay, the city was frequently the scene of unrest, from the time some of its garrison had
deserted to the cause of the revolutionary party of Dom Miguel in
May 1823 until the final defeat of the Miguelites in 1834.

In August 1827 Lord Porchester disembarked at Lisbon at the
start of his exploration of Portugal, which was to occupy him for
several months. His itinerary is outlined to give some idea of the
extent of one visitor's exploration of the country at this period. His
first tour took him to Mafra, Torres Vedras, Obidos, Alcobaça, and
Batalha (this was before Beckford's description had been published), and on through Coimbra – with, naturally, a detour to
the ridge of Busaco – to Oporto, where he met Mr Waterhouse
(presumably Southey's old friend), John Crispin the Consul, Mr
Kingston his banker, and Edward Whiteley the chaplain. An excursion was made to Amarante, Vila Real, and Lamego, returning by
the Douro to Oporto.

Porchester continued his journey via Barcelos and Ponte de Lima,
before skirting the coast and crossing into Galicia, where, accused of
spying, he was briefly imprisoned. On his release, he made his way
back to Oporto via Braga and Guimarães, and then took ship to
Lisbon.

Riding south to the Algarve, his route led from Setúbal
to Monchique and Lagos, from which he visited Sagres and Cape
St Vincent before turning east through Silves, Faro, and Tavira.

Finding sequestered Mértola in a ferment of revolt, he hurried on through Beja to Evora, where he was again incarcerated briefly, which probably saved him from lynching by a reactionary Miguelite mob.

In November 1835 George Borrow landed at Lisbon, on the first stage of his Peninsular perambulations, which were to continue intermittently for the next four and a half years, only a few weeks of which were spent in Portugal.

In 1846 Thackeray briefly berthed at Lisbon, *en route* from Cornhill to Cairo on a Peninsular and Oriental steamship.

In 1853 John Mason Neale, compiler of Murray's *Handbook for Travellers in Portugal*, was quartering Lisbon. He refers to a certain Mr Smith, the British Consul at the time, who might be found at his office on the Caes do Sodre, while the Vice-Consul, Mr Meagher, was in the Rua Nova de São Caetano. 'From the latter gentleman every kind of courtesy will be experienced', was Neale's succinct comment, which left his readers in little doubt as to what to expect from the former functionary.[12]

He refers to the fact that the Inglesinhos had produced a guide to Lisbon, 'an interesting little work', which might supplement his own description of the city, as would an *Itinerario Lisbonense*, and recommended the map produced by the Society for the Diffusion of Useful Knowledge. At least, he assured the intending tourist:

> The dirt, the beggars, and the dogs which the descriptions of travellers have led the stranger to expect, are gone . . . and the visitor can enjoy his solitary ramble either on the quays or in the town, not only without danger from robbers, but also without being exposed to those importunities to which he would be liable under similar circumstances in our own metropolis.

Perhaps the Revd Neale closed his eyes to these natural hazards?

They are now, 140 years later, no more prevalent than one might expect in certain purlieus of a port and capital, but it would be foolish to assume that the visitor, whether on his solitary ramble or otherwise, is entirely secure, and one should take natural precautions. Having been forewarned, let us start our own exploration of Lisbon.

NOTES

1. Sebastião José de Carvalho e Mello (1699–1782), returning to Lisbon from a diplomatic mission to Vienna, having previously held the post of Minister Plenipotentiary in London, soon became a dominant figure in Portuguese politics. He was created Conde de Oeiras in 1759 and Marquês de Pombal in 1777. On the death of Dom José he was disgraced, and retired to the town from which he took his title.

2. See Chapter 1.

3. Author of *Travels through Portugal and Spain* (1775), *A Tour in Ireland in 1775* (1776) – which made him so unpopular there that his portrait was painted on the interior of Dublin chamber-pots – *A Trip to Paris* (1792), and a book on chess.

4. During the French occupation some years later, Junot ordered the destruction of all stray dogs, which caused protestations, as they were considered useful as scavengers.

5. He returned there in 1794 and 1799.

6. See Queluz.

7. Herbert Hill (1749–1828) had been chaplain at Oporto from 1778, and moved to Lisbon in 1782. He remained there until 1807, before retiring to England, where he married late but happily. In addition to his normal duties, he had acted as chaplain to the force of British troops stationed in Portugal from 1797 to 1800 under the command of Major-General Simon Fraser.

8. The Falmouth-Lisbon packet had been established as early as 1702.

9. Henry Brougham, when secretary to a British mission to Portugal in 1806, reported home that Strangford was 'too flighty and uncertain in his movements to gain my confidence . . . My temper has been tried perpetually by his infinite childishness in doing business, and indeed in doing anything else . . . there is a defect about him which I can still less pardon than his want of commonsense. I mean his *total want* of that first-rate quality which gives a man's word the right to be believed'. In November 1807 Strangford had followed the Court to Brazil, when in the face of General Junot's army, it had hurriedly embarked for its long exile in Rio, escorted by Sir Sidney Smith's squadron.

10. Sir William Erskine committed suicide here in April 1813.

11. There is a good chapter on Beresford in Rose Macaulay's *They Went to Portugal, Too* (see Bibliography).

12. William Smith was consul there from 1834 until his death in 1865.

6

Lisbon: the Bairro Baixa

Several roads converge on the Rotunda or Praça Marquês de Pombal, a busy roundabout dominated by a statue of that dynamic if dictatorial statesman, from which the wide Avenida da Liberdad, a garden-flanked but otherwise undistinguished thoroughfare, descends a gentle slope to approach the Bairro Baixa.

Beyond the lower end of this street extends the Rossío, a large rectangular square officially known as the Praça de Dom Pedro IV, for in its centre stands a statue of that king. It was cast at Marseilles to represent Maximilian of Mexico, but by the time the ship transporting it to Mexico had put in at Lisbon, news had arrived of his assassination. A deal was made by the authorities concerned who, after affecting a few cosmetic changes, were able to congratulate themselves on having acquired a royal statue on the cheap.

The undulating pattern of the tesselated pavement of white limestone and black basalt, both materials being readily available in the vicinity of Lisbon, caused it to be named 'Rolling Motion Square' by the English, and also, at one time, 'Turkey Square', after the birds (although known as *peru* in Portuguese) formerly displayed for sale there. These characteristic pavements are said to have been invented early in the nineteenth century by the engineer Pinheiro Furtado. They must have been a distinct improvement on the former surface of the streets, described by Richard Twiss several decades earlier as 'very badly paved with small sharp stones, which renders walking almost impracticable'. And yet one is still not surprised to see so many shoe shops in the city.

The Rossío was once the scene of public executions, *autos-da-fé*, bull-fights, carnivals, and what not; but its café-lined pavements are now largely occupied by loungers sunning themselves, particularly on its west side, which provides a good view of the castle of São Jorge dominating the former Mouraria, or Moorish quarter.

To the north is the restored Teatro Nacional, partly built on the

51

site of a mid-fifteenth-century palace, later occupied by the Inquisition, whose victims heard their sentences read in adjacent São Domingos, in which Fray Luis de Granada (whose *Guide for Sinners* was first published in Lisbon in 1556) is buried. The church, largely rebuilt after 1755 and re-roofed after being gutted by fire several decades ago, is still impressive in its half-calcined state. It was near this seat of the Holy Office that in 1492 the Portuguese Jews, preferring exile to forcible conversion, assembled prior to their expulsion.

Close by, in the Paço dos Condes de Almada, took place the conspiratorial meetings of the 'Restauradores' in 1640 before the overthrow of the Spanish establishment and proclamation of Portuguese independence after sixty years of occupation.

Immediately south of the Rossío is an area known as the Baixa or lower town, laid out on a grid pattern after the earthquake under the aegis of Pombal. Manuel da Maia (assisted by Elias Sebastian Pope, an Englishman) and Eugénio dos Santos de Carvalho, were primarily responsible for the rebuilding, until succeeded in 1760 by Charles Mardell. Carlos Mardel, as he later signed himself, and who was probably of Hungarian origin, arrived at Lisbon in 1733 and died there in 1763.

The Rua Augusta, the principal street of the Baixa, leading directly to a triumphal arch, is flanked by the Ruas do Ouro and da Prata, formerly allotted to the gold- and silversmiths of Lisbon. According to one earlier traveller, they frequently worked on the ground floor close to their doors, and made 'a most intolerable noise'.

It was here late in 1836 that George Borrow found himself among a group of men whose appearance suggested they were neither Portuguese nor European: indeed, they were the Jews of Lisbon, to whom he introduced himself by pronouncing a *beraka* or blessing, and was welcomed immediately as 'a powerful rabbi'. Capitalizing on their mistake, Borrow was able within a few days to know 'all that related to them . . . in Lisbon'. But disillusioned, he chose to describe the community in those paragraphs excised from some later editions of *The Bible in Spain*, as likely to give offence, as 'a vile, infamous rabble, about two hundred in number', who 'principally depend for their livelihood on an extensive traffic in stolen goods'; and, although it was said that there is honour amongst thieves, in his opinion, this was 'certainly not the case with the Jews of Lisbon'.

Near the upper end of the Rua do Ouro is the incongruous

Elevador, a passenger lift designed by Gustave Eiffel, which ascends directly to the Carmo (see Chapter 8).

All three streets debouch on to the Terreiro do Paço or Black Horse Square, as it is invariably called by the English, after the equestrian statue by Machado de Castro which embellishes it, erected to commemorate the generosity of Dom José to the victims of the Great Earthquake. The west side of the square was the emplacement of the royal palace, which was entirely burnt out in that catastrophe. Although it is said that some of the melted silver plate was recovered from the calcined ruin, its more valuable library, including rare musical manuscripts, was reduced to ashes.

Flanked on three sides by ranges of arcaded buildings in the 'Pombaline style', the square is best seen from the water-lapped quay; but although imposing in extent, many would agree with Sacheverell Sitwell that it does not deserve the encomiums that have been lavished upon it: certainly not since it has been used as a parking lot.

In the past, most travellers arriving either by sea, from Cacilhas on the far shore of the estuary, or from Aldeia Galega (re-named Montijo, and where the Madrid road ended), would have stepped ashore here from their launches and ferries. And it was from here too, on 23 April 1662, that young Catherine of Braganza and her suite embarked with all pomp on the *Royal Charles*, bound for Portsmouth and marriage to Charles II.[1]

It was in the estuary here – familiarly referred to as 'Jackass Bay' by the ribald English mariners – that Sir John Jervis's squadron cast anchor in December 1796, which did much to revive England's languishing prestige, further stimulated by his defeat a few weeks later of a larger Spanish fleet off Cape St Vincent.

It was from here, late in November 1807, that Dom João VI, escorted by Sir Sidney Smith's squadron, set sail for Brazil on the approach of Junot's army, the advance guard of which entered Lisbon only hours later. It has been estimated that between eight and fifteen thousand people embarked, the convoy weighing anchor with treasure worth 80,000,000 *crusados* and half the money in circulation, amid cries of 'Death to the Prince, who abandons us' from the menacing Lisbon mob.

Only nine months later, the populace were execrating the embarkation of Junot's troops – 24,000 men – who, after their defeat at Vimeiro, were being escorted back to La Rochelle in British transports, as agreed by the disgraceful terms of the Convention of Cintra, by which they were allowed to take with them their 'personal property'. In the event, this meant most of their spoil, even if Adam Neale, Physician to His Majesty's Forces, who was there at the time, was of the opinion that although the Portuguese raised a great outcry, 'the clamour was groundless'.

They certainly did attempt to smuggle many valuable articles of plunder on board; but so great has been the vigilance of General Beresford and Lord Proby, that they have in a great measure been foiled in their attempts, and forced to relinquish their booty, which has been placed in the public stores, till claimed by the individuals from whom it was cruelly wrested.

Nevertheless, they

contrived one mode of eluding the British vigilance: it is the active employment of two mints, in which they have converted a large quantity of church-plate into French crowns and Napoleon d'ors. All this specie they are permitted, by the construction of the articles of the convention, to carry off to France. You will allow that this piece of Gallic finesse has been rarely surpassed.

The Rua Alfândega leads past the splendid Manueline portal of Nossa Senhora da Conceição Velha, built on the site of a synagogue, to approach the so-called Casa dos Bicos, named after its conspicuous façade of diamond-shaped bosses. This sixteenth-century residence of the Albuquerque family was restored a decade ago, when the two upper floors, with their balustraded windows and balconies, were entirely reconstructed, following the design depicted in early engravings and *azulejo* panoramas of Lisbon.

On the hill behind rears the cathedral (see Chapter 7).

NOTES

1. It was not until January 1693, after several years of widowhood, that she returned to Lisbon, dying at the Palácio da Bemposta in 1705.

7

Eastern Lisbon

From near the lower end of the Rua da Prata in the Cidade Baixa, the transverse Rua da Conceição (not that in which stands the church of that name), leads towards the foot of the Castelo hill. From here, a gradual ascent brings one to the *Sé* or cathedral, recognizable by its low, battlemented towers.

In December 1383 Bishop Martinho Anes was flung unceremoniously from the north tower by the populace, enraged by his Spanish sympathies. (Not knowing of his death, Clement VII appointed him a cardinal seventeen days later.) With the accession of Dom João I, and his marriage to Philippa of Lancaster, life among the chapter was less turbulent, and her chaplain Robert Payne even found sufficient leisure to translate Gower's *Confessio Amantis* into Portuguese.

The earlier church, dating from the time of Afonso Henriques, and of which the English crusader-priest Gilbert of Hastings was the first bishop,[1] had been to a great extent rebuilt in the Romanesque style after minor earthquakes in the 1330s and 1340s, but the convulsion of 1755 caused further damage. The plain capitals of its barrel-vaulted interior, with its low lantern, are relieved by rose-windows in the apses, while the Gothic ambulatory chapels contain the tombs of João Anes, the first archbishop, who died in 1440. Dom Afonso IV and Dona Brites lie in the *capela-mór*, restored after a fashion in the eighteenth century, when Baroque organs were installed. Owing to the constricted site, the cloisters were constructed beyond the apse (as are those at Leiria). Apparently the crypt served as an armoury for an abortive rising against the Salazar regime in March 1959.

Skirting the north flank of the cathedral, the climb continues past the ruinous Limoeiro, a former royal palace in the courtyard of which flourished the lemon tree which gave it its name. It later housed the Mint, and served as a prison; and it was here in October

1383 that João, the Master of Avis, having just assassinated Andeiro, the lover of Leonor Teles, Dom Fernando's widow, was acclaimed regent.[2]

Further uphill is the Castelo de São Jorge, the ruins of which, although insensitively restored by the municipality, provide both plunging and panoramic views of the lower city, as do its tree-shaded terraces and rampart walks. The Moorish citadel and casbah, built on the site of the Phoenician settlement and Roman *oppidum*, was surrounded by walls and later converted into a palace. It remained the principal royal residence until the time of Dom Manuel, who preferred more palatial accommodation adjoining the Terreiro do Paço. By the seventeenth century it was much decayed, although used partly as a prison. Two British inmates were Colonel Sir John Milley Doyle, in 1823, for scheming against Dom Miguel, and a decade later, Sir John Campbell, the Miguelite general.

At the upper end of the Rua do Limoeiro is the Largo das Portas do Sol, a narrow promenade commanding a roofscape of the labyrinthine district known as the Alfama, which is described later in this chapter, although steps descend steeply into it from here.

Off this terrace is the Espírito Santo Foundation, established by a banker with the commendable idea of preserving the traditional skills of Portuguese craftsmen in the decorative arts. While its workshops may be visited also, the adjacent palace of the Counts of Azurara houses its museum. Here are displayed superb collections of furniture and silver, views of Lisbon by Alexandre Noël and of Oporto by Carlos van Zeller, several Arraiolos carpets, Castelo Branco embroideries, and Indo-Portuguese tapestries; the sicupera-wood doors, Jacaranda and box-wood cupboard, and japanned furniture are all admirable specimens of Portuguese cabinet-making.

Shortly, a lane descends and climbs again to approach São Vicente de Fora (*fora*, or formerly lying outside the medieval walls), built in the Italian Renaissance style by Felipe Terzi and Baltasar Alvares between 1582 and 1627, but departing from the Vignolan pattern in that the façade is flanked by square corner towers and the upper storey is pierced by windows. The original dome fell in 1755, but the coffered barrel vault of the well-proportioned interior is notable, together with the great eighteenth-century organ skulking behind the high altar. The great *retabulo* of the Infante by Nuno Gonçalves stood in São Vicente until its translation to the Museu de Arte Antiga.

It was here in 1787 that Beckford first met Gregorio Franchi, then a choirboy, who became his protégé and remained his close friend.

Eighteenth-century *azulejos* depicting La Fontaine's *Fables* embellish the cloisters, while the adjacent *portaria* preserves a fine ceiling by Vincenzo Baccerelli of Florence, and tiled scenes of sieges of Lisbon and Santarém. In the refectory, now a Braganza Pantheon, are the remains of several members of that dynasty, many formerly displayed in an embalmed state. Among them are Catherine of Braganza, and the last king, Dom Manuel II. As a gracious gesture Carol II of Rumania (1893–1953), deposed in 1940 but who spent part of his exile at Estoril, together with Mme Lupescu, his morganatic wife, are also lying here.

Downhill, beyond the Feira da Ladra, is Santa Engrácia, an ambitious structure, in plan a Greek cross with rounded extremities and framed by square towers, designed by João Nunes Tinoco to replace a church demolished in consequence of some ineffable act of sacrilege said to have occurred there in 1630. He was succeeded in 1690 by João Antunes, but its construction later hung fire to such an extent that the expression 'obras de Santa Engrácia' came to be applied to any never finished work. At one time the shell was put to use as an artillery magazine; and only in 1966, with the completion of its ballustraded cupola, was the phrase invalidated, although some considered this addition a mere expedient. Flawed or not, on its termination the church was proclaimed by the Salazar regime – in the customary manner of dictatorships – to be the 'National Pantheon'.

The splendid interior, with its four ribbed semi-domes of coloured marbles set in contrasting patterns, is at least spatially imposing; and here are sheltered the cenotaphs of Vasco da Gama, Afonso de Albuquerque, Nun'Alvares Pereira, the Infante Dom Henrique (Henry the Navigator), Pedro Alvares Cabral, and Luis de Camoens.

Near the waterfront stands the Museu de Artilharia, a somewhat antiquated accumulation of militaria, where a maquette of the Lines of Torres Vedras provides some interest in the modest section devoted to the Peninsular War.

Being in the vicinity of the Santa Apolónia railway station, the indefatigable tourist may find a green-roofed taxi to take him to the Museu do Azulejo, the only building of importance in the riverside suburb of Xabregas. Installed in dependencies of the secularized convent of Madre de Deus, founded in 1509 by Dona Leonor, the widow of Dom João II, it contains an outstanding collection of tiled pictures, while in the church are the exuberantly carved and gilt frames surrounding André Gonçalves' paintings of the Life of Saint Francis. Dutch tiles of *circa* 1710 depict rustic scenes; those in the sacristy come from the factory of Rato, and date from about 1780. Rooms off the cloister display a variety of other *azulejos*, including some caricature *singeries*. On an upper level is a chapel dedicated to Santo António, with tiles representing scenes from his life; and the richly gilt *coro alto*. Among paintings here are the curious fifteenth-century Flemish *Panorama of Jerusalem*, in which are set scenes of the Passion; and lastly, an *azulejo Panorama of Lisbon*, thirty-six metres long. This is both a remarkable work of art and also of historical interest as a fairly accurate record of numerous architectural features from a period not more than twenty-five years prior to the Great Earthquake.

The Largo do Chafariz de Dentro is the main square of the **Alfama**, but this intricate area is probably best visited as a separate shorter excursion, when feeling fresh and energetic, and with a detailed map in hand.

Although it is now unlikely that one will be stoned by urchins, as was Rose Macaulay when climbing to the castle in 1943, for merely ignoring their importunities, one is advised, nevertheless, to beware of dextrous bag-snatchers, who can only too rapidly make their escape among its passages and wynds.

Apart from being a characteristic survival of old Lisbon, with its maze of narrow alleys and breakneck flights of steps clambering up the lower slopes of the hill, the Alfama is otherwise of slight interest. Tourists intent on discovering those quaint corners bright with hanging washing which appear to quicken the pulse of some sentimental travellers in search of the picturesque, will no doubt find what they want.

NOTES

1. Gilbert had introduced the Sarum Use to Lisbon, where it was followed until 1536.
2. See Estremoz.

8

Lisbon: the Bairro Alto

Exploring any part of Lisbon other than the Bairro Baixa, requires stamina, for as George Borrow remarked – and he was physically tougher than most visitors, and not one to complain overmuch – 'the streets are in general precipitously steep'.

Consider the occasional use of a green-topped taxi to get you about, or when returning home, exhausted by a switchback stroll through the maze of narrow streets, some of which – known as *travessas* or *becos* – are quite likely to peter out as steps. A few British-built, yellow-liveried, Edwardian-looking trams will be seen threading their way along the wider thoroughfares, their place being taken on some of the steeper inclines by characteristic rack-railways or funiculars.

The Rua do Carmo climbs from the Rossío to the Chiado (officially the Rua Garrett), long one of the more fashionable promenades and shopping streets, and still retaining a charming *fin de siècle* café. In 1988 part of the district was severely damaged by a fire said to have been provoked by an arsonist hoping to claim insurance, but rebuilding is slowly under way behind the remaining façades, which are being preserved wherever possible.

Uphill to the right are the ruins of the Carmo convent, founded by the Constable Nun'Alvares after the battle of Aljubarrota, and where he took the Carmelite habit and died. Shattered in the earthquake of 1755, it later harboured a chemical manufactory, and now shelters archaeological and architectural relics, among them the tomb of Dom Fernando I, and the canopied effigy of Rui de Meneses.

To the south of the Chiado, a few paces behind the eighteenth-century church dedicated to the Mártires (those Crusaders who died when Lisbon was taken from the Moors), is the Teatro São Carlos. This replaced the former opera-house by Giovanni Carlo Bibiena, destroyed in 1755 only seven months after its inauguration. Designed in 1792 by José da Costa e Silva on the lines of its namesake at Naples, its rusticated *porte-cochère* and pilastered façade have similarities also to La Scala at Milan. According to the story, it was here, during his visit to Lisbon, that Byron was struck by an irate husband who assumed that the susceptible foreigner was making advances to his wife, as no doubt he was.

The building was turned into a casino during the Peninsular War, and William Grattan of the Connaught Rangers describes 'that sink of profligacy and nest of sharpers, the San Carlos gambling-house . . . the constant resort of all the idlers in Lisbon', although it is possible that this may have referred to a neighbouring establishment.

From the Praça de Luis de Camoes the Rua do Alecrim – meaning rosemary in Arabic – descends rapidly towards the Tagus; and it was in this street stood the mansion commandeered by General Junot, in which the 'Convention of Cintra' was signed in fact.

It is probable that the assembly rooms of the British Factory were also close by, although at an earlier date they stood near the lower end of the parallel Rua das Flores; and it was here that Richard Twiss would have attended the harpsichord recital given by Mrs May, wife of a prominent member, which impressed him as equalling anything he had ever heard on that instrument 'for the rapidity of execution, and the delicacy and taste' with which she played 'the most difficult pieces'. On another occasion Twiss attended an Italian opera at the royal palace at Belém, at which no females performed, nor actresses, and where

> instead of women, they have eunuchs, dressed exactly as women are; so that, from the stage, they appear to be really what they represent. But the dancing between the acts being likewise by men with great black beards and broad shoulders, dressed in female apparel, was a disgusting sight. The jealousy of the queen is said to be the cause of this uncommon exhibition.

Not only jealousy, but religious mania, a presage of her insanity, was also in evidence, according to Richard Croker, in Lisbon in December 1780. He complained that 'The balls given by the members of the British Factory are all that can be found', for the rigid piety of the queen 'had been the occasion of shutting up all places of amusement; neither opera nor plays are permitted, even at this festive season'.

The Rua do Misericordia climbs north from the Praça de Luis de

Camoes to São Roque, an outwardly unpretentious Jesuit church containing a chapel dedicated to the Baptist, which, resplendent with its lustres, is a notably extravagant example of Italian workmanship of its period. An opulent confection of lapis lazuli, agate, porphyry and ormolu, it was designed in part by Luigi Vanvitelli, and blessed by Benedict XIV before being dismantled and shipped out from Rome, and installed here only eight years before the earthquake, which surprisingly it survived. It caused a sensation at the time, although the cost was crippling, and its artistic value was therefore much exaggerated by the Portuguese, which it still is.

An inscription near the pulpit describes the career of Sir Francis Tregean, a Cornish recusant buried here in 1608, at which time Father Henry Floyd, Fludd or Flood, the chief visitor of the Inquisition for the English community and a zealous converter of souls, made Sao Roche his lair. It was at 'St Rocco' that Richard Twiss repaired to hear a three-hour-long musical *função*, for which he had a penchant, during which he was astonished to see that the female members of the congregation, 'having all white muslin veils and black silk cloaks . . . remained squatted on the ground' throughout, which was then the custom.

Further uphill stands a mid-eighteenth-century palace designed by Ludovice, the architect of Mafra, now housing the Lisbon branch of the Port Wine Institute, where, in comfort but at a price, an extensive range of vintage ports may be sampled.

Thus stimulated, and before descending by funicular to the Praça dos Restauradores, cross to the nearby Miradouro de São Pedro de Alcantara for the view towards the Castelo de São Jorge, and explore part at least of the grid of narrow lanes to the west, forming the throbbing core of the Bairro Alto.

During the day its street life is characterized still by *varinas* or fishwives, balancing creels on their heads and crying their wares; Gallegan knife-grinders still play their plaintive pan-pipes to announce their presence: sellers of lottery tickets and boot-blacks are more likely to be in evidence in the more populated streets and squares. Twiss, when referring to another street-market near the Arsenal, stated that fish was 'procured from Oporto, by men employed for that purpose, who perform the journey in four days on foot, taking the shortest route, without regarding the common roads', and 'vegetables, fruits, tortoises, monkeys, parrots, and Brasil birds' were also to be found on sale there.

As dusk falls, the *casas de fado* and other shadier dens of entertainment and night life proliferate. The *fado* is promoted as being as 'typical' of Portugal as *flamenco* is of Spain, and its devotees claim that on occasions performances rise well above the perfunctory. Its origins are disreputable, probably deriving from the libidinous *lundum*, a dance introduced from the Congo into Brazil, where it became a natural activity amongst the slave population. From Brazil also came the *modinhas*, those lascivious songs which Beckford considered 'the most seducing, the most voluptuous imaginable, the best calculated to throw saints off their guard and to inspire profane deliriums'. Traditionally, these songs and dances were taken over by the less than virtuous residents of the port quarter and the Alfama – some of them slaves before their emancipation in 1761 – to entertain their less than fastidious clients.

Among earlier *fadistas* known to polite society were Caldas Barbosa, a Brazilian mulatto, whose compositions were hardly delicate, and, in about 1840, Maria Severa, who became the mistress of the bull-fighting Conde de Vimioso. During the second half of the century the *fado* became increasingly popular, gaining a status parallel to the cancan, but only comparatively recently has it been considered decent; but with respectability and professionalism much of its former spontaneity has been lost.

At a slightly higher level stand the dependencies of the former Colégio dos Inglesinhos, founded in 1628 but only vacated by the seminary in 1973. The irascible Consul Maynard had a bee in his bonnet about them, referring to the 'implacable malice of the English Seminary to our Religion'. A century and a quarter later, when Lisbon was invested by the French, held at arms' length by the Lines of Torres Vedras, Father Edmond Winstanley was offering his services to Wellington as chaplain to the military hospitals in the vicinity, and willing to accommodate any Irish sick and wounded within his walls. (Winstanley remained with the army until after Waterloo, when he returned to Lisbon.) George Borrow visited the place out of curiosity, although by then the buildings were rather dilapidated. Hospitably escorted round by the Rector, he was even taken up to the roof, which provided a 'very grand and noble' view; but as he assured the readers of *The Bible in Spain*, he did not visit it 'in the hope of seeing busts, or books, or fine prospects, – I visited this strange old house to converse with its inmates; for my favourite, I might say my only, study is man'.

Those with sufficient stamina may make the longer circuit by descending the Calçada do Combro, leading west from the Chiado, passing Santa Catarina or Dos Paulistas, notable for its painted vault, the elaborate wood-carving in the apse and of the Baroque organ-case, and stucco-work by Giovanni Grossi of Milan.

The street continues steeply downhill, debouching into the Largo de São Bento, dominated by the Palácio da Assembleia da República or Parliament building, which since 1834 has occupied the much extended dependencies of the former convent of São Bento da Saude or dos Negros. It was here that the humanist George Buchanan, after lecturing at Coimbra, was confined by the Inquisition for several months in 1552.

Near by, at the corner of the Travessa do Pasteleiro, stood the convent of the English Bridgettine nuns after 1760, and where they remained until returning to Syon a century later. The community had moved to Lisbon in 1594, and their hospitality is often referred to by earlier travellers, among them Baretti, who remarked that visitors were 'used by them with such endearing kindness, that their parlatory is in a manner never empty from morning till night. The poor things are liberal to every body of chocolate, cakes, and sweetmeats . . .'.

Twiss likewise found them 'very chatty and entertaining', and regretted that they were separated from him by a grill. Young Robert Southey, as might be expected, disapproved, being convinced that, despite their generosity, 'a nun is as miserable in herself as she is useless to society . . .'. Apparently their company was so popular with members of Admiral Norris's squadron, stationed in the Tagus in 1735, that the abbess had to ration the number of visitors.

Further west extends the district of Lapa, formerly known as Buenos Aires, on the sunny hill-slope of which, as remarked by William Graham in 1820, 'all persons of condition reside'. Among them had been the Revd Herbert Hill, when visited by Southey; and Byron briefly, for several of the hotels patronized by the English were situated there. This comparatively sequestered area grew to become a diplomatic enclave, and the British Embassy has been accommodated since 1940 in the Palácio Porto Covo at a lower reach of the steep Rua Domingos à Lapa.

The Calçada da Estrela climbs past the Parliament building towards the late-eighteenth-century Basilica da Estrela. Although repeating several of the faults of Mafra, the decorative appearance of the exterior is far more effective than its frigid interior, however well

proportioned. As with several other Portuguese churches and convents, it was commissioned in fulfillment of a vow depending on the
birth of an heir, in this case to the devout and melancholy Dona
Maria I, whose tomb it shelters, together with that of her confessor.[1]

On the far side of the adjacent gardens is the discreet entrance
to the cypress-shaded Cemitério dos Ingleses, known to the
Portuguese as the cemetery 'Os Ciprestes'. (The Cemitério dos
Prazeres – of the Pleasures – lies a short distance to the west.) Permission to establish this heretical graveyard was given in 1717 on
condition that it was called the 'Hospital of the English Factory',
although in fact the terms of the treaty of 1654 allowed them to have
their own burial-ground. The Dutch Factory acquired the adjoining
plot, and the two were surrounded by a wall, and it was here that
many members of the non-Catholic Anglo-Portuguese community,
together with Scandinavian and Dutch Protestants (among them
the diamond merchant and Consul, Daniel Gildemeester *père*; see
Sintra), were interred. An absorbing hour may be spent deciphering
the names on its evocative tomb-slabs and monuments. The earlier
cemetery chapel was replaced in the late nineteenth century by the
present church of St George.

A neighbouring building bearing the name 'Hospital', which
had been reconstructed in 1793 by Gerard de Visme, is now the
Parsonage. When Junot entered Lisbon in 1807, some of the bolder
spirits among the British who remained were by his order arrested
and imprisoned here, but apparently they succeeded in making
themselves so unpleasant that he let them out again. The present
Hospital stands above the old Jewish graveyard, to the north.

Among the more eminent buried in the Cemitério dos Ingleses
are Dr Philip Doddridge, the hymn-writer and non-conformist
divine, who died only thirteen days after his arrival in Lisbon in
1751. (His friends had subscribed £300 towards the cost of the
journey – a third of it from Lady Huntingdon – but in vain.) Three
years later, the author of *Tom Jones*, Henry Fielding, was buried
there. His gravestone was replaced by a tomb in 1830 'on a spot
selected by guess', according to Wordsworth's daughter Dorothy
(Mrs Edward Quillinan), who visited the cemetery in 1846. In 1879
this was in turn replaced.

Lying here in unlikely juxtaposition are Abraham Castres, Envoy
at the time of the Great Earthquake; Thomas Barclay, an Irishman
killed in a duel in 1793 (who two years earlier had been nomi-
nated American consul in Morocco by Washington at the request of

Jefferson); Thomas Horne, Beckford's agent and banker; Prince Christian August von Waldeck, who died at Sintra in 1798 after commanding the Portuguese army for only a year; and more recently, in 1944, Nicholas Horthy, the exiled Regent of Hungary.

There is little else of interest to see in this area except, just north of the Largo do Rato, the reservoir known as the Mãe d'Agua, distributing the waters of the Aguas Livres aqueduct, which strides into the city from the north-west, commencing at Canecas, almost twelve miles away. Built in the second quarter of the eighteenth century, this aqueduct was long one of the 'lions' of Lisbon, and thus visited by numerous travellers, among them Baretti, who suffered an unexpected and unwarranted 'lapidation' from the denizens of the district (as did Rose Macaulay in the Alfama two centuries later). George Borrow was so impressed as to suggest that one 'should devote an entire morning to inspecting it'.

It was near here, from its foundation by Pombal in 1767 until 1835, that the Royal Factory of the Rato was producing porcelain in emulation of the Buen Retiro factory, inaugurated eight years earlier at Madrid. Tómas Bruneto of Turin was its first director, but it was not until 1824, when the Vista Alegre factory was set up near Aveiro, that the production of porcelain was firmly established in Portugal.

The Rua da Escola Politecnica leads from the Largo do Rato to the Miradouro de São Pedro de Alcantara, referred to above.

NOTES

1. During the Peninsular War its dependencies served as a military hospital; they are now the headquarters of the Instituto Geográfico e Cadastral.

9

Western Lisbon and Belém

An unhurried visit to the Museu Nacional de Arte Antiga is indispensible, for in no other collection can one appreciate the vigorous individuality of the arts of Portugal. Partly housed in the former palace of the Counts of Alvor, flanking the Rua das Janelas Verdes ('of the Green Shutters'), it is frequently referred to by this name. At some distance from the centre, it is reached conveniently by taxi, although a clanking tram shuttles there from Black Horse Square.

The collection of Portuguese paintings is extensive, but the Museum also contains important sections devoted to furniture, fabrics, glass (largely from the Marinha Grande and Vista Alegre works), ceramics, metalwork, and sculpture. The treasury is resplendent with magnificent examples of the art of the goldsmith, remarkable among which is the Monstrance of Belém (or Custodia dos Jerónimos), dating from 1506 and designed by a certain Gil Vicente, using the first gold brought back from the Indies by Vasco da Gama. Not surprisingly, English influence is seen in several silver tea-services and tankards originating in Oporto.

The Portuguese were the first Europeans to import Oriental porcelains from Macau, from Japan between 1550 and 1640, and from Goa (which, when copied in faience, was known as *porcelana da India*), but fine examples from factories in operation throughout Portugal in the eighteenth century are also displayed.

Among Japanese screens are the *Biombos* Namban, depicting the Namban-jin or 'Barbarians from the south', as the Portuguese traders arriving at Nagasaki in the 1540s were named; another pair of screens shows them setting sail from (probably) Goa for Japan, and their disembarkation; and a third, which was presumably made after the Portuguese were forced to leave the country in 1639 (for neither their costumes nor their ships are so well characterized, and the artist may well have not seen them in person).

A *Holy Family* by Mabuse, Bosch's *Temptation of St Anthony*, and the elder Cranach's *Salome*, are overwhelming among the paintings; but so is the *St Jerome* by Dürer, dated 1521, offered to Rui Fernandes de Almada, then living in Antwerp, and later seen hanging in the conventual library of the Jerónimos at Belém. Outstanding among canvases by Portuguese masters, other than the anonymous, are several by Frei Carlos, Francisco Henriques, Gregorio Lopes, Cristovão Lopes, Cristovão de Morais, and Cristovão de Figueiredo, even if they pale in comparison with the superb *Retable of the Infante*, painted in the late 1460s by Nuno Gonçalves for the chapel of St Vincent in the *Sé*, and later moved to Sao Vicente de Fora.

The patron saint of Lisbon is shown receiving the homage of Dom Afonso V, while many of the sixty portraits depicted on its six panels – of the royal family and Court, and representatives of several communities, among them Cistercian monks from Alcobaça, rabbis, knights, fishermen, etcetera – have been identified with more or less certainty.

Paintings by more recent Portuguese artists, comparatively little known abroad, include several by Domingos António de Sequeira, who after spending several months in prison for having painted an allegory of *Lisbon sheltered by Junot* (cf. Oporto), was commissioned by Dom João VI to design the monumental silver service now at Apsley House, presented to the Duke of Wellington by a grateful monarch. Representative works by Josefa 'de Obidos', Francisco Vieira Portuense, Vieira Lusitano, and 'Morgado de Setúbal' are also to be seen; while a portrait of Marianne of Austria, wife of Philip IV of Spain, attributed to Diego de Velázquez de Silva (or Diego da Silva Velázquez, as the Portuguese prefer to call him), reminds us that although his mother was a Velázquez, the artist's father was of Portuguese origin, the Silvas having only settled in Seville earlier in the sixteenth century.

About a mile further west, beyond the graceful Ponte 25 de Abril spanning the estuary here,[1] stands the Quinta de Baixo or Palácio de Belém, the official residence of the Portuguese President. Acquired from the Conde de Aveiras by Dom João V in 1726, it was also known as the Quinta 'dos Bichos' or beasts, for Moroccan lions were formerly mewed up in cages in its courtyards. Curiously, Baretti referred to it as the 'Paço de Vaca', the palace of the cow! Its Picadeiro or *manège* now houses the Museu dos Coches.

This assembly of extravagantly carved and gilded coaches – to which those at Vila Viçosa are a pendant – require little more than a cursory inspection, although the intricacies of their construction may fascinate the amateur of these cumbersome and creaking vehicles. Of historical interest are the plainer travelling-coach of Philip III of Spain, and that of Dom João V; while impressive on account of their fine workmanship are an eighteenth-century *sege*, and two carriages constructed in London in the 1820s.

Among a collection of liveries, harnesses, and bull-fighting gear are the saddle and saddle-cloth of the 5th Marquês de Marialva, Beckford's friend, who had the hereditary title of Grand Master of the Horse. Beckford himself at one time seriously considered renting the palace, but in 1794 he chose instead the *quinta* of São José de Ribemare at adjacent Alges. During his previous visit Beckford had remarked that he would 'much rather bask the winter away in some snug palace at Lisbon with a view of the Tagus and a garden well filled with early flowers and orange trees, than traverse the windy plains of Castille, exposed to the inconvenience of hoggish inns and the wearisome paces of mule drivers', which in the event he was shortly to do.

Some distance uphill is the pretentious but uncompleted pile of the Palácio da Ajuda. Crum Watson, author of *Portuguese Architecture*, found it one of those buildings, like the Palácio das Necessidades,[2] which it was 'impossible to admire . . . great masses of pink-washed plaster pierced with endless windows, and without any beauty of detail or of design'. It is hardly worth the climb, unless one is a connoisseur of the furniture and decoration of the time of Maria II, 'da Gloria', and her second husband, Ferdinand of Saxe-Coburg-Gotha (a cousin of our own dear Prince Albert), of Dom Pedro V, married to Stéphanie of Hohenzollern-Sigmaringen, and of Dom Luis, married to Maria-Pia (daughter of Victor Emmanuel II of Italy), who as queen dowager lived here until her death in 1911.

Few will have sympathy with the ostentatious accumulation of inferior objects selfishly acquired at the expense of the Portuguese people in an epoch which could ill afford such extravagance, and can only concur with the opinion of that fastidious traveller Richard Ford, when visiting the finer equivalent in Madrid, that 'Nothing is more tiresome than a palace, a house of velvet, tapestry, gold, and bore . . .'.

It was in the balustraded botanic gardens of the former palace on this site – a wooden construction run up after the 1755 earthquake, and partly burnt down in 1794 – that Beckford was bewitched briefly by a blue-eyed Irish girl.

It was in the 'the Prince's Park, a large enclosure above the suburb of Belem', now that of Monsanto, that Wellington's reinforcements, after disembarking from their transports, would encamp while awaiting marching orders.

In July 1809 a ruined house here served as Captain Sherer's regimental mess, where 'round a rudely constructed table of casks and planks, seated on portmanteaus, stones, or knapsacks', they enjoyed their evenings far more than 'at a board better provided, and in the most commodious mess-room'.

From there they would make their way into town, 'walking amid a concourse of people, differing in feature, complexion, and dress, so widely from the natives of England', passing such curious foreign sights as 'long strings of loaded mules; the cabriolets; the bullock-cars . . . watercarriers; the lemonade-sellers; and, above all, the monks and friars in the habits of their orders'. Several churches would be visited, mostly decorated 'in a tawdry and offensive taste; and [with] a profusion of badly-executed carved work, gilt and painted', which 'quite fatigued the eye'. At São Vicente, Sherer and his companions were 'received with the most flattering politeness', and presented with fruit and wine by the good fathers. Their ramble took them to a horse-fair 'near the gardens of the Salitre', and to 'Gold Street', where Sherer bought some cheap but delicately wrought trinkets; to the Largo de Sao Paulo, where they dined, before attending a comedy 'not unlike our *Beggar's Opera* at a theatre in the Rua das Condes, followed by a ballet, in which 'Madame Brunet, a handsome woman, and a graceful dancer, formed the chief attraction'. He ended the full day by 'taking an ice at the Grotto, a very excellent coffee-room', perhaps that of Lahmeyer's hotel.

A few minutes' walk west of the coach museum stands the Mosteiro dos Jerónimos, a splendid example of the Manueline style of architecture, which has impressed every traveller in the past, even if covered by scaffolding to repair its roof, as seen by Baretti, or sheltering some 500 orphans, when visited by Borrow.

On its site had stood the former mariners' chapel of Restelo, founded by Henry the Navigator, and its name was changed to Belém or Bethlehem. The departure of Vasco da Gama's fleet from the adjacent quays in 1497 and their fortunate return two years later, inspired Dom Manuel to expend every effort in making the monastery, which he dedicated to Santa María, a worthy memorial to Portugal's thanksgiving. The first master of works was Diogo Boitac (responsible for the *Igreja de Jesus* at Setúbal), who was succeeded by João de Castilho, while Nicolas Chanterène, the French sculptor, was also working there. After a lull, its construction was resumed by Diogo de Torralva and Jerónimo de Ruau, son of the better known Jean de Rouen.

Extensive restorations were undertaken in the nineteenth century, when a dome was added to the south-west tower and the fabric extended by dependencies in a mock-Manueline style (which had to be rebuilt after its partial collapse). The connecting arch overshadows the exuberantly carved west portal, with its portrait statues by Chanterène of Dom Manuel and his second wife, Dona Maria; their tombs, together with those of Dom João III and Dona Catarina (their sarcophagi borne by elephants: an exotic touch) rest in the *capela-mór*.

The interior, its boldly soaring columns bearing Renaissance decoration in low relief and supporting vigorously ribbed vaulting, is indeed imposing, as is the sacristy, vaulted from a single pier. The south transept shelters the tomb of the unfortunate Dom Sebastião, who lost his life in the Quixotic expedition to Morocco; to the north lies his great-uncle Henrique, the Cardinal-king, who succeeded him. Unusual is the incorporation of confessionals in the north wall of the nave, which alternate with others opening on to the abutting cloister, each bay of which is divided by three columns supporting traceried arches, while a single column sustains the vaulting of the upper storeys.

When visited by Baretti, a walled garden and olive groves extended up the hill behind, dotted with cells and chapels 'belonging to several paultry sinners of low condition who have repented, and are allowed to live there in perfect idleness; which way of consuming time is by them termed Vida celeste, a heavenly life'. Figs flourished here, as did 'many Brasilian plants . . . particularly that called Banana'.

The nineteenth-century addition houses the Museu Nacional de Arqueologia and adjacent Museu da Marinha. Among the extensive collections one might expect of a country with such a long seafaring history are a range of ship models, navigational instruments and other marine equipment, and furniture from Dom Manuel II's yacht, the *Dona Amélia*, dismantled in 1938, in which the royal family had set sail from Ericeira in 1910 for exile in England.

Of interest too is the Indo-Portuguese sculpture from the Oratory at Goa, founded in 1682, and one of Luis Frois, a missionary who died at Nagasaki in 1597; also a plan of that city depicted on a seventeenth-century screen. Among the paintings is one illustrating the *Action of Bocca Tigris* against Chinese pirates in 1810, several views of Macão, and a portrait of Sir Charles Napier, who scattered Dom Miguel's fleet off Cape St Vincent in July 1833.

The annexe displays two ceremonial galliotes or royal barges, one embellished by Pillement, some Merryweather fire-engines, the seaplane in which Gago Coutinho and Sacadura Cabral flew from Lisbon to Rio in 1922 (three years after Alcock and Brown's flight across the north Atlantic), and facsimiles of charts and portolanos, notably José Costa da Miranda's map of the Atlantic of 1681.

When I was last in Lisbon, dust was billowing from an adjacent site, where a huge 'Cultural Centre' was being built at immense cost, and, I was told, many were wondering to what purpose. Why such extravagance when other monuments are crumbling away, was the general complaint; and museums whose contents are more deserving of preservation, are left in a state of penury. This is the fashion in many capitals when culture languishes, when cultural values depend on the inflated figure a painting may fetch, and the mere number of visitors to a museum is what counts. Public money is squandered by presumptuous politicians ambitious to leave some durable trophy of their transitory presence by inaugurating prestigious buildings, very few of which redound to their credit. Why has Portugal, a poor country, to imitate the pretensions of Paris, I was asked, where Pei's glass pyramid in front of the Louvre has destroyed Classical perspectives; where Pompidou's pop-culture factory collects dirt and rusts; not to mention the mammoth arch at La Défense and the new opera-house . . . *basta*!

One such monument, typical of the taste of the times, rose up on the bank of the Tagus in 1960 to commemorate the quincentenary of Henry the Navigator's death, carved on which is a colossal sword, its hilt in the form of the Cross of Avis – fit companion to the colossus perched on its plinth across the estuary.

The Torre de Belém, its distinctive profile glistening in the early morning sun, as when I first saw it, cannot disillusion. It is considered by many as the classic example of Muslim decoration applied to Manueline architecture. The architectural historian Albrecht Haupt, writing in 1888, saw likenesses to the Temple of Gujerat in

the Punjab, although Francisco de Arruda, responsible for its construction, had been no further afield than the Portuguese posses-
sions in the Maghreb. It was after his return to Lisbon that he was
commissioned to build this bulwark of the Restelo on a new plan,
completed by 1520. Although formerly surrounded by water, it
later became stranded on the sandy shore, but the new retaining
wall, when covered at high tide, enables one to imagine its original
state.

Its main external features are the foursquare tower embellished
with *ajimece* windows and Moresque balconies, and the advanced
platform, its battlements bearing the shields of the Order of Christ,
below which a rope moulding is carved. At each landward corner,
and surmounting the tower, are circular sentry-boxes or casemates
topped by segmented or melon-shaped domes: others line the platform. Wide vaulted passages lead from an interior patio to gun
emplacements whose cannon would have been on the optimum
level to hole the hulls of any enemy vessel rash enough to come
within range. Below were the store-rooms, magazines, and water-
lapped dungeons, for it also served as a state prison. Note the
columns supporting armillary spheres, the device of Dom Manuel,
and the delicacy of the carving on the seaward balustrade of the
tower, before ascending to the upper oratory and wall-walk and
clambering on to the flat roof for the panoramic views it commands.

NOTES

1. See Chapter 3.
2. This former palace, standing between the hill of Buenos Aires and
   Belém, has served as the Foreign Office since 1916. Its name derives
   from having been built on the site of the chapel of Nossa Senhora das
   Necessidades ('of the needy').

10

Northern Lisbon

The hillside Parque de Eduardo VII was laid out in honour of the State visit of Edward VII and Queen Alexandra in 1903.[1] Built into a former quarry is the Estufa Fria or 'cool' greenhouse, through the bamboo roof and lush foliage of which the sunlight shyly filters. Both this and the contiguous glass-house or Estufa Quente, protect varied tropical and sub-tropical plants, many from Portugal's former colonies; and with their rivulets, flamingo pool, banana trees, cacti, ferns and other exotic vegetation, these hot-houses, when not too sweltering, are an unusual and interesting refuge.

A short distance down the far side of the hill extend the headquarters of the Gulbenkian Foundation, together with its museum. Calouste Sarkis Gulbenkian (1869–1955), born at Scutari into an already wealthy Armenian family, studied at King's College, London, and acquired British nationality in 1902. He lived for some time in Paris, and for the last thirteen years of his life in Portugal. Was it not for the indifference and crass obtuseness of the British fiscal authorities, his fortune, largely due to his five per cent interest in the Iraq Petroleum Group of companies, would have been left to the country of his naturalization, where in London the Foundation still has an important branch. In the event, he chose to leave his art collections and the whole of his very considerable estate to the Foundation he had set up in Lisbon, where it funds work of a charitable, artistic, educational and scientific nature.

An orchestra was established in 1962, seven years after his death, and the museum inaugurated seven years later. Its contents, of a consistently high quality, mirror that connoisseur's eclectic tastes. His acquisitive activities ranged from Greek coins (for which he had a passion) and Italian bronze medals to illuminated manuscripts and French book-bindings; from Chinese jades and porcelains and Japanese lacquer boxes, *inros* and *netsukes* to massive silver epergnes by Germain and other *orfèvres*; from *objets de virtu* and

73

furniture by the major *ébenistes* to the exotic art of René Lalique. Several, but by no means all the European Schools are represented in over 100 choice paintings – there are none by Portuguese or Spanish artists – among which are no less than nineteen canvases by Guardi.

A few paces away stands the Palácio Azambuja, now the Spanish Embassy. It was formerly known as the Palácio dos Meninos de Palhava, being the residence of those 'youths of straw', Dom João V's bastards. Beckford, curious to visit it, was stunned by the fustiness and gloom of its principal apartments, hung with damask of deepest crimson: 'No glasses [mirrors], no pictures, no gilding, no decoration but heavy drapery; even the tables are concealed by cut velvet flounces, in the style of those with which our dowagers used formerly to array their toilets', which caused him to philosophize on the lengths to which nurses, equerries and chamberlains would go to stifle every lively and generous sensation in the princelings they educate, 'to break a human being into the habits of impotent royalty'.

The bastards were conceived in the convent of **Odivelas**, some two or three miles north, largely rebuilt since 1755, and now of slight interest, although preserving the partly mutilated tomb of Dom Dinis, its founder, and that of Maria Afonso, his natural daughter. Philippa of Lancaster died there of the plague in 1415, later being buried at Batalha.

This fashionable convent became an irregular haunt of Dom João V. The result of the peculiar penchant of this philoprogenitive sovereign – commonly known as the *freiratico* or nun-lover – were Dom António, born in 1714 to a French nun; Dom Gaspar, a future archbishop of Braga, born two years later to another inmate, Magdalena Máxima de Miranda; and Dom José, who ended his days as Inquisitor-general, who was born in 1720 to Madre Paula Teresa da Silva (1701–68), the royal mistress for a decade from 1718.

They were a turbulent lot – the nuns – who caused such a commotion in October 1713 that they were 'only subdued by the Duke of Cadaval after a pitched battle', so reported the British Consul. Nevertheless, Madre Paula was an excellent musician, and (as suggested by Sacheverell Sitwell) at one time may well have been a pupil of Domenico Scarlatti, as was the legitimate Infanta Maria Bárbara. And when the nuns were not otherwise occupied, they confected *marmelada* or quince jam, for the quality of which the convent had to keep up its reputation.

General Dumouriez, although writing several decades later, was convinced that most convents still followed the example of that of Odivelas. The nuns, 'Throwing aside their professional habits, covered with rouge, with patches, and diamonds', were 'little more than cloistered prostitutes', who 'excited and practised the most refined gallantry, and passed for the most attractive favourites of the Portuguese nobility'.

In the Campo Grande, some distance beyond the Gulbenkian Foundation, stands a tasteful modern building known as the Torre do Tombo, its name being that of a tower of the Castelo São Jorge, in which the National Archives were originally held. Among the more important of the many historical documents preserved here is the Treaty of 1494 ratifying the division of the Atlantic and adjacent territories between Portugal and Spain; among letters, some signed by Vasco da Gama, Magellan, et al.; and among other bibliographical rarities, the vividly illustrated *Livro das Fortalezas* of Duarte de Armas.

The neighbouring Palácio Pimenta houses the Museu da Cidade, containing much valuable graphic material concentrating on Lisbon's history, ranging from Dirk Stoop's engraving of the *Embarkation of Catherine of Braganza from 'Black Horse Square'*, showing a fountain then embellishing the emplacement of the statue, to views of Lisbon by Robert Batty, James Holland (some of whose sketches had illustrated *Jenkins' Landscape Annual for Portugal*), Isias Newton, and George Atkinson. Of particular interest are those made before 1755, and a vista drawn the following year by C. Lempière, apart from projects for the reconstruction of the ruined capital.

Further afield are the Museu do Trajo (costumes) in the Quinta Palmela, and the Museu de Teatro; while in the same district is the Quinta de Fronteira, with its remarkable formal gardens, shellwork, and *azulejo*-panelled basins, and their tiles of *circa* 1670 depicting knights on prancing chargers very similar to Velazquez's equestrian portraits in the Prado.

NOTES

1. In earlier centuries the king would have been known as Dom Duarte, the usual, but not immediately obvious, Portuguese for Edward.

11

Queluz – Mafra – Sintra

The royal palace at **Queluz** is an irregularly planned rococo building of *pedra lioz* and rose stucco, constructed by Mateus Vicente de Oliveira for the Infante Dom Pedro only three years before the Great Earthquake, which it survived undamaged; for fear of future tremors, only single-storey extensions were added later. The entrance courtyard had been designed in miniature emulation of the Cour du Marbre at Versailles, but that is about the only similarity between the two palaces.

Being on the road to Sintra, it was visited by many making that popular excursion, among whom were British officers in Lisbon during the Peninsular War. Among them, in July 1809, was Captain Sherer, while waiting for his regiment to march. Normally enthusiastic about what he saw, he condemned the apartments at 'Caluz'[*sic*] as 'neither magnificently or elegantly decorated', except for some handsome mirrors, finding the furniture 'in a tawdry and wretched taste'. Apparently General Junot had refurbished the palace not long before – even decorating it with Imperial eagles – as a suitably regal residence for Eugène de Beauharnais, whom it was intended would become King of Portugal. But he had then chosen to occupy it himself, until obliged by Wellington to decamp. Naturally, Junot took the precaution of removing all that was valuable before quitting the place.

Neither did Sherer much care for the gardens 'laid out in a formal, quaint style, trees, hedges, and box, being tortured into every possible variety of shape . . . clumsy statues, defaced busts, and ill-designed fountains', to complete the unflattering picture. The gardens had been laid out by Jean-Baptiste Robillon (who at one time had worked with Thomas Germain, the Parisian silversmith) with formal parterres, urns and topiary, balustraded steps, and a canal lined with blue and white *azulejos* decorated with maritime scenes. I disagree with Sherer: they still have much charm, even if the lead statuary has been burnished by restorers, and the patina of ages removed.

In 1760 Dom Pedro married his niece, the future Dona Maria I, who was soon to exhibit incipient madness. It is difficult to imagine the gloom which must have permeated this palace during the last decades of her long life. Beckford, when attending one of the hushed fêtes got up as a distraction, during which the Infanta Carlota Joaquina insisted on him running a race down the avenue of catalpas and orange trees with her youthful maids of honour, describes his sensation of horror at hearing the queen's agonizing wails.

Her grandson Dom Pedro IV (1798–1834) was born and died in the circular King's bedroom, decorated with paintings depicting the exploits of Don Quixote. Apart from the richly gilt Hall of Mirrors, which did impress Sherer, the Sala dos Azulejos with its Mafra-like bird-cage and red lacquer screens from Macão, and the coffered Sala das Meriendas, embellished by Goyaesque picnic scenes, are delightful.

Some distance beyond **Belas** (where the Infante Dom Manuel held court in 1735 after twenty years of self-imposed exile in Austria), the pink marble quarries of Pero-Pinheiro are skirted as **Mafra** is approached. Well may one's pulse quicken on the first glimpse of the grey towers of what Beckford fancifully described as 'the palace of a giant': indeed it is a colossal pile, totally different in scale and conception to that at Queluz.

The immense bulk of the convent entirely dwarfs the village at its feet, for its main west front alone is 220 metres in extent, twelve longer than the Escorial near Madrid, with which it has been compared, largely on account of their colossal dimensions. Mafra has been likened to a monastic palace: the Escorial to a palatial monastery.

The Italianate portico is framed by twin steeples, referred to by Beckford as being in a 'pagodaish' style; while above the crossing of the church rises a Baroque dome. Built out from either end of the flat façade are two huge pavilions surmounted by squat onion domes, which have certain similarities to the towers of the royal palace 'da Ribeira' at Lisbon, demolished after 1755. These towers, together with the church and the aperture frames, are constructed in the local limestone, which when exposed to storms from the Atlantic – only seven miles distant – is darkened by lichen. The rest of the building is mainly of brick, plastered over; the decision to resort to this material no doubt being made on account of the colossal expense of using masonry throughout.

Its construction was the result of a vow made by Dom João V, preoccupied by the absence of a male heir. The birth of Maria Bárbara in 1711, three years after his marriage to Maria-Ana of Austria, was followed in 1712 by that of Dom Pedro, who, in spite of having used consecrated 'nappies' sent by Pope Clement XI, did not survive infancy. While anxiously awaiting the arrival of the Dom José, not born until June 1714, the king had committed himself to rebuild entirely the Capuchin friary at Mafra as a thanks offering should Heaven vouchsafe him an heir, and the site was cleared in expectation.

Frederico Ludovice,[1] as he is known to the Portuguese, was entrusted with the design of the votive church and monastery, which was to include royal quarters among its dependencies, but these in time grew to take up a significant proportion of the whole. Work began in 1717, but gradually and inexorably the original plan was extended: expense being no object. In 1730 the church was consecrated, but it took only another five years for the rest of the structure to be virtually completed. This would house not just the thirteen monks of the Order of Arrábida as originally intended, but an extra 280; and half as many novices in addition.

Up to 20,000 labourers, masons, carpenters, gilders, and a variety of other artisans were employed on its building and embellishment, their numbers rising in the peak years of 1729 and 1730 to as many as 45,000. A hospital was run up for their care, and a military contingent 7,000 strong was stationed there to control this huge workforce, when not themselves active on the site. Various estimates have been made as to the eventual cost, which is hard to compute; but it was certainly enough to hasten the financial ruin of the country, in spite of the riches of Brazil flooding in.

Like many travellers curious to see this wonder, Baretti, who visited it in 1760, was not entirely happy about several features of the edifice, however magnificent as a whole: for instance, the porticoes seemed either too small for the statues that embellished them, or the statues were too large for the porticoes. There were still some 200 craftsmen on the site, and Baretti got into conversation with one of them, Eugene Nicholas Egan, a diminutive Irishman, who was busily occupied constructing the huge organs, having been chosen to carry out that intricate work by David Perez, the composer, and Caffarello, the castrato. Egan confided to Baretti that his

Travelling in Portugal in the eighteenth century.

John of Gaunt, Duke of Lancaster, dining with Dom João I.

The *pelourinho* passed on ascending towards the castle, Elvas.

The Roman temple at Evora, with (right) the cathedral lantern.

View of Lisbon before the Great Earthquake of 1755.

Early view of the Torre de Belém (detail).

The cloisters of the Jerónimos, Belém.

The Sala das Pêgas in the Palácio Nacional, Sintra.

Early view of Sintra and its *serra*.

Roofscape at Tavira, in the Algarve.

The British camp near Vila Velha, by Major Thomas St Clair (19 May 1811).

A drawing by Major Thomas St Clair of *The Passage of the Tagus near Vila Velha de Ródão* (16 April 1812).

The tomb of Dom Pedro I at Alcobaça.

The Capelas Imperfeitas at Batalha, seen from the south-east, with (left) the Capela do Fundador.

The kitchen, Alcobaça.

The interior of the university library, Coimbra.

Pastime in Portugal, or A Visit to the Nunnerys, after T. Rowlandson (April 1811).

Lieutenant Colonel Frank Wilson's drawing of Wellington's headquarters at Freineda, with the village house as it still is.

The west window of the church at Tomar overlooking the Claustro de Santa Barbara.

On the lagoon near Aveiro.

Terraced vineyards in the Douro valley.

British shippers conferring in the Rua Nova dos Ingleses, by J. J. Forrester (1834).

Early nineteenth-century view of Oporto from Vila Nova de Gaia, with the roofs of several port shippers' *armazéns*.

A view of Ponte de Lima in the 1830s, by George Vivian; very similar today.

A view looking east over Marvão.

salary was not so great as he had been lead to expect, but that there was enough left to pay him anything at all is a wonder.

Egan introduced Baretti to his inventive friend the bell-ringer, who was delighting the Court by the variety of chimes he could ring. Each clock-tower contained over fifty bells, among them carillons cast at Malines in 1730; and the story is told that when the Flemish bell-founders expressed some doubt as to Dom João's ability to pay their price, he shamed them by sending an advance double the amount demanded. The clock mechanism is exhibited now as it was to Baretti:

> So many wheels! So many springs, pivots, rods, some of brass and some of steel . . . yet both the money and the ingenuity has all been squander'd to produce nothing else but some bell-music, which must prove disgustful if it lasts more than three minutes.

Baretti referred to the refectory as 'a glorious thing', with a table extending along the centre long enough to seat 150 at each side. And he could not help noting that set on the table before every two seats was a white earthenware 'mug' [? jug] containing about two bottles of wine, and a trencher of Brazil-wood holding six figs, two bunches of grapes, and two lemons. He did not stay to watch them tuck in, but was assured that each friar was supplied also with three good dishes 'fat or meagre as the day happens to be' and 'a weaten loaf that weighs about a pound', all of which cost the crown an immense amount. And no wonder, he concluded, considering that with 'thirty-two good teeth for each mouth, there are above four-teen thousand teeth a-going twice a day the whole year round', and then there was 'the additional expence of their morning chocolate, their cloaths, their firing, their great consumption of wax in the church and in the cells', etcetera.

Baretti would have liked to have spent more time in the Library, a magnificent Baroque hall, eighty metres long, and even Beckford was not allowed much time by his nimble conductor to examine its contents. Southey remarked that the friar who accompanied him had suggested that 'it would be an excellent room, to eat and drink in, and go to play afterwards', as though the refectory was not enough; but then Southey was prejudiced, condemning them as 'the most ignorant and blackguard of all the monastic orders'. Byron, who considered the monastery a fine example of 'magnificence without elegance', when admiring the room, was asked if 'the *English* had *any books* in their country'.

Note the *trompe l'oeil* panelling in the audience chamber, and the hardwood floors of several galleries. The principal corridor along the west front, off which opens the royal oratory, provides a good view of the well-proportioned church with its comparatively sober ornamentation. Its main decorative feature is the skilful use of the highly polished marbles, including the rosy-hued variety from neighbouring Pero-Pinheiro: only the larger-than-life statues in the vestibule, the imported work of Italian sculptors, are of Carrara marble. Claude de Laprade was responsible for several statues in the church itself. The original painted altar-pieces were replaced by marble reliefs by Alessandro Giusti, who remained at work here for twenty years until blindness forced him to hand over to his pupils. Together with Vieira Lusitano, Giusti had set up a school at Mafra for young artists, architects and sculptors, several of whom played a part in the rebuilding of Lisbon.

Beckford was impressed particularly by the fine execution of the Corinthian capitals, carved with precision and sharpness, although he had seen others far better designed. Later, when attending Vespers, he refers to two 'shabby-looking Englishmen' – in fact Mr Burn, the codfish merchant, and Sir John Swinnerton Dyer[2] – who were gaping at him, and so he took care 'to behave in a dignified devout manner'.

To the north of the church was the 'palatial' suite of Dona Mariana, Dom José's wife; to the south, his own; but in comparison to the rest of the building which may be explored, many will agree with Beckford, who was 'soon weary of wandering about forlorn unfurnished apartments', and considered them the dullest and most comfortless he had ever seen; but then it was customary to store away the gorgeous furniture when royalty was not in residence.

Regular Canons of St Augustine were encloistered here for two decades from 1772; but in 1808 General Junot was in occupation, to be followed soon after by no less than seven British regiments simultaneously. On 7 November 1810, because it lay within the Lines of Torres Vedras and was thus protected from Masséna's marauders, it was chosen by Wellington as providing suitably splendid quarters in which to give a convivial dinner and dance for his officers when celebrating Marshal Beresford's investiture as Knight of the Bath.

But Mafra fell on evil times. Lord Porchester, passing that way in 1827, found a detachment of British troops under Sir Edward

Blakeney in possession.[3] Late in 1835 George Borrow was appalled to find it 'abandoned to two or three menials' and exhibiting an aspect of solitude and desolation, due to the religious orders having been dissolved only a few months earlier and their properties put to secular use whenever possible; the dependencies were later to serve as a military school.

In October 1910 it was at Mafra that Dom Manuel II spent his last night on Portuguese soil before embarking on the royal yacht riding at anchor off neighbouring Ericeira, and sailing to exile in England.

Sintra, or Cintra as it was perhaps better known to the English, having been often so described in both poetry and prose, lies on the northern slope of the Serra de Sintra some eight miles west of Queluz and fourteen south of Mafra. The bosky summit of this range, rising to over 500 metres, is frequently obscured by sea mists, as Southey experienced, when after 'panting all day like a frog in a dry ditch', he returned from the excursion wet and cold, having been enveloped in cloud on making the ascent.

The Royal Palace, with its two conical oast-house-like chimneys, dates in part from the early years of the fifteenth century, its arabesque balustrading and *ajimece* or two-light windows being incorporated later. It was here in 1428 that Dom João I received the Burgundian envoy;[4] and in 1578 Dom Sebastião held his last audience here before setting off on his African expedition, which ended in the disaster of Alcazar-Kebir (or Alcácer-Quibir). In 1683 the impotent Dom Afonso VI died of apoplexy at Sintra, and the apartment in which he had been confined for nine years is still shown, where – like a wild beast in a den – his incessant pacing is said to have worn away the tiled floor.

The rambling pile was being radically restored after earthquake damage when seen by Baretti. Beckford, when referring some decades later to the apartments then being prepared for the reception of Queen Maria, had good reason to complain of the 'swarm of sign-post painters' then employed in daubing the ceilings, and the upholsterers covering the walls with light silks and satins. He would have condemned likewise the repellent nineteenth-century redecoration of the chapel.

Many of the rooms preserve their colourful *azulejo* decoration of *Mudéjar* inspiration. Notable are the Sala dos Brasões, its magnificent *artesonado* dome embellished with prancing stags supporting the blazons of noble families; the vine-leaf motif in the bedroom of Dom Sebastião; the mermaids playing their musical instruments in the Sala das Sereias; the compartmented ceiling of the Sala das Pêgas, covered with painted magpies, each bearing in its beak the device POR BEM, a curious decoration said to have been suggested to Dom João I to satirize the chattering Court gossips after Philippa had surprised him surreptitiously embracing one of her ladies-in-waiting. Equally fine is the Sala dos Cisnes, with its green and white *azulejos*, and polychrome roof painted in octagons and adorned with twenty-seven gold-collared swans.

Uphill from the palace stands the former Hotel Lawrence, where Byron put up in 1809 when apostrophizing Sintra as a 'Glorious Eden'; it is also perhaps that referred to some fifty years earlier as 'the English inn . . . because it is chiefly kept up by a society of English merchants'. After a change of proprietor it is mentioned by Beckford as a 'clean snug inn' being run by 'a most flaming Irish Catholic'. In 1811 Captain Thomas Henry Browne refers to it as being a good hotel, but the charges were 'enormously high, owing to the great influx of Englishmen and other strangers to visit this beautiful spot'. The families of several members of the Factory at Lisbon had summer residences there, where, according to Southey, they idled away their time in visiting their idle acquaintances.

The road leading ahead passes the former **Palace de Seteais** ('of the Seven Sighs'),[5] virtually completed by 1787 for Daniel Gildemeester *père*, the Dutch Consul, whose son sold it a decade later to Beckford's friend the 5th Marquês de Marialva (who had previously lived in what is now the Quinta do Marquês de Velada, nearer Ramalhão).

It is likely that it was here that Beckford was entertained by Marialva during his last visit to Portugal, when at a dinner party he found himself sitting opposite the *bacalhau* merchant Mr Burn (who was to quiz him at Mafra a month later), who 'like a limpet to a rock' sat beside Mrs Hake (whose name Beckford writes as Aik, no doubt deliberately), 'one of the most lively and flippant of the Factorial ladies'. This fond couple, so he had been told, had been active among the British community in spitting their venom at him, and no doubt Beckford was gratified when Mme Gildemeester confided to him her low opinion of such guests, little more than a swarm of insects 'unworthy to crawl upon the hem of her garment, and whom she would shake off with a vengeance at the first opportunity'. Beckford himself referred to them as 'the scrubs and scrubesses of the English Factory'.

By 1835, according to James Alexander, the place was barely

furnished, the pictures on the walls being generally Rowlandson's burlesque English scenes and incidents. It is now a luxury hotel of some charm.

Further along the road to Colares is the **Quinta de Penha Verde**, in which Sir Benjamin Keene spent two delicious summer months in 1748, and where, two centuries earlier, João de Castro, a former viceroy of India, had retired and planted the first orange trees in Europe.

Nearby is the **Quinta de Montserrate**, built by Gerard de Visme, a prosperous English merchant, who entertained William Hickey here 'in a manner never surpassed and seldom equalled'. Beckford, who rented it in 1794, the year he made his excursion to Alcobaça and Batalha, described it as 'a beautiful Claude-like place, surrounded by a most enchanting country'. Lady Craven, who also remarked on its glorious situation, nevertheless thought it 'a Vile Planned house', for De Visme was 'gothicizing' it. After De Visme's death in 1798, Beckford, during his third and last visit to Portugal, bought the estate and may well have indulged in dabbling with further improvements to the villa, and landscaping; but not long after his return to England it became ruinous, and in Byron's words, 'the most desolate mansion in the most beautiful spot I ever beheld', a 'fairy dwelling', where

giant weeds a passage scarce allow
To halls deserted, portals gaping wide . . .

Rose Macaulay, writing in the mid-1940s, conceded that both De Visme and Beckford 'are at least absolved from the barbarous orientalism of the Montserrate of today, constructed in a Moorish delirium by the Visconde Cook of 1856'. This was Sir Francis Cook, first Visconde de Montserrate, who had commissioned the artist William Stockdale, advised by William Nevill of Kew, to lay out its luxuriant gardens with their exotic plants, tree-ferns, palms, and conifers; its eucalyptus are said to be descendants of the first of their kind in Portugal, where unfortunately they are fast becoming ubiquitous. The contents of the mansion were auctioned off in 1948, when the property was sold to the State, who allowed the structure to deteriorate.

The road on, with its 'endless perspectives of flowery thickets between stems of poplar and walnut', reminded Beckford of Savoy and Switzerland, or 'without a violent stretch of fancy', to believe himself in the Gardens of the Hesperides 'and to expect a Dragon under every tree'.

Nearby **Colares** is reputed for its red wine, 'a sort of half-way excellence between port and claret' to young Southey's taste.

From there – shunning the sophisticated delights of coastal Cascais and Estoril – the circuit of the richly clad Serra de Sintra is continued by passing below the Convento dos Capuchos, better known as the **'Cork Convent'** from the slabs of cork which line the damp walls of its rock-cut atrium. The hermitage was a curiosity visited frequently by English ladies and gentlemen, so the hospitable friars told Baretti. Beckford, who clambered up to it on more than one occasion, once entertained its prior at Ramalhão, who 'contrived to toss off the better half of three bottles of port in a twinkling, and soon gulped down an equal quantity of claret and madeira'. No wonder his 'flaming nose and juicy forehead' beggared description. But by 1811 only a handful of friars remained in residence.

Along the crest of a bold ridge lies a ruined fortress of Moorish foundation, while the main massif is crowned by the **Castelo da Pena**. On a clear day the views it commands compensate for the distraction of this Gothic eyrie, a grotesque architectural confection encasing the cloister and chapel of a former Hieronymite monastery. The superb position prompted Ferdinand of Saxe-Coburg-Gotha (consort of Dona Maria II and a cousin of Prince Albert), to commission a certain Baron von Eschwege to design a baronial pile, and work was started in about 1840. After the queen's death in 1853 a *feteira* or fern-garden was laid out in the surrounding woods, complete with rustic cottage and 'Moorish' pavilion, to gratify Ferdinand's mistress, a German singer named Haensler, who he entitled the Condessa d'Edla.

The road from Sintra to Lisbon passes near the *quinta* at Ramalhão rented by Beckford during the summer of 1787, where he would trifle away the whole morning 'surrounded by fidalgos in flowered bed-gowns and musicians in violet coloured accoutrements, with broad straw hats . . .'. Five years later it was acquired by the obnoxious and intriguing widow of Dom João VI, Dona Carlota Joaquina, who in 1822 retired there after having refused to take the oath to the Constitution. She would have been expelled from the country had not ten doctors declared expediently that she was unfit to travel. Nevertheless, she survived for another eight years, hatching conspiracies meanwhile, and it was from here in 1833 that her reactionary brother Don Carlos of Spain proclaimed against his niece Isabel II, an ill-judged action which precipitated the First Carlist War in Spain.

Was it this *quinta* referred to by Osbert Sitwell as having been rented by Ronald Firbank earlier this century?

NOTES

1. Johann Friedrich Ludwig (1670–1752), born at Ratisbon, had trained at Augsburg and Rome before visiting Lisbon in 1701, where he worked for the Jesuits. His team included António, his son; Carlo Battista Garbo, a Milanese who had settled in Portugal some twenty years earlier; Custódio Vieira; and Manuel de Maia, later responsible for the construction of the Aguas Livres Aqueduct.
2. Probably Colonel Sir John Swinnerton Dyer, 6th baronet.
3. This was part of a force commanded by General Sir William Clinton, which Canning had sent out at the request of the Portuguese government to prevent any foreign intervention in the internal affairs of Portugal, where there had been an Absolutist rising in support of Dom Miguel against his brother Dom Pedro.
4. In his train came Jan van Eyck, to paint the portrait of Dom João's only daughter, the Infanta Isabel. This must have pleased Philippe le Bon, who married her in Bruges the following year. It was to celebrate the occasion that the Burgundian duke, emulating that of the Garter, founded the Order of the Golden Fleece. Another, presumed, portrait of Isabel may be seen in the polyptych by Van der Weyden in the Hôtel-Dieu at Beaune.
5. It was long assumed that the 'Convention of Cintra' was signed in this mansion, but the document, although dispatched from Sintra, was actually ratified in Lisbon: nevertheless, the name has been associated with this disgrace to British arms ever since the publication of Byron's vitriolic lines in *Childe Harold*.

12

The Lower Alentejo:
Beja – Serpa– Mértola

Beja, a thriving agricultural town in the centre of the rolling wheat belt of the Baixa Alentejo, as Pax Julia was the capital of a Roman *conventus*, the others in Lusitania being at Mértola, Mérida, and Santarém. At **Aljustrel**, twenty-five miles south-west, were the extensively worked copper mines of Roman Vipasca; while forty-five miles due west, on a height near the coast at **Santiago de Cacém**, stood Roman Mirobriga (from which the castle keep of Beja may be discerned on a clear day, although it is not so easy to pick out Santiago from Beja).

The Moors corrupted the title Pax Julia to Beja, and walled the place, which remained in their hands until 1162. Its later history is comparatively uneventful. In 1808 it was sacked by Colonel Maransin's marauding French troops. More recently, largely in reaction to centuries of exploitation by landowners whose huge estates or *latifúndios* were similar in extent to those in Spanish Andalucía, it became for a time a stronghold of Communism; and it was here in January 1962 that General Humberto Delgado planned his abortive revolt against the Salazar regime.

The most conspicuous building in Beja is the forty-metre-high *torre de menagem* of its castle, completed early in the fourteenth century on what were Roman foundations. Close by is the Ermida de Santo André, its cylindrical buttresses similar to those of São Bras at Evora; deconsecrated Santo Amaro, preserving several Visigothic capitals and columns; and to the east of the castle, Renaissance São Tiago. The covered market in the central Praça da República was once the Misericórdia.

Beyond the east end of this square stands the former convent of Nossa Senhora da Conceição, founded in 1467 on what was probably the site of the forum. Above its west door is an *ajimece* window removed from the demolished palace of the Dukes of Beja, which was connected to the convent by a brick-built gallery. Its balustrades may have influenced the design of those at Batalha.

It has been assumed that it was from this convent that Mariana Alcoforado wrote the five reproachful letters to Colonel Noël Bouton, Comte de Saint-Léger and later marquis, known as the Chevalier de Chamilly, who during the latter part of the war with Spain in the 1660s had made her his mistress, and then deserted her. These *Letters* were published first in French in 1669, followed after nine years by their English translation, which gave the reputed 'Portuguese Nun' a certain notoriety.

The Baroque chapel, and the *azulejos* in the cloister and chapter-house, some of *Mudéjar* design, are notable; among the paintings is a portrait of the worthy Manuel do Cenáculo Vilas-Boas, the bibliophile Bishop of Beja before his translation to Evora.

There is little else to be seen in Beja, for the dependencies of the convent of São Francisco have suffered the fate of so many others since 1834 of conversion to barracks. Remains of Roman occupation may be seen at the partly excavated site of the first- to fourth-century villa at **Pisões**, some five miles to the south-west.

Near a spur of the vine-covered Serra Abelheira, south-east beyond the Guadiana, stands ancient **Serpa**, so-named in the *Antonine Itinerary*. Considering that it had a Roman mint, few relics of its past have survived, except a ruined castle, stretches of wall and, among medieval gateways, the Porta de Beja, abutted by the remains of a huge *nora*, a form of chain-pump, and aqueduct. Gothic Santa Maria contains mid-seventeenth-century *azulejos*; Santo António, similar to Santo André at Beja, preserves a small cloister.

A lonely winding road leads south over the wooded hills to *Minas de São Domingos*, whose ancient copper mines, rediscovered in 1857, were then exploited by the British company of Mason & Barry until 1965. Once worked by the Romans, they are an extension of those known to the Phoenicians at Rio Tinto and Tharsis – recalling the names of Tartessos or Tarshish – lying beyond the Spanish frontier, which here follows the course of the Chanca.

Bearing west, the road descends steeply into the rocky gorge of the Guadiana; the arabized form of the Roman river Anas being Wadi-anas. Impressively sited on its far bank rises the small town of **Mértola**, dominated by its partly Moorish castle. A curious pier-like structure, once thought to be the remains of a Roman or Visigothic bridge, extends from the water's edge, but it is more likely the relic of a Moorish *nora* – as at Serpa – in which Roman masonry had been incorporated.

Founded in remote antiquity, Roman Julia Myrtilis was by AD 440 in Suevic hands. Numerous early Christian inscriptions, some in Greek, suggest that the river-port – conveniently placed to export the ore from both São Domingos and Aljustrel – continued to flourish in the sixth century, and was briefly subject to Byzantium. Carved on a tombstone found here, dated AD 525, is a so-called 'Moorish' arch, which would confirm that this horseshoe form of construction was in fact used in the Iberian Peninsula at least two centuries *before* the Moslem occupation. Mértola was in their hands from 712, and was held briefly by the Ibn Qasi prior to 1146, when the invading Almohads wintered here before marching on Seville. It was not reconquered until 1238.

The fine vaulting of the battlemented Igreja Matriz, formerly a mosque, is probably contemporary with the late-thirteenth-century castle keep. Much excavation and restoration is under way in Mértola: both a forum and *cryptoporticus* have been uncovered not far west of the church, while the foundations of a Roman villa lie below the Town Hall, with its small museum. Other museums, devoted to Mértola's successive eras of occupation, are promised: that illustrating the Islamic domination will be near the southern prow of the *enceinte*, and Paleo-Christian remains will be displayed *in situ*, to the north.

13

The Algarve:
Vila Real de Santo António to Sagres

From Mértola the road south climbs steeply before winding across the cistus-covered ridges of the Serra do Malhão – 'great waves', as Southey dramatically described them in 1801 when making his excursion to the Algarve – eroded by tributaries of the Guadiana, which, deep in its rocky valley, forms the neighbouring frontier. Descending for the last time, with the coast basking in the distance, the road approaches **Castro Marim**, Roman Baesuris, dominated by its huge castle, which in 1319 became the first headquarters of the Order of Christ, where it remained until transferred to Tomar 130 years later. The fortress was damaged in the earthquake of 1755, and only the ruins of its church survive within the *enceinte*.

Adjacent **Vila Real de Santo António**, a tunny-fishing centre and the easternmost town of the Algarve, lies on the estuary of the Guadiana opposite Spanish Ayamonte, to which ferries ply frequently, although they may be superseded with the completion of the international bridge a short distance upstream. An earlier riverport, which may well have been of Phoenician foundation, was engulfed by the sea in about 1600, and Vila Real, built to replace it, was run up on a grid plan after 1774, largely on Pombal's initiative. The ashlar masonry used in part of the new town's construction was transported from Lisbon at ruinous expense, not long after which some perfectly adequate quarries were fortuitously 'discovered' in the vicinity, which suggests that local jobbery was thriving.

Captain Richard Croker, who passed through the place in 1780, thought it 'by no means an unpromising introduction to Portugal: the houses are uniformly and neatly built; being painted white, with green windows', but at that time the paint would have been hardly dry.

The next town of consequence along the coast is **Tavira**, which the

author of Murray's *Handbook* considered one of its pleasantest. It
still is, but admittedly my impression may have been influenced by
the succulent red mullet I savoured there.

Tavira's early history is vague. At one time it was claimed to be
the site of Roman Balsa, but this is now thought to be further west,
near **Luz**. In 1239 it was captured from the Moors, and flourished
with the export of the melons, carobs, almonds, and figs of its rich
hinterland, and also of the scarlet kermes dye, which was then
sought after. In the mid-seventeenth century Tavira suffered a temporary decline, partly due to frequent visitations of the plague, and
the port silted up.

The sanguinary *copeja*, or seasonal slaughter of its tunny shoals,
still takes place in the estuary of the Gilão, but it is not a pleasant
sight. The river, which bisects the town, is spanned by a fine old
bridge and flanked by several eighteenth-century houses, a picturesque feature being their Oriental-looking triple-gabled roofs. In
the older *enceinte* are the Misericordia, with a good portal, and
Santa Maria do Castelo, rebuilt in the mid-eighteenth century, but
retaining the Gothic doorway of its predecessor, said to have been
constructed on the site of a mosque. Tavira's other monuments are
not outstanding, but for me the port has a special charm, which I
hope will not evaporate.

The same cannot be said of many other places through which the
coast road passes. The N270, bearing inland, is a more agreeable
route, as it winds up through fruitful hills to **São Bras de Alportel**.
From there, descend past Estoi (see below) for Faro.

The unexciting main road runs parallel to the shore, here fringed
by extensive sandbanks. One of these, the Cabo de Santa Maria, off
Olhão, with its flashing lighthouse, is the most southerly tip of
Portugal. **Olhão** itself is no longer the curiosity it once was, when its
predominant architecture, a medley of cubical, marshmallow-like,
flat-roofed dwellings, would invite comparisons with North Africa.

Faro, a straggling modern town, and the prosperous capital of the
Algarve, is of slight attraction, although its walled *enceinte*, or
Vila-a-Dentro, deserves exploration.

Until its forum was discovered below the cathedral, it had been
assumed that the Roman town of Ossonoba was centred on the
extensive second- to seventh-century Roman villa of Milreu at **Estoi**,
seven miles inland, where excavations had uncovered several fine
portrait busts, a temple converted into a Paleo-Christian basilica,
and third-century baths.

In 1249 Santa Maria de Harune, as Faro was then known, was wrested from the Moors by Dom Afonso III, and continued to prosper, perhaps partly on account of the commercial activity of its large Jewish community, one of whom, Samuel Gascon, had installed a printing-press there in 1487, only a few years before their expulsion.[1]

During the Spanish occupation, the Algarve was raided intermittently by the English, notably in 1596, when the Earl of Essex, finding Faro undefended, landed a contingent of troops, who naturally pillaged the place. Essex had the forethought to rummage the episcopal library, for Jeronimo Ossorio (who had moved his see from Silves to Faro only three years before his death in 1580) had the reputation of being the 'Portuguese Cicero'. Some 200 volumes of theology, many mutilated by the Holy Office, were sacked up. At a later date Essex donated the indigestible tomes to the infant Bodleian, a gesture that was considered very generous from a Cambridge man.

The city suffered severely in the earthquakes of 1722 and 1755, after which much of the rebuilding was due to Francisco Gomes de Avelar, a later energetic bishop. The Renaissance cathedral, preserving the squat tower of an older church, is embellished with *azulejos* and a splendid red and gilt chinoiserie-painted organ, while notable among its monuments is the lion-supported tomb of Bishop Pereira da Silva. The present incumbent is said to resent visitors (whatever their Faith) entering his cathedral merely to satisfy their aesthetic curiosity; it may be closed therefore except within circumscribed hours, although pressure is being built up to make him reconsider such a retrograde step.

South of the apse is a former convent, its undulating roofs similar to those at Tavira, with a museum in its two-storeyed cloister displaying a mosaic from Milreu among other archaeological treasures. On the far side of a deserted square beyond the Arco de Repousa stands São Francisco, with an ornate *capela-mór* and *azulejos* of 1762. The ecclesiologist may also wish to visit two other churches off the Largo do Carmo, both retaining features of interest.

On approaching **Almansil**, the increasingly busy stretch of main road passes the church of São Lourenço, the whole interior of which is plastered with blue *azulejos* attributed to Policarpo de Oliveira Bernardes; but there is little else to stop for.

Inland lies **Loulé**, reputed for its disproportionately large and ornate chimneys, a curious conceit of popular architecture; while nearer the shore extends an attractive wooded district now the haunt of golfers, several courses having been laid out in recent years. Near the more westerly of these, at **Vilamoura**, another Roman villa has been excavated.

The road now skirts several resorts strung out along the coast, promoted for its denticulated rocks and sandy beaches. Among them is **Albufeira**, which formerly had some attraction, but rampant over-exploitation has already spoilt much of this part of the Algarve. Few who have visited it in the past would recognize the conurbation of **Portimão**, not that it ever had much in its favour.

It is preferable to drive north from Albufeira to **São Bartolomeu de Messines**, and from there to bear west along the sunny southern slope of a range of low hills towards Silves.

Comparatively little remains of **Silves** to remind one of its illustrious past apart from its walls, its ruined castle, and cathedral, all built with a dark red sandstone which has been vividly described as the colour of congealed blood. The Arab chronicler Idrisi stated that the town – Shalb or Xelb – possessing a river-port and shipyards and surrounded by a strong wall and with well-furnished bazaars, was populated largely by Yemenites who spoke a very pure Arabic, composed poetry (both the upper and lower classes), were eloquent of speech and elegant in manners.

This civilized oasis was also at the centre of the mid-twelfth-century Ibn Qasi revolt against the Almoravids. It remained in Moorish occupation for another century, having in 1189 survived a frightful three-month siege and sacking by a force of Crusaders, some of them from London, which had landed at the mouth of the Arade. In 1596 it was again pillaged, this time by Essex, but by then the bishopric had been transferred to Faro, and there was little to cart away. Severely shaken in 1755, it was described not much later as one of the most desolate and deserted places in Portugal.

The former cathedral ('old and unremarkable' in Southey's eyes), had been constructed on the site of a mosque, as were most churches of importance in the south, and it retains several curious architectural features, although it was not improved by post-earthquake restorations. At a higher level, surrounded by gardens, are relics of the castle, the parapet walk of which provides a pleasant panorama of the surrounding orange groves and almond orchards.

Alvor, on the coast west of Portimão, and perhaps the Carthaginian Portus Hannibalis, had also been attacked by the above-mentioned Crusaders, who in true Christian fashion massacred all those who had taken refuge there. It was here too that Dom João II died, after futile attempts to relieve his dropsy by taking the waters of **Caldas de Monchique**, whose springs, the efficacious properties of which were reputed by both Romans and Moors, lie inland on the sunbaked southern slope of its Serra. Its summit, the Foia, rising to a height of 900 metres, is the highest peak in the Algarve.

From 1578 until 1755, when it was virtually razed, the provincial capital was **Lagos**, perhaps because it had become a favourite residence of Henry the Navigator, being conveniently near Sagres. It was here that this mercantile prince established a company trading with the newly discovered territories in Africa. In the mid-1570s Lagos was the main port of assembly of troops and transports for Dom Sebastião's suicidal Moroccan campaign; and it was off the coast here in 1759 that Admiral Boscawen defeated a French squadron commanded by De la Rue.

Southey, arrested for not having the courtesy of waiting on the *corregedor*, which was then the routine convention for travellers on arrival at any place of consequence, became one of the first tourists to patronize the local handicraft industry, buying an aloe-fibre work-bag as a curiosity for his wife.

Part of the mid-fourteenth-century walls survive beside the water-front avenue, but more considerable stretches with their bastions, rise further west. On the promenade is the former customhouse, below the arches of which African slaves were herded for auction. Adjacent is Santa Maria, with its Manueline windows and the richly embellished chapel of Santo Antonio, preserving *albarrada azulejos*, but its painted vault dates from after the earthquake. Note the tomb of Hugh Beatty, colonel of an Irish Regiment, who died here in 1789.

In the museum congregate miscellaneous archaeological collections, but they have not yet cast sufficient light on whether or not Lagos was the successor of Roman Lacobriga: its site may well have been on Monte Molião, admittedly no great distance away.

The road undulates over the hills towards **Sagres** and the Cabo de São Vicente, *onde a terra se acaba e o mar começa* – where the land ends and the sea begins – in the words of Camoens. Although the peevish author of Murray's *Handbook* suggests that 'Probably no person will wish to visit Sagres twice', the site has a special fascination, and the Pousada do Infante offers good accommodation on this wild and windswept promontory.

The presence of Henry the Navigator, who died at Sagres in 1460, is strongly felt still, but it is not easy to disentangle fact from legend. It would appear that this half-English prince, with his well-developed spirit of curiosity, decided to set up an observatory and school of navigation here after leaving nearby **Raposeira** – as if that village was not sufficiently isolated and 'remote from the tumult of people and propitious for the contemplation of study'. He engaged the assistance of the most reliable cosmographers and cartographers, among them Jaume Ribes, a Chueta from Mallorca (Judah Cresques before his conversion in 1391), whose father, Abraham, had compiled the famous *Catalan Atlas* in about 1375.

Among the first of several expeditions the Navigator initiated of which there is a definite record, was that of 1421, when the West African coast was explored as far south as eight degrees latitude north, for he desired 'to have knowledge of that land, but also of the Indies and the land of Prester John, if such might be'. The occupation of the Canaries took place in 1424 (but these islands were later disputed with Castile, who acquired the group by treaty in 1479); in 1425 Madeira was settled; in 1430 the Azores were rediscovered, having been sighted some eighty years earlier, although not colonized until 1445; the island of Arguim was reached in 1443; and only a few weeks before his death, Prince Henry was in a position to grant to the Order of Christ at least the spiritual dominion of the Cape Verde islands.

The headquarters of Portuguese maritime exploration was then transferred to Lisbon, and Sagres decayed. In 1597 the Vila do Infante, Dom Henrique's former residence, was sacked by Drake, and what remained of it was shattered in 1755.

On **Cape St Vincent**, with its beckoning lighthouse, fishermen with their long rods now perch perilously, as far below them pound the surging Atlantic breakers. The awesome iron-bound headland, the Roman Promontorium Sacrum, and the south-western extremity of the European mainland, takes it present name from the legend that relics of that martyr had been brought here in the eighth century. These were later translated miraculously to Lisbon in a boat guided by a pair of ravens, and lie in the cathedral dedicated to him; while the ravens now figure in the city's arms.

More historical events have been the several naval engagements fought off the barren coast, among them the defeat of Sir George Rooke by Admiral Tourville in 1693; an attack on the Spanish fleet by Rodney in 1780; the rout in February 1797 of another Spanish fleet of twenty-seven men-of-war by Nelson and Admiral Jervis (created Earl of St Vincent for his victory), commanding a mere fifteen vessels; and in 1833, during the War of the Two Brothers, when a Miguelite squadron was trounced by Sir Charles Napier, for which action he was entitled Count Cape St Vincent.

A slow and uninteresting road winds north at some distance from the coast and away from the Algarve via **Odemira**.

Avoiding the tubular jungle of the tanker terminal of **Sines**, a by-road climbs to **Santiago do Cacém** (with a *pousada*), dominated by the ruins of a Moorish castle rebuilt by the Templars. Here also is the extensive site of Roman Miróbriga Celticum, only partially excavated, and of a pre-Roman *oppidum* in occupation since the eighth or ninth century BC.

NOTES

1. Presses were set up in Lisbon and Leiria five years later by Rabbi Eliezer and Abrao Samuel d'Ortas respectively.

14

The Upper Alentejo:
Marvão – Portalegre – Castelo de Vide

An attractive alternative entrance to Portugal may be made by diverging off the main Madrid-Badajoz highway at Trujillo, for Cáceres, and on via Aliseda towards Valencia de Alcántara and the frontier. I have a preference for the detour from Aliseda to Albuquerque, there bearing north-west.

In May 1705 both Albuquerque and Valencia de Alcántara were besieged by Anglo-Portuguese troops, capitulating to the Earl of Galway and to General Fagel respectively. During 1762, when a Spanish army invaded the Trás-os-Montes, Valencia was seized by forces commanded by General John Burgoyne,[1] who captured the French General Dumberry there. Both towns threatened the Portuguese frontier, here formed by the serrated ridge of the Serra de São Mamede and the contiguous Serra de Marvão, rising dramatically from the rolling *meseta*.

The road passes between these ranges to cross the frontier. On entering the first Portuguese village, a right-hand turning makes a steep ascent up the flank of a massive hill to its wind-buffeted summit and **Marvão** itself, nestling within its thirteenth-century ramparts, which are practically intact. Several outworks were added later. Understandably, the site has been fortified since remote antiquity, for the easily defended eyrie dominates the district. The castle on its rocky outcrop provides several distant and plunging views, among them, far to the north-west, of the Serra da Estrela, in which the Torre, the highest peak in Portugal, rises to 1,025 metres. The Pousada de Santa Maria at Marvão can provide a comfortable base from which to explore the area.

From the valley floor, the road to Portalegre climbs over the Serra de Mamede, known to the Romans as the Herminus Minor, passing near **São Salvador de Aramenha** (Herminum) the largely unexcavated site of the *oppidum* of Ammaia, later a Roman settlement.

John Mason Neale, the querulous author of Murray's *Handbook to Portugal*, was unfairly dismissive of **Portalegre**, in suggesting that 'no traveller can be recommended to extend his excursion hither unless induced to do so by some particular object', for although its long history is unexceptional, the place is not without interest. It was important enough in 1299 for Dom Dinis to besiege it for five months during the dynastic feuds of that period.

In June 1704, during the War of the Succession, in the absence on sick leave in Lisbon of their commander, Colonel James Stanhope, his regiment, together with the Portuguese garrison, was surprised and captured after a brisk bombardment by a Spanish force under Colonel d'Asfeld (who was later to become a Marshal of France). During the Peninsular War it often served as winter quarters for British troops. Military bands would play raucously in the cloisters of nunneries to entertain their inmates. Races were organized; occasionally hunts were got up between Portalegre and Castelo de Vide; and even cricket was played at some cantonments. Some officers preferred less strenuous pastimes. Captain Sherer recorded that he spent much of his time here in the library of the hospitable canon on whom he was billeted, which contained not only handsome editions of the classics but also a good selection of French authors.

A century and a half ago an enterprising Yorkshireman, who had been importing cork from Portugal, acquired a small factory at Portalegre, and that entrepreneur's son, George Wheelhouse Robinson, continued what was a flourishing business until his death in 1931. The work of the cork-strippers, and life in the district several decades ago, has been described entertainingly by Huldine Beamish (see Bibliography).

In the lower town stands the convent of Nossa Senhora da Conceição or that of São Bernardo, now occupied as a training centre for military police, who were pounding around the cloister when, courteously escorted by the officer on duty, I was allowed to visit the church. It retains several features of interest, among them the tomb of its founder, Jorge de Melo, Bishop of Guarda, possibly sculpted by Chanterène *circa* 1540, and some very fine *azulejos*.

The walled upper town is dominated by the pinnacled towers of the cathedral, notable for its massive pilasters and architectural altarpieces, the *azulejos* in its sacristy, and the pediments in its cloister. Richard Russell was the incumbent for several years before 1682.

Little remains of the castle at **Crato**, to the west, destroyed by Don Juan de Austria in 1662, but its Igreja Matriz contains good altars and *azulejos*. A branch of the Knights Hospitaller known as the Grão Priorado, or Order of Crato, had its headquarters here after 1350, having moved from Leça do Bailio, near Oporto. The last of its Grand Priors, the bastard son of the Infante Luis and Violante Gomes, seductively named 'The Pelican', was Dom Antonio, in 1580 a serious rival to Philip II in his claim to the Portuguese throne.

South of Crato lies **Alter do Chão**, probably the Albelterium of the *Antonine Itinerary*, with a restored mid-fourteenth-century castle, the Solar de Vasconcelos, and a Renaissance fountain.

West of the town, near **Vila Formosa**, a road following the line of its Roman predecessor brings one to an imposing six-arched Roman bridge spanning the Seda.

Just north of Crato is the charmingly named village of **Flor da Rosa**, where the church and dependencies of a large fortified convent founded by the father of Nun'Alvares Pereira, the great Constable (*O Comdestabre* or *Condestável*) of Portugal, is being restored. It was a far-flung family, the Constable being one of the thirty-two illegitimate children of a certain Alvaro Gonçalves Pereira, Prior of the Portuguese branch of the military Order of the Hospitallers of St John, but I have not attempted to climb any further into the ramifications of that particular fruitful tree.

From Flor da Rosa a cross-country road leads north-east to **Castelo de Vide**, a beautifully sited old spa on the slope of a spur of the Serra da São Mamede. Although containing few outstanding buildings – Baroque Santa Maria, the former Torre palace, and the Town Hall, with its Salão Nobre decorated by Ventura Porfírio, are worth a mention – it is an agreeable place, freshened by numerous fountains, possessing several small chapels, and preserving its medieval *Judiaria*.

Its Anglo-Portuguese garrison, although they had repelled a Spanish assault in June 1704, capitulated to the Duke of Berwick's threat that he would put to the sword all those who continued to resist and 'leave the women exposed to the brutality of the soldiers'.[2] If they surrendered they would be allowed 'to keep their equipage and there would be no plunder'. In the event, the Portuguese dumped all their remaining gunpowder into a well rather than hand it over to the enemy. In the following year the castle was seriously damaged by an explosion.

From **Alpalhão**, the road north descends beyond **Nisa** towards the Tagus, crossed at **Vila Velha de Ródão**, where it forces its way west through vertiginous cliffs. The river here was long provided with a bridge of boats, which during the Peninsular War formed a vital link in Wellington's lateral lines of communication, and the view of 'The Passage of the Tagus' was one reproduced frequently in prints of that period. The local museum contains artefacts from now submerged riparian sites, dating back to Paleolithic times.

For Castelo Branco and the Beira, see Chapter 18; for Abrantes and Tomar, to the west, see Chapter 17.

NOTES

1. John Burgoyne (1722–92), also a successful dramatist, had a varied career. He was given supreme command in Canada later, but capitulated at Saratoga in 1777. He also managed the impeachment of Warren Hastings.
2. James Fitzjames (1617–1734), a natural son of the future James II and Arabella Churchill, and created Duke of Berwick in 1687, had been Captain-General of Franco-Spanish armies from early 1704.

15

Northern Estremadura: Torres Vedras – Vimeiro – Roliça – Obidos

Some twenty-eight miles north of Lisbon lies the vinous town of **Torres Vedras** (probably deriving its name from *turres veteres*, the complex of prehistoric fortifications on the neighbouring Castro do Zambujal). Although it has a ruinous castle, in itself the place is of slight interest. However, its name is irrevocably connected with the lines of redoubts stretching across the twenty-five-mile-wide neck of the peninsula on which Lisbon stands and which so successfully kept Masséna at arm's length during the winter of 1810–11.

It was in October of the previous year, less than three months after the battle of Talavera, that Viscount Wellington, as he had been recently entitled, leaving his small army encamped near Elvas to recruit its strength, returned briefly to Lisbon to make contingency plans to protect the capital in the event of any future French designs to reoccupy it. He had recognized already, after the battle of Vimeiro, the defensive possibilities of this hilly district, and with Colonel Richard Fletcher, his chief engineer, had ridden over the area, selecting suitable ridges for this purpose, while Major José Neves Costa noted down the intricacies of the terrain. Although Wellington had an excellent military survey of the immediate vicinity of Lisbon, compiled by General Sir Charles Stuart in 1799, he had no detailed map of the country further north.

Throughout 1810 the Portuguese were engaged in constructing two roughly parallel lines of batteries and forts, the arduous task being undertaken with the greatest secrecy. Local peasant labour and Lisbon militia regiments were supervised by Captain Mulcaster, together with some 150 British NCOs and eighteen engineers.

The impressive series of redoubts, 152 in all, were mounted with almost 450 guns. The more northerly line extended from **Sisandra** on the coast to **Alhandra** on the Tagus.[1] A second line passed just north of **Mafra** to meet the river near **Póvoa de Santa Iria**. Both flanks were protected by naval flotillas.

Headquarters was sited at **Pero Negro**, a central point between the two lines and conveniently near the viewpoint of Monte Socorro. By a simple system of semaphore posts on commanding heights, a message could be sent to any part of the front within minutes, while lateral roads laid out behind the lines enabled troops to be moved rapidly to whichever area might be threatened. A written order took less than an hour to reach any unit.

This complex of defensive positions was manned by Wellington's Portuguese militia and *ordenança*, and Romana's Spanish troops (variously estimated at 29–33,000 men in all), supported by 2,500 British gunners and marines. Thirty-four thousand British front-line regulars would remain concentrated behind the Lines ready for deployment wherever required.[2]

The Allies made their strategic retreat from Busaco exactly a year after work on the Lines had been initiated. Meanwhile a 'scorched-earth' policy was also put into effect, the local population north of the Lines, together with their livestock, being herded south into what was basically an entrenched camp over 500 square miles in area. During the second week of October 1810 Wellington himself entered its outworks, leading his troops into secure and well provisioned territory.

It was not always easy to convince the peasants that they must retire from their villages, and Wellington had no compunction about ordering his cavalry commander to inform the local magistrates that 'if any of them stay, or if any of the inhabitants have any communication with the enemy, they will be hanged'. The threat had its effect, and before long he was to report that

> The people of Portugal are doing that which the Spaniards ought to have done. They are removing their women and properties out of the enemy's way, and taking arms in their own defence. The country is made a desert, and behind almost every stone wall the French will meet an enemy.

No wonder, when Masséna apprehensively approached the largest redoubt, just south of **Sobral**, designed to hold twenty-five guns and 1,500 men, it did not take him long to be convinced of the impregnability of these formidable works, which he had no idea would be obstructing what he confidently expected to be a triumphant march on Lisbon. Any attempt to take them by frontal attack would be folly indeed; and thoroughly frustrated, he ordered his army to dig in.

The fact that the French were able to subsist where they did for so long is little short of miraculous, for although they were used to living off the land, the army was cut off entirely from any regular supplies, as confirmed by Wellington when writing to Lord Liverpool on 21 December:

> It is certainly astonishing that the enemy have been able to remain in this country so long; and it is an extraordinary instance of what a French army can do. It is positively a fact that they brought no provisions with them, and they have not received even a letter since they entered Portugal. With all our money, and having in our favour the good inclinations of the country, I assure you that I could not maintain one division in the district in which they have maintained not less than 60,000 men and 20,000 animals for more than two months. This time last year I was obliged to move the British cavalry only from the district which they now occupy with their whole army, because it could not be subsisted. But they take everything, and leave the unfortunate inhabitants to starve.

In their desperate search for corn and any other food or drink hidden from them, the French would thrust their bayonets or ramrods into the earthen floors of peasant houses and, if this had no positive result, they then poured water on the ground. As this would sink first into any spot lately disturbed, the ingenious practice quite frequently led to the discovery of buried hoards of produce, linen or other treasures, at least until the Portuguese realized that the British too had picked up the habit.

By early March 1811 sheer starvation forced Masséna and his shrunken army, ravenous and demoralized, to retreat from a position between Santarém and Rio Maior to between Tomar and Leiria. He then retired precipitately north, with the intention of concentrating on the Mondego, little realizing that the far bank of that river was defended by Portuguese militia under the command of Colonel Nicholas Trant (a British officer in the Portuguese service, later engagingly described by Wellington as 'A very good officer, but as drunken a dog as ever lived'). Not wishing to risk a battle while astride that torrent, Masséna attempted to disengage, but was only able to hasten his retreat by destroying all his remaining wheeled transport except caissons and gun-carriages, and hamstringing all animals no longer serviceable.[3]

The bedraggled 'Army of Portugal', harried continually by guerrillas, limped north-east towards Celorico. It was then deflected past Almeida, into which Masséna threw a garrison before leading his straggling troops across the frontier into equally hostile Spain.

Wellington, who had followed close on their heels, set up headquarters near the border at Freineda. Beresford was ordered south to invest Badajoz and keep an eye on Soult. The disastrous campaign had cost Masséna dear: between 25,000 and 30,000 men killed, wounded, picked off by vengeful Portuguese peasants, and otherwise prevented from taking part in any further fighting; and in addition he had lost some 9,000 horses and virtually his entire wagon train.

The contest was resumed early in May, with the sanguinary battles of Fuentes de Oñoro and Albuera (see Chapter 19).

The direct road north from Torres Vedras, to Obidos is one of the worst I have yet discovered in Portugal – at least in an area where one might have expected better communications – and it is still marked on recent maps as having a wretched surface; but no matter, for Vimeiro, a small village not far to the north-west off the road to Peniche, is our next target.

It was here that the second battle between the British and French took place during the Peninsular War, the first having occurred at Roliça, further north. But to explain the circumstances of these two engagements, they must be described in chronological order.

During the first few days of August 1808, an expeditionary force commanded by Lieutenant-General Sir Arthur Wellesley, the future Duke of Wellington (which, for convenience, I have named him throughout), landed in heavy surf at the mouth of the Mondego near Figueira da Foz, west of Coimbra, where Admiral Sir Charles Cotton had posted some 400 marines. An additional contingent under General Sir Brent Spencer disembarked soon after, but although together mustering some 14,000 men, they were short of mounts. To have attempted an undisturbed disembarkation further south would have been much more difficult, for the French occupied the fortifications at Peniche, and the mouth of the Tagus was far too close to Junot's base.

They marched south under a blistering sun, and were soon joined by 1,600 Portuguese auxiliaries commanded by Trant, lent by

General Bernardino Freire, whose Portuguese army awaited further developments near Leiria.

By 14 August the British had entered Alcobaça, and were approaching Obidos, a fortified village which the French under General Delaborde had surprisingly given up, having retired a short distance further south to a position at the far end of a horseshoe of hills not far beyond the village of **Roliça**. Another French army, commanded by General Loison, approaching from Rio Maior, was expected to converge hourly with Delaborde's force.

Before dawn on 17 August the Allies, divided into three groups, moved ahead, Wellington leading the main body into the centre of the horseshoe, where their scarlet lines and glittering arms must have made a splendid display in the morning sun. But Delaborde was too experienced and wary a general to take this bait, realizing that a pincer movement was also in progress and that his flanks were threatened, and withdrew to a more defensible ridge; but Wellington had also ordered his two wings to repeat their encircling manoeuvre.

It was at this juncture that Colonel Lake accidentally entered a gully with his four line companies, which, pressing ahead, found themselves unexpectedly behind the French front, precipitating a more general engagement (in which poor Lake was killed, and buried later where he fell; a monumental cross marks the spot). The whole British line swarmed up the ridge and penetrated interme-diate defiles, and taking advantage of their numerical superiority, they carried the French position in spite of stubborn resistance. Nevertheless, skilfully screened by his more numerous cavalry, Delaborde was able to extricate his demoralized battalions, although forced to leave three of his five guns on the field.

Learning that Loison was by now close at hand, and that the expected transports bringing additional brigades from England had already dropped anchor at the mouth of the Maceira, Wellington did not press the pursuit. His elated troops were ordered south-west across the hills towards **Vimeiro**, where, bivouacked in line of battle on adjacent ridges, they would cover the landing of these reinforcements.

August Schaumann of the King's German Legion (later to become Deputy Assistant Commissary-General in the British ser-vice), described the disembarkation at adjacent **Maceira Bay**, where 'guns, wagons, some of which were being fitted together, moun-tains of ship's biscuits, haversacks, trusses of hay, barrels of meat and rum, tents, some of which were already up, and dragoons busy catching and saddling their horses' were part of the animated scene; while amongst the dust and din, officers both naval and military were shouting conflicting directions. The cavalry had their problems, for owing to the long sea journey the horses had lost the use of their legs, and the moment a trooper attempted to mount one of them, it 'folded up its back legs like a dog, or rather dropped his hind quarters on the ground'.

The strength of the combined British forces was now brought up to 17,000 which, according to regulations, required a general officer senior in rank to Wellington, who, although showing promise in the eyes of the military establishment in London, was after all a mere 'sepoy general'. Indeed, Sir Harry Burrard, who had sailed with these transports (but who had not seen action for a decade), if not jealous of Wellington's reputation for distinguished service in India, was perhaps piqued to learn of the latter's recent success, for which he could hardly claim any credit.

Fearing that Wellington might steal a further march on him, Burrard promptly pulled rank, disallowing any advance on Lisbon until Sir John Moore, with an additional 10,000 men, had joined the expeditionary force, even if this meant waiting a fortnight (which earned him the epithet of 'obtuse pig' from Schaumann). Wellington must on no account take chances, particularly as the French were doubtless concentrating against them: it was certainly not the moment to beat them in detail. Meanwhile, Burrard would remain on board another night.

With only a few hours of *de facto* command remaining, Wellington was rowed back to shore, thoroughly disillusioned by the outcome of their conference. But before dawn he received intelligence that an enemy force, commanded by General Junot in person, was approaching rapidly from the direction of Torres Vedras. Although there was no sign of the French until nine in the morning, soon after, the glint of arms and clouds of dust were noticed to the east rather than south, and this required an immediate change in his dispositions.

Battalions armed with rifles were deployed in advance of Vimeiro hill as a skirmishing line[4]; other battalions were placed on the reverse slope of its crest, for this now appeared to be their main objective, and twelve guns were positioned ready to rake the massed French columns as they approached the British in line.

The first volleys were fired at a range of slightly over 100 yards, and this was repeated every fifteen seconds as the flanks of the line wrapped round the head of the advancing column: 900 muskets were firing into a dense mass, unable to deploy into line, and only capable of replying with 200 of the 1,200 arms at their disposal. Inevitably, the French recoiled, broke, and fled. Another column now came within range, but again their formation was against them even though they had overwhelming numerical superiority: 1,200 facing 695. Once the French reached the summit they were subjected to devastating volleys, and their ranks disintegrating, they stumbled back downhill panic-striken, leaving the accompanying artillery to be captured. A second attack in similar formation, this time by grenadiers, was met in addition by artillery, including howitzers firing the newly invented shrapnel shell, and dreadful carnage ensued both here and soon after in other parts of the battlefield.

By midday it was all over, with the French streaming away to the south. Burrard, who had eventually landed, only to find the battle in full swing, condescendingly allowed his junior to 'carry on'; but once the outcome was in no doubt, refused stubbornly to permit Wellington, still with a large body of fresh troops at his disposal, to follow up the victory by turning a retreat into a rout. Some 2,000 French trapped in a cul-de-sac of hills were even allowed to escape.

The following day Burrard was in turn superseded, with the arrival from Gibraltar of General Sir Hew Dalrymple, who once only in his long career – he had entered the army back in 1763 – had been in command of troops in combat. While the 'gentlemen' (as Wellington called them) were debating what to do, General Kellermann rode up under a flag of truce to propose an armistice, which Sir Hew cheerfully granted.

Meanwhile, there were bloated bodies to bury under a blazing August sun. Captain Harry Ross-Lewin reported that the churchyard at Vimeiro contained heaps of legs just amputated there by surgeons, together with a large dish full of severed hands.

According to Adam Neale, Junot had the 'effrontery', on returning to Lisbon after his defeat, 'to announce that he had obtained a decisive victory over the English, and actually to force the inhabitants . . . to illuminate splendidly on the occasion'!

When the terms of the subsequent 'Convention of Cintra' became known in London, an uproar naturally ensued, and it was demanded that the generals concerned should face a Court of Enquiry. This was largely because it had been agreed by Dalrymple that Junot and the remaining French troops in Portugal would be transported back to La Rochelle in British ships, together with their 'personal property', which in many instances was merely valuables plundered from the Portuguese. The fact that thousands of lives, British, French, and Portuguese, were saved, and the destruction of an immense amount of property avoided, was of minor concern. However, the result was that Sir Hew was relieved of his command, and Sir Harry was retired. Wellington was exonerated from any blame.

The events which led up to the winter retreat of Sir John Moore from the windswept plains of León and across the snowbound Galician mountains to La Coruña – the 'Dunkirk' of its day, when a high proportion of the disposable British army was saved from destruction and capture – have been recorded frequently, and need not be detailed here.

The melancholy dispatches had reached England only a few weeks before Wellington, the fêted victor of Roliça and Vimeiro, and who retained the confidence of the nation, was appointed to take command of all British forces remaining in Portugal, the great majority of which were stationed in the vicinity of Lisbon, where reinforcements were awaited with impatience.

On 22 April 1809 he was back in Lisbon. Within three weeks he had swept General Soult from Oporto by a remarkable *coup de main*, as described in Chapter 26.

Meanwhile General William Carr Beresford, a rigid disciplinarian, was reorganizing the Portuguese military establishment, which although it caused resentment among a minority of officers, was to have an invigorating effect on the rank and file, who were to prove themselves a most valuable complement to the Allied forces. One important innovation was the integration of a Portuguese infantry battalion in each of five British brigades.[5]

After viewing the Atlantic rollers breaking on the beach at Maceira Bay, we may leave the field of Vimeiro, and head for **Peniche**. Situated on the sandy neck of a rock-bound, flat-topped peninsula, and with its fishing harbour, canneries and dockyards, guarded by its Fortaleza, it is a lively place even if its monuments, with the possible exception of the painted ceiling-panels of the Misericordia, are not memorable. And the circuit of the peninsula may be made via Cabo Carvoeiro if only for the distant view of the offshore Berlenga islands.

Peniche was attacked by Drake and the Prior of Crato in 1589, but its defences were formidable.[6] General D'Urban, when inspecting the place in December 1809, noted that nearly 100 heavy guns were in position in its different works, and perhaps with the drama of La Coruña in mind, had suggested that it was perfect 'for the Embarking of the British Army, should it ever be necessary to do so in the Face of the Enemy'.

In more recent years Peniche was the site of the main political prison used by Salazar's repressive secret police, the PIDE (Polícia Internacional e de Defesa do Estado); and it was from here in January 1960 that Alvaro Cunhal, the Communist leader, together with nine others, made their escape, using the age-old device of tying sheets together.

(Less than two years later, an even more spectacular escape was made by seven Communists, this time from Caxias, nearer Lisbon, who, commandeering an armoured Mercedes presented to Salazar by Hitler, rammed the prison gates and got away unscathed by machine-gun fire.)

Driving east, at **Atouguia da Baleia** ('of the whale'), a town of medieval importance, we pass the church of São Leonardo, containing good Romanesque capitals. Before long we obtain a view of the low range of hills beyond Roliça, to the south-east, the assault of which has been described above.

Ahead rise the aqueduct and battlemented walls of **Obidos**, out of season a charming village of narrow, cobbled lanes, the far end of its *enceinte* dominated by an ancient castle built by Dom Dinis, and now a *pousada*. In the main square stands Santa Maria, preserving a Renaissance portal, early eighteenth-century *albarrada azulejos*, the tomb of João de Noronha, carved by Chanterène, a retablo by João da Costa, and notable ceiling paintings. Others depict the *Mystic Marriage of St Catherine*, by Josefa d'Ayala y Cabrera, who although born in Seville *circa* 1630, spent most of her life in this village, where she died (and was buried in São Pedro), and is therefore usually referred to as Josefa 'de Obidos'. Adjacent to the church is the museum, housing a good local collection, with relics recovered from the field of Roliça, among other objects, and displaying a maquette of the Lines of Torres Vedras.

Conspicuous in the valley below the walls is the ungainly church of Senhor da Pedra, built on an unusual hexagonal plan, but never completed. This is passed on the road to **Caldas da Rainha**, an ancient spa whose warm sulphur springs Dom João V found

restorative. During the Second World War it was the temporary
forced residence in Portugal of refugees from Nazi-occupied
Europe. Caldas is also a garrison town, from which a detachment
made a premature advance on Lisbon in March 1974, only to be
turned back. Its yellow and green pottery is remarkably crude.

Although described only sixty years ago as 'almost impossible for
cars', a good road now climbs across a range of hills before descending gently to Alcobaça.

NOTES

1. Alhandra in particular was to suffer during the blockade and, when
   liberated, exhibited a sad picture of destruction, with houses gutted,
   and soldiers and sailors boiling their kettles in the streets, shattered
   mahogany furniture being used as kindling.
2. Numerous remains of masonry and earthworks are recognizable along
   the more northerly line, and their exploration can provide an interesting excursion. The less energetic can survey the maquettes in either
   the military museum in Lisbon or in that at Obidos, while detailed
   maps and descriptions are found in Wyld's folio *Atlas* of 1841, Eliot's
   Treatise on the Defense of Portugal, and Jones', *Journal of Sieges*,
   among other studies.
3. See Chapter 19.
4. A monument rises adjacent to the village.
5. General Benjamin d'Urban, writing in December 1809, and referring
   to the 4th and 10th Regiments of Portuguese infantry, commanded by
   Colonels Campbell and Oliver respectively, who deserved the highest
   credit, stated enthusiastically that he had 'never seen an English brigade move with more steadiness and precision', while only days later he
   was commenting that Colonel Elder's progress in training the 3rd Regiment of Chasseurs was perfectly wonderful.
6. António, the Prior of Crato – a bastard of the Infante Luiz, born in
   1531 to Violante Gomes, engagingly known as 'the Pelican', and the
   daughter of a *Converso* family – had disputed the succession at the
   death of Dom Sebastião.

16

Alcobaça – Aljubarrota – Batalha – Leiria

Alcobaça, lying snugly at the confluence of the fruitful valleys of the Alcoa and Baça, is dominated by an edifice masking the finest example of medieval architecture of its size in Portugal: or, in Lady Holland's liberal opinion, 'by far the best and least disgusting convent I ever saw'.

The place was at one time known for its cotton chintzes, and from the mid-eighteenth century cambrics were being manufactured there under the guidance of Scottish and Irish managers. But as early as 1787 William Stephens was reporting that its products were 'trifling', although every exertion was being made by one of the inspectors to improve it. He was of the opinion that

> The situation of this fabric near the Convent where the Monks encourage Idleness by example and by distributing their superfluous provisions, makes all efforts of the managers ineffectual, and weakens their command over the workmen.

He may well have been correct in his assumption, although in fact the community were reputed to be 'improving' landlords.

Stephens was an interesting character. In 1769 he was developing a glass factory founded twenty years earlier by John Beare among the pinewoods of **Marinha Grande**, some fifteen miles north.[1] He instructed his employees in music and dancing, and concerts were frequent, and he had even fitted up an opera-house there, where performances were given every month of Portuguese and Italian operas, with his artisans singing many of the parts. William died in 1802, and it would have been his brother who entertained the Hollands there in 1805, and who in 1826 left the business to the State.

The Cistercian **Abbey of Alcobaça** was founded in the mid-twelth century by Afonso Henriques as a thanks-offering for the capture of Santarém from the Moors, and the original structure was completed by 1223. Its mitred abbot, the senior of his rank in Portugal, was a person of influence, being *ex officio* high almoner and precentor to the king. One of them, Vasco Tinoco, has been identified in the *Retablo of the Infante* by Nuno Gonçalves.

In 1725 its west front was cloaked by an indifferent Baroque façade, and onion-domed belfries were added, although the deep-set Gothic portal with its rose-window is still evident; and in 1770 the interior was embellished by rococo *talha* designed by William Elsden, then working at Coimbra.

In 1773 the abbey was visited by Richard Twiss, who records that he dined and supped with above twenty of the superiors in a private room, 'and in the evening the bottle went as briskly about as ever I saw it do in Scotland; so that with the aid of some musical instruments, we spent a very agreeable day'. In the following year the anti-clerical Major Dalrymple, having accepted their hospitality, ungratefully commented that it was a shame 'that the celestial pastors should possess so much worldly wealth, thereby wallowing in sloth and idleness, a nuisance to society'.

In June some twenty years later, William Beckford was entranced by the sight of 300 monks then in residence, including servants or lay-brothers, and 'living in a splendid manner', but his *Recollections of an Excursion to the Monasteries of Alcobaca and Batalha*, in which his visit is so inimitably described, was not published until 1835. Southey was dismissive, as usual, when writing up his expedition: 'so monstrous a medley . . . a huge patched pile'; and insinuated it was not for nothing that 'most of the young women near were dressed in the monks' old hats'. Lady Holland was impressed by its library, noting that it contained 'many gifts from travellers and several from inhabitants of the British Islands'; while in December 1809 General D'Urban, rarely given to hyperbole, described it, as 'splendid'.

But within a year the abbey and its dependencies were ransacked by the French under D'Erlon. The destruction was quite deplorable. William Tomkinson, entering Alcobaça with the British cavalry, found the damage exceeded anything he had ever seen. Not only had its two fine organs been wantonly smashed, but the enemy had

burnt what they could, and destroyed the remainder with an

immense deal of trouble. The embalmed kings and queens were taken out of their tombs, and I saw them lying in as great preservation as the day they were interred. The fine tessellated pavement, from the entrance to the altar, was picked up, the facings to the stone pillars were destroyed to the top, scaffolding having been erected for that purpose . . .

There must have been little left to pillage in the anti-clerical riots of 1834.

The abbey was later the object of the equally rigorous attentions of 'restorers', who in attempting to re-convert the interior to its original Cistercian purity, stripped it bare: 'one of the worst and most disgraceful works of vandalism of our times', condemned Sacheverell Sitwell, a shade too sweepingly. At least nothing now detracts from the grandeur of the interior, remarkable for its great length as compared with its width, an impression accentuated by the girth of the piers and the narrowness of the intermediate bays. A curiosity is that the shafts stand on bevelled corbels at some distance from the ground throughout the length of the nave, presumably to provide extra space for the stalls once ranged there.

Placed foot facing foot in the transepts lie the finely carved tombs of Dom Pedro I and Inês de Castro, both attended by six angels. It was said that the king had ordered this unusual disposition so that, at the Resurrection, the first object to meet his eyes would be the form of his beloved mistress. Their tombs are inscribed with the words *Até ao fim do mundo* – until the end of the world. On the foot of Dom Pedro's is carved the Wheel of Fortune, and the Day of Judgement embellishes that of Dona Inês.

Briefly, the romantic tragedy took the following course. Inês Pires de Castro, the daughter of a Gallician nobleman, had been brought up with her cousin Doña Constanza, a daughter of the Duque de Peñafiel. When in 1340 Constanza went to Portugal to marry Dom Pedro, Dom Afonso IV's son, Inês followed in her suite. The Infante, on first setting eyes on this 'heron-necked' beauty, conceived an uncontrollable passion for her; and although Inês was later exiled from Court, on Constanza's death in 1345 she returned to Portugal and set up house with him. To legitimize the several children she bore, Dom Pedro married her at Braganza in 1354, or claimed to have done so.

The Court faction, jealous of the Spanish influence they considered she had on the heir to the throne (for her brothers had political pretensions), eventually extracted from Dom Afonso his tacit permission for her 'removal'. But although the Dom Afonso weakened on seeing his grandchildren, who were at the time staying with their mother near Coimbra, the nobles most concerned were not to be thwarted, and in 1355 murdered her in cold blood. Not surprisingly, Dom Pedro raised the standard of revolt, but influenced by the Archbishop of Braga, he became reconciled with his father, ostensibly. But later, on his accession, he had two of those involved in her assassination hunted down and executed. He also swore before the Cortes that their marriage was a reality, and had her body exhumed and enthroned beside him to receive the homage of the nobles before being placed in the royal tomb he had ordered to be made for her here.[2]

Off the cloister opens the chapter-house, the monks' hall (with their dormitory above), and the sensational tiled kitchen, Beckford's 'most distinguished temple of gluttony in all Europe', dominated by its immense oblong-shaped pyramidal chimney. It now stands silent and empty, but here, if his memory served him right,

> ran a brisk rivulet of the clearest water, flowing through pierced wooden reservoirs, containing every sort and size of the finest river-fish. On one side, loads of game and venison were heaped up; on the other, vegetables and fruit in endless variety. Beyond a long line of stoves extended a row of ovens, and close to them hillocks of wheaten flour whiter than snow, rocks of sugar, jars of the purest oil, and pastry in vast abundance, which a numerous tribe of lay brothers and their attendants were rolling out and puffing up into an hundred different shapes, singing all the while as blithely as larks in a cornfield.

Only seven years later, Southey, while grudgingly admitting that the culinary department was 'most magnificent', was only too quick to condemn the 'empire of Alcobaça' as being miserably mismanaged, suggesting that no subjects in Europe were more ready or had more cause to fling off their yoke, for the Bernardines 'take a fourth of the whole produce, and compel the people to send their corn to the convent-mills, their olives and grapes to the convent-presses'.

Adjacent stood the huge refectory: an 'immense square of seventy or eighty feet; linnen foul and greasy', as noted Beckford with disapproval in his *Journal*. Opposite its entrance is a charming lavatory containing a Renaissance fountain; and also off the cloister is the Sala dos Reis, displaying statues of kings, a group representing the Coronation of Afonso Henriques, and an immense cauldron said to have been captured from the Spanish at Aljubarrota.

Overlooking the town are relics of a Moorish castle. Baron Taylor, the French dilettante, when sketching the scene early last century, was informed by an old woman that the Moorish chief to whom it belonged returned on one night of every year 'for the purpose of keeping a kind of Witches' Sabbath, and demanding twelve virgins as an annual tribute . . . However, there is not much danger in him now', she reassured him, 'for the *frades* prevent his injuring us; but still any young women who visits the ruins by herself runs the risk of losing her senses, and I have even known some who have died from so doing'.

A short distance to the west of Alcobaça, at **Vestiara**, off the Nazaré road, is a church with a notable portal; but **Nazaré** itself, being on the 'tourist circuit', is best avoided during the summer, when it is crowded with trippers.

Its fishermen, said to be of Phoenician origin, carry on their hard life unconcernedly. Their boats, with their colourful painted eyes, are indeed picturesque, even if now hauled up the beach by tractors rather than teams of oxen. The sardines drying on their wire frames; the chequered shirts and black stocking caps of the men; the impassive groups of black-shawled women, with their thickly pleated skirts and heavy gold earrings, still provide an unusual spectacle.

Driving east from Alcobaça, the main road shortly traverses **Aljubarrota**, a village giving its name to the decisive battle of August 1385, although in fact this took place nearer Batalha, in an area not then encumbered by pines. João, Master of Avis, and his right hand, the Constable Nun'Alvares Pereira, after marching from **Porto de Mós**, had here redeployed their troops (including a small contingent of English archers), to await the approach of Juan I's Castilians. Juan, on the death of his father-in-law Dom Fernando, had invaded Portugal to settle his claim to the crown by force of arms, in spite of mounting opposition, for although there had been dissidence among the nobility and the Church, the population as a whole supported Dom João.

Although caution had been agreed, individual hotheads amongst the undisciplined Spaniards forced the issue by indulging in harassing attacks, and soon both sides were engaged in a general mêlée. Although the Castilians were superior in numbers, they faltered on seeing the royal standard go down, and the whole army disintegrated, Juan himself galloping off the field to seek the transient security of the castle at Santarém.

Without undue exaggeration, Dom João I was able to claim that 2,500 enemy men-at-arms had been killed, apart from a high proportion of those members of the landed aristocracy of Portugal who had opposed his accession.

The road too closely skirts the honey-tinted **Abbey of Batalha**, correctly Santa Maria da Vitória (in honour of Dom João's victory), which is undoubtedly one of the masterpieces of Portuguese architecture, although lacking the austere grace of Alcobaça's interior. Certain details recall the English perpendicular style, while the nave reminded Beckford 'of Winchester in form of arches and moulding, and of Amiens in loftiness'.

Afonso Domingues, at first responsible for its construction, was succeeded by Master Huguet, who was there from 1402 until 1438. By then work had started on the octagonal chapel behind the apse, intended as a mausoleum for Dom Duarte, Dom João's eldest son. Although additional cloisters were later added, the initial impetus was lost with the death in 1521 of Dom Manuel, more preoccupied with the erection of his own magnificent mausoleum at Belém.

In 1788 William Burton Conyingham, who had visited Portugal not long before, commissioned James Kavanagh Murphy to make measured drawings of the abbey.[3] His *Plans, elevations, sections and views of the church at Batalha* (including an imaginative reconstruction of the Capelas Imperfeitas), although considered by Beckford to be the work of a 'dull draftsman', had some influence on James Wyatt, who on three occasions used designs based on them.

In his *Excursion*, Beckford devoted far fewer pages to Batalha than to Alcobaça, partly because he did not so much appreciate its exuberant ornamentation, but this he kept to himself when being shown round by the enthusiastic prior, realizing that 'to entertain any doubts of the supreme excellence of Dom Emanuel's scollops and twistifications amounted to heresy'. Perhaps too, although there 'was no want of the utmost cordiality' in his reception, his hosts were very much poorer, although producing an

> immense platter, containing a savoury mess of fish and rice and vegetables delicately fried after the Italian fashion, caraffes of wine, baskets of ripe and fragrant fruit, pomegranates, apricots, and oranges . . .

Several tombs were mutilated by the French; and General Picton's regiment was quartered there briefly also, which cannot have improved its state; but it survived comparatively unscathed, until 'restorers' got to work. The compiler of the *Handbook to Portugal* was justifiably indignant when he saw what was going on, describing some of its new fittings as being 'in the most wretched modern taste' and the glass outrageously restored by a Frenchman in 'so abominable a character that they would be scouted by any gin-palace in England'. The fabric fell later into the hands of the State, and was gutted of most of these accretions. Part of the cornice of the unfinished chapel was then added, and the chapter-house of this 'battle abbey' was chosen later as a suitable site in which to place the Portuguese 'Tomb of the Unknown Soldier', suspended above which is a shattered *Crucifixion* found at Neuve-Chapelle in Flanders.

The nave is twelve metres loftier than that of Alcobaça, which exceeds it in length by almost thirty metres; they are very similar in width. Below the elaborate star-vaulting of the octagonal lantern of the Capela de Fundador is the double tomb of Dom João and Dona Philippa, whose effigies lie tenderly hand in hand. Above them are twin canopies carved with the arms of Avis and Lancaster. Their mottos, *Por Bem* (as at Sintra) and *Yl me plet*, are carved repeatedly around the tomb, which is comparatively undamaged, although the embalmed body of the founder was exposed by troops retiring from Busaco; Colonel Leach, who should have known better, admitted to having cut off a button from the royal robes as a memento.

Their younger sons lie along the south wall, each altar tomb (among them that of Henry the Navigator, with an indifferent effigy) decorated with their personal device and the Order of the Garter, founded by Edward III, Philippa's grandfather. The remains of Dom Fernando, the 'Infante Santo', were only returned from Fez three decades after his death in 1443. They had been left as a hostage for the surrender of Ceuta, which was never made, during the ill-fated expedition against Tangier.

Remarkable is the unsupported vault of the chapter-house, and the elaborately convoluted 'vegetable' tracery in the Claustro Real, in which Sacheverell Sitwell recognized the poppy, cardoon and artichoke. From the lavatory, with its delicately foliated tracery, there is a memorable diagonal view across the cloister, with its secular cypresses, towards the upper parapet and clerestory.

Even more extraordinary is the exotic west portal of the octagonal

'Capelas Imperfeitas', which has no direct communication with the church, where interwoven among its lace-like carving is seen the obsessively repeated motto of Dom Duarte: *leauté faray tam yaserey*, loyal I shall ever be. Some idea of their intended elaboration may be gauged from the profuse ornamentation of the truncated bases of the octagon's upper storey, still open to the sky. The tomb of Dom Duarte and Leonor of Aragón, mutilated by the French, lies opposite the portal.

Ten miles to the north – beyond the site of Roman Collippo, near **São Sebastião do Freixo** (Azóia) – rises the royal castle and palace of **Leiria**. The town itself, although of medieval importance (it was here, at a Cortes held by Dom Afonso III in 1254, that the Commons were first represented in Portugal), is now of slight interest, nor is its cathedral of great moment.

When retiring from Busaco, several English troopers, knowing that the French were close behind and that convent doors would hardly protect their inmates, broke them down, and out came the nuns 'as thick as a flock of sheep and set off for Lisbon', some of them jumping up behind the dragoons, clasping their gallant deliverers tightly round their waists. And just in time, for when William Grattan of the Connaught Rangers passed through the place some months later, he found it little more than 'a heap of ruins'.

A stiff climb brings one to the castle, the loggia of its splendid main hall providing a fine plunging view, while that from the *torre de menagem* extends across the pine-forests surrounding Marinha Grande towards the distant Atlantic.

For Tomar, to the south-east, and Conímbriga to the north-east, see Chapters 17 and 20 respectively.

I would suggest visiting Tomar from Leiria (or vice versa) rather than taking the direct road from Batalha. This preferable route leads one past the well-sited castle of **Ourém Velha**, in which Dona Mécia López de Haro, Dom Sancho II's queen, was held captive when carried off from Coimbra in 1246 by a band of barons headed by a brother of the Archbishop of Braga, and very probably with her connivance.

By taking this road, **Fátima** is given a wide berth, a detour which I would certainly *not* recommend to anyone unless he or she is curious to investigate the massive commercialization of a cult, where one of the more deplorable manifestations of the theocratic regime of Dr Salazar is incarnate.

The wretched story is briefly told. In May 1917 three dull-witted peasant children claimed to have witnessed visions of the Virgin on that desolate plateau. Two of them did not survive the age of twelve, yet their infantile delusions were seized on and pilgrimages expediently organized by the ecclesiastical authorities eager to emulate the fervour of Lourdes and reap the fruits of devotion. Ten years after the alleged apparitions, these pilgrimages were described as being 'attended by real hardship, as the country is wild and accommodation practically non-existent'. Once Salazar was in power, he imposed on the gullible peasantry, exploiting the fact that over half the population was then still illiterate, and superstition rife; notably north of the Tagus.

A woman, ostensibly possessed of the Devil, was burned alive in Portugal as late as 1933; infanticide was frequent, and apparently the inexplicable stoning of trains, and witchcraft, were not uncommon phenomena.

The cult was catching. Rodney Gallop, when writing at the time on the folklore of Portugal, retold an incident which took place in a remote area of the Beiras where the railway crossed into Spain. One day a small girl, who had been minding her flock, rushed breathlessly into her village with the tidings that an image of 'Nossa Senhora' had fallen from Heaven and landed just beside her. With great excitement its parishioners assembled and, although at first the priest was sceptical, with the local *Filharmónica* at their head, they proceeded to the spot to bring back the miraculous image to their church. There, sure enough, was the picture: a Queen of Spades, blown from the hands of a card-playing traveller in a passing train.

But to return to Fátima. Vast sums were spent on the erection of a basilica, consecrated in 1953 and hallowed by Paul VI's presence in 1976. Like the basilica of Our Lady of Peace erected in the Ivory Coast not long ago, it is little less than an affront to any instinct of veneration. Its sixty-five-metre-high tower is buttressed by a hemicycle surmounted by statues of sundry saints, below which extends an immense esplanade, still occasionally thronged by credulous congregations. What Hilaire Belloc wrote of Lourdes at the turn of the century can as well be applied here, when he condemned it as 'detestable in its accommodation, and to make it the more detestable there is that admixture of the supernatural which is invariably accompanied by detestable earthly adjuncts'. I have heard it described recently as a 'Spiritual Disneyland'.

NOTES

1. Apparently the sand used at that time was brought 'from ye Isle of Wight, and the barilla from Alicant, and the potash from Russia or North America; so that except the pines and salt of tartar from Oporto, none of the rude materials are the produce of Portugal'.
2. Dom Pedro never remarried, but Teresa Lorenzo, a Galician and one of his mistresses, bore him a son, João (1358–1433), later appointed Master of the Order of Avis, who in 1385 acceded to the throne as Dom João I.
3. James Kavanagh Murphy (1760–1814) had been among those architects consulted in 1786 concerning additions to the House of Commons. His drawings of Batalha, and his pedestrian *Travels in Portugal*, were not published until 1795.

17

The Ribatejo:
Santarém – Tomar

Santarém, set on a commanding height overlooking the Tagus, and formerly one of the strongest fortresses in Portugal, is interesting more for its historical associations than for the majority of its surviving monuments.

Roman Scallabis derived its present name from Santa Iria, or Irene, a nun of Tomar who, accused of unchastity, suffered martyrdom in AD 653, her body being flung into the Nabão. After floating down the Tagus (some say in a marble coffin), it was here washed ashore, her innocence then being indisputably established by miraculous apparitions. They were a credulous lot, and were singled out in the proverb: *Quem burro vae a Santarém, burro vae e burro vem*, The ass who goes to Santarém, ass he goes and ass he returns. Others have suggested that this referred more specifically to the seminarists.

It is likely that Afonso Henriques' trouncing of the Moors at the Battle of Ourique in July 1139 took place at neighbouring Vila Cha de Ourique, rather than at Ourique in the Alentejo, some distance south-west of Beja; and it was after this victory that he assumed the style of 'King of the Portuguese'. Eight years later, by night attack, he seized Shantariya, as its name had become distorted by the Moors; and although the Almohads made a desperate attempt to recapture it in 1181, Dom Sancho I was able to repel their repeated assaults.

Dom Dinis died at Santarém in 1325, and it was here in 1357 that the murderers of Inês de Castro were executed. Being conveniently near Almeirim, a royal summer residence, it was the scene of several gatherings of the Cortes during the next two centuries.

In 1704, during the early stages of the War of the Succession, the Archduke Charles of Austria, after suffering an attack of dysentery, was obliged to spend several uncomfortable weeks in shabby quarters here, and in the words of the late David Francis, had 'little to do

except to beg for money, to try to silence the quarrels of his court-
iers, and by way of diversion to play at cards with the servants and to
shoot at the bats and swallows in the evenings'.

In 1811, recognizing its strength, Masséna occupied Santarém
briefly after being frustrated by the Lines of Torres Vedras. But
before retiring further, he naturally sacked the place. Captain
William Bragge recorded that eleven convents and eight churches
fell victim to the French, who were guilty of 'the most wanton
Mischief'. What was left of the town became the last stronghold of
the reactionary Miguelites in 1833.[1]

From the central *largo*, overlooked by the many-windowed seminary built for the Jesuits by João Nunes Tinoco, the Rua Serpa
Pinto leads towards the church of Graça, with a portal imitating that
of Batalha and a very fine rose-window, and containing the tombs of
both Pedro Alvares Cabral, the discoverer of Brazil, and of Pedro de
Meneses, a governor of Ceuta.

The tomb of Duarte de Meneses, who died in Africa, is preserved
in the former church of São João de Alporão, perhaps built on the
site of a mosque, and now a museum; but the only relic it was said to
contain of that former governor of Alcácer-Ceguer was a single tooth.

At the far end of the steeply scarped promontory, embellished by
the gardens of the Portas do Sol, once perched the Moorish citadel,
which had so long dominated this stretch of the Tagus valley. Its site
still provides both an impressive plunging view and a wide *coup
d'oeil* over the undulating wooded pastures of the Ribatejo.

It was from near **Almeirim**, on the far bank, that Captain Joseph
Moyle Sherer, stationed there in February 1811, passed whole morn-
ings watching the French through his telescope. From here he could

> see a troop of their dragoons exercising on the plain below the
> town; there a general officer riding out with his staff; here some
> field officer visiting his guards and picquets, and there several
> of their men washing and cleaning their arms and appointments
> on the very brink of the stream. You constantly heard the sound
> of their voices; and, on a still day, might readily distinguish what
> they said. We often, indeed, conversed courteously with their
> officers, until the prating imprudence of some individual caused
> such intercourse to be forbidden, most properly, I admit.

Even with a naked eye, he could discern 'their picquets posted,
and their fatigue parties felling trees to form abbatis, digging

entrenchments, or constructing breast-works; while . . . forage
parties, detachments, or orderlies, were constantly going out and
returning'; until, on 5 March, the enemy retreated precipitately to
the north.

The Casa dos Patudos at neighbouring **Alpiarça**, the former home
of José Relves, the politician who had proclaimed the Republic in
1910, is now a musuem containing miscellaneous collections of
paintings – many by his contemporaries, and some of doubtful
attribution – ceramics, furniture, and Arraiolos carpets. Of particular interest is an anonymous portrait of Domenico Scarlatti, said to
be the only one known of the composer.

In the vicinity is a large earthwork identified as Moron, which
Decimus Junius Brutus made his military base *circa* 138 BC before
leading his troops north to the Lima.

The Tagus may be re-crossed at **Golegã** – note the church with its
good Manueline portal – before reaching a turning for **Abrantes**,
itself of slight interest.

British troops found winter quarters here late in 1704, but are
said to have had a hard march here, subsisting largely on chestnuts,
the only food to be found in plenty. In 1807 it was captured by
General Junot *en route* for Lisbon, for which facile exploit Napoleon
dubbed him Duc d'Abrantes. Wellington concentrated his forces
here two years later, before marching east to Talavera, and it
remained an important base throughout the war, even passing into
proverb: *Quartel General em Abrantes; tudo como dantes*, Headquarters at Abrantes; everything as before.

It is worth making a short detour along this riverside road as far as
Tancos, if only for the picturesque view of the castle of **Almourol** on
its island site. Rebuilt by the Templars in 1171, it was referred to in
Francisco de Moraes' *Cronica de Palmeirim de Inglaterra*, translated by Southey, correcting Anthony Manday's Elizabethan version of the romance.

Some twenty miles north, charmingly situated on the tributary
Rio Nabão, lies **Tomar**, a small town of much character, dominated
by the huge Convento de Cristo. It succeeded Roman Sellium or
Nabancia, which stood downstream on the left bank near Santa
Maria dos Olivais. This church was almost entirely rebuilt since the
burial there in 1195 of Gualdim Pais, Grand Master of the
Templars, and its founder.

Tomar's history was bound up with the fortunes of the military
and monastic orders that became its overlords, and even when the

Templars in Portugal were suppressed, this was enforced only nominally. In 1319 their extensive properties were handed over to the knightly Order of Christ, whose headquarters were transferred here from Castro Marim in the Algarve in 1356. From 1417 until his death, the Grand Master was Henry the Navigator, and in 1492 its mastership passed to Dom Manuel and remained a royal perquisite.

But although the influence of the Order waned, the town was to flourish in the eighteenth century with the establishment of a Royal Hat Factory, and then a cotton mill, which by the 1850s employed 300 hands.

A road winds up the umbrageous hillside past Nossa Senhora da Conceição, the perfect proportions of which are the delight of architectural historians, who have attributed it to Diogo de Torralva, the Spanish son-in-law of Francisco de Arruda; but the design owes much to the influence of Serlio.

On entering the monastic *enceinte* of the Convento de Cristo, steps ascend to the richly decorated south portal of its church, an addition by João de Castilho, in which he incorporated Renaissance detail into the Flamboyant Gothic design, and which leads directly into Diogo de Arruda's short nave. Within the abutting Charola, the sixteen-sided Templar church, its plan typical of those of that Order, rears the impressive central octagon, sustained by piers preserving remains of paintings in the Flemish style. That any have survived is remarkable, for the place was sacked repeatedly by the French. Colonel Frazer of the Royal Horse Artillery, most surprised that he had never heard the convent mentioned – its architecture 'so fine, and the whole pile of buildings so noble' – was equally distressed to find canvases 'torn in pieces, and many carried away; the organ broken, and altars thrown down, fireplaces made in the cloisters, and everything broken and defaced . . . in wanton barbarity'.

The upper level of the Great Cloister, probably designed by Diogo de Torralva but completed by Filippo Terzi, leads to a gallery overlooking the smaller Claustro de Santa Barbara, which provides the best view of the sensational window of the chapter-house. This lavishly decorated aperture, constructed while Diogo de Arruda was supervising the works, is perhaps the most striking example extant of the Manueline style at its most fantastic. The Cross of the Order of Christ surmounts the royal arms and the armillary spheres of Dom Manuel, which are connected by a writhing mass of carved ropework, seaweed and coral-stems. A transverse rope with its cork floats, the chain circling one huge buttress, and the colossal buckled Garter which binds the other (very likely symbolizing the English Order presented to Dom Manuel by Henry VII), the head and shoulders of an old man supporting, Atlas-like, the roots of a tree-stump which protrudes from the base of the grated window and the spiralling, furled sails within the circular window of the upper choir . . . the whole anonymous masterpiece displays both an incomparable fertility of imagination and mastery of the mason's craft.

It is worth ascending to and following the narrow wall-walk, and skirting the dependencies to view the noble Aqueduto dos Pegões, its ogival arches spanning the valley, and descending through cypress-shaded gardens to regain the older town centre.

Here, in the Praça da República, near the foot of the castle hill, stands São João Baptista, with its Manueline doorway; while secreted in a neighbouring lane is the former Synagogue of Tomar, now the Museu Abraham Zacuto.[2] Its vaulted chamber shelters Hebrew inscriptions and Jewish tombstones collected from sites throughout Portugal; while discovered below the floor of an adjacent house during its restoration is a women's ritual bath.

Take the N113 from Tomar to Leiria for Batalha. The N110 leads north through delightful country past hill-top **Penela**, dominated by the extensive ruins of its ancient castle, to approach Conímbriga, for which see Chapter 20.

NOTES

1. I have not been able to peruse an anonymous description – possibly by a certain John Gordon Smith – entitled *Santarem; or Sketches of Society and Manners*, published in 1832.
2. Named after Manoel Alvares, alias Abraham ben Samuel Zacuto or Zacutus Lusitanus (1452–c.1515), who carried out astronomical and mathematical researches for the Bishop of Salamanca until 1480. In 1492 he took refuge in Portugal, where he remained as Court astronomer until forced to seek asylum in North Africa after 1497.

18

Beira Baixa:
Castelo Branco – Covilhã – Belmonte

Situated north of the Tagus and between the Serra da Estrela and the Spanish frontier, this province has a charm of its own, and yet is not often visited except by travellers driving south from Guarda. I have as yet to venture along the tortuous roads traversing the lonely Serra de Alvelos, between Castelo Branco and the writhing river Zêzere.

The more open country to the east, nearer the Spanish frontier, although it saw comparatively little actual fighting during the Peninsular War, was an area in which the Allied armies spent several winters in cantonments, and this made me curious to explore it. The district is said to harbour a dispersed Crypto-Jewish community, but I have made no enquiry as to their whereabouts, should they still exist.

The administrative and commercial capital of the Beira Baixa is **Castelo Branco**, a town of ancient origin, refounded by the Templars in the thirteenth century. It was attacked during a Spanish invasion in 1704, when it surrendered at discretion to General de Thouy, and again in 1762. In 1807 it was sacked by General Junot, and by Marshal Victor in 1809. In April 1812 it was briefly in Marmont's hands, who withdrew on hearing of the fall of Badajoz. Shortly after, when writing from near here, Major-General Le Marchant (killed when leading his heavy brigade of cavalry at Salamanca only three months later), expressed his

> deepest regret at the melancholy affects of the ravages committed by the enemy on the helpless inhabitants . . . not a vestige of clothing, furniture, meat, grain, wine or oil have they left them; everything carried away or destroyed. Little do you, who have never witnessed the horrors of war, comprehend its destructive effects.

However, according to Sherer, once the word got around among the peasants further away from the passage of the retreating French that British discipline was strict and that their troops paid for everything, they would bring in a steady supply of bread, milk, eggs, poultry and excellent country wine.

The surviving monuments of Castelo Branco are understandably few. São Miguel served as a cathedral for just over a century, until 1881, when the diocese became extinct. The gardens of the former Bishops' Palace, embellished with a wealth of topiary, Baroque statuary, urns and obelisks, an *azulejo*-lined water-tank, and a parterre adorned with box arabesques, is worth seeing. Likewise, the adjacent palace, now a museum, if only for its collection of *colchas*, the traditional embroidered bedspreads of the district, displaying Persian, Indian and Oriental influences in their design; while the school of embroidery established here has done much to keep their manufacture alive.

The main road north approaches the Serra da Gardunha, passing through country which caused General D'Urban to compose one of his rare lyrical paragraphs, for he found it

the most beautiful Garden imagination can conceive, every inch of it covered with Vineyards, Corn-fields, Groves of Chestnut, Olive, Cork and Oak, intersected by streams, interspersed with beautiful villages and splendid Mountains whose Tops are in the Clouds.

To the east, on the site of Roman Egitana, lies **Idanha-a-Velha**, the seat of a bishopric from AD 569 and the legendary birthplace of Wamba, elected 'king of the Goths' in 672. Although sacked by the Moors, by the twelfth century it was controlled by the Knights Templar. The present village takes up only a small part of the massively walled *enceinte*, in which a medieval watch-tower rises on the podium of a Roman temple, while a Roman bridge spans the little river Ponsul. The restored Palaeo-Christian basilica at present houses a quantity of carved and inscribed stones while the site continues to be excavated. Relics of both a baptistery and a bishop's palace are pointed out also.

Neighbouring **Monsanto** is visited more for its picturesque position on the granite boulder-strewn slope of a castle-crowned hill, the walls of many of its dwellings being formed by the boulders themselves, in the interstices between which the villagers have contrived to build their humble homes.

The main road is regained at **Penamacor**, retaining a large part of its medieval fortifications. It was here in 1584 that the first of several imposters claiming to be Dom Sebastião held court, sustained by the Messianic hope of the superstitious peasantry that this king, killed at Alcazar-kebir six years earlier, might still be alive and would lead them against the intrusive Spaniards. It was the unlikely birthplace in 1699 of António Nunes Ribeiro Sanches, of Marrano descent, who became physician to the Empress Anna of Russia and later to Catherine II.

The road winds north-east over the hills to **Sabugal**, with its castle, and a bridge over the Côa, where in April 1811 Masséna's rearguard was badly mauled by the pursuing Allies, and would have been annihilated had it not been for the crass incompetence of Sir William Erskine.[1]

An earlier castle may be seen at **Sortelha**, as we bear west across country to reach the main road near Covilhã, conspiciously sited on the lower slope of the Serra da Estrela, with the Torre looming above.

Covilhã's monuments are negligible, but its thick brown blankets are snug. It has long been a textile centre. In 1677 the British Consul in Lisbon was reporting to London that nine men and two women had been lured from Colchester by the Portuguese ambassador in order 'to teach the people to card and spin in the English way', and in spite of the Consul's attempts to persuade them to return home, these weavers had made their way to Covilhã. But they were only the first batch to arrive, being followed by others who in addition had smuggled over their looms. Naturally, the Consul was most concerned, reiterating in his dispatches that unless they were recalled, the English export of cloth to Portugal would soon be ruined.

However, they appear to have run into difficulties of another sort not long after, for in 1704 Colonel John Richards (who in 1709 was to lose his life when the castle at Alicante was blown up) had remarked that the industry was not flourishing, largely on account of the Inquisition's interference with the New Christian entrepreneurs and artisans. Nevertheless, by the mid-nineteenth century it revived, with some 150 looms in operation, manufacturing brown woollen cloth.

Covilhã served as a cavalry base during part of the Peninsular War, with General Sir Stapleton Cotton (1773–1865) in command.[2] Balls were got up to enliven the long winter evenings, and it would appear that the local females were passionately addicted to dancing. Indeed, Commissary Schaumann of the King's German Legion, who obviously had an eye for the girls, refers to 'barbarously brilliant' balls, at the same time emphasizing that as regards morals he had never come across 'such a Sodom and Gomorrah as that place was. The girls and the women of the higher as well as the lower classes were practically all disreputable. Pure virgins were rare . . . .'.

But organizing a dance was not always so easy; indeed, on one occasion all the ladies inexplicably declined the invitation. On making enquiries, the reason was soon explained. Apparently, on Junot's invasion, a certain French corps had spent several days there, and had given a dance, perhaps to ingratiate themselves, for they were cordially loathed. The wives of the local gentry refused to attend the function; and in order to avoid trouble, they sent instead 'their chambermaids and other working-class girls . . . decked in their mistresses' fine clothes and jewels'. Unfortunately, someone revealed the ruse and, to avenge the affront, the French officers arranged between themselves that the moment the quadrille was over, at a blast of a trumpet, they 'would fall upon the women and overpower them – a plan which was actually carried out, amid the most terrifying shrieks'.

Not unnaturally, the ladies of Covilhã suspected another such outrage from the British troops. However, once reassured that this was unlikely to occur, they relented and tripped along, and the ball was a great success. Pyramids of cakes, apples, melons and grapes stood on shelves around the ballroom, and the street leading to it was lined with men bearing straw torches. Once the band had struck up, and wine, punch and grog distributed, there was no holding them.

Spanish, English and German dances were executed amid the most appalling tumult. The ladies were beside themselves with joy. Some of them, in order to facilitate their movements, had pinned up their dresses tightly in front of them, so as to outline their figures very sharply behind, while others had pinned them behind, producing the reverse effect, [and those who were not dancing] swarmed like locusts round the buffet, and after stuffing themselves with all they could, actually began filling their pockets.

Schaumann was assured that one fat monk, among other clerics who had not been invited but who had nevertheless squirmed their way in, had had 'no less than twenty-four cups of tea and twenty-four biscuits, and that he was coming back for more . . .'.

Continuing north-east, the road skirts **Belmonte**, commanded by its ineptly restored castle. Adjacent stands what was probably the *domus municipalis* or council-house, for it has several similarities to that at Braganza. São Tiago contains the Cabral chapel, preserving an image of the Virgin which travelled round the Cape of Good Hope with Pedro Alvares Cabral when on his expedition to India. Cabral, who was born at Belmonte *circa* 1467 and is buried at Santarém, was to discover Brazil in 1500.

Just north of the town rises the **Torre Centum Cellas**, one of the more imposing and well-preserved ruins of Roman origin extant in Portugal, although no convincing answer has been given as to its precise use. It may have been part of an important villa, but during the Middle Ages its upper storey was altered, and it later served as a watch-tower.

From here the road continues up the narrowing valley towards high-lying Guarda (see Chapter 19).

NOTES

1. Wellington was incandescent, but perhaps not entirely surprised. On learning of Erskine's arrival in the Peninsula, he remarked that he had 'generally understood [him] to be a madman, to which his military secretary had responded: no doubt he is sometimes a little mad, but in his lucid intervals he is an uncommonly clever fellow; and I trust he will have no fit during the campaign, though he looked a little wild as he embarked'. Erskine (1769–1813) later committed suicide in Lisbon, but was buried at Brozas, near Alcántara, in Spain.
2. Later Lord Combermere.

Beira Alta and the Côa valley

If entering Portugal from Salamanca and Ciudad Rodrigo, the frontier is crossed at **Vilar Formoso**. It was just south of this highway, straddling the border, that the hard fought two-day battle of Fuentes de Oñoro took place, described by Wellington as 'the most difficult one I was ever concerned in and against the greatest odds'.

During the first week of May 1811 headquarters had been set up at Freineda, some five miles west; and at first the Allies – 34,500 infantry (including 11,500 Portuguese) and 1,860 cavalry – together with forty-eight guns, were disposed behind a low ridge dividing the river Tourões and the rivulet of Dos Casas. Wellington's left flank pivoted on Fort Concepción, an imposing Vaubanesque stronghold some nine miles north, near Aldeia del Obispo, in Spain, and well worth the detour. The bulk of his forces were positioned in and around the granite-walled village of **Fuentes de Oñoro**, just within Spain.

Masséna, having received reinforcements and reassembled and re-equipped his crippled army after their disastrous retreat from the Lines of Torres Vedras, and intent on restoring his tarnished reputation, was marching south-west from Salamanca with 48,000 men. But over-confidently, and not having yet learned his lesson from Busaco, he repeated the error of making an impetuous frontal attack on the imperturbable British lines awaiting him. After severe hand-to-hand fighting in the maze of granite-walled alleys of Fuentes, from which the Allies were dislodged briefly by sheer weight of numbers, the French were driven back. Next day an informal truce was made to enable the place to be cleared of dead and wounded.

Meanwhile, Wellington extended his right flank southwards towards **Nave de Haver**; and it was against this comparatively weak sector that Masséna next concentrated, forcing the Allies to swing back at right-angles, pivoting on Fuentes, now at the centre of their front, to face south. Eventually the French had to give up the struggle from sheer exhaustion, and retired to lick their wounds, while Wellington, on one of the rare occasions during the whole war, ordered his troops to 'dig in'.

Masséna was relieved of his command shortly after, and replaced by Mortier.

(It is not the place here to describe the much bloodier battle between Beresford and Soult, which occurred only eleven days later at Albuera, south-east of Badajoz, in which the casualties were some 6,000 and between 7–8,000 respectively.)

The modern highway drives directly west from Vilar Formoso towards Guarda, on several occasions crossing the older main road descending past the ruins of **Castelo Bom** into the boulder-strewn gorge of the Côa and entering **Castelo Mendo**, with remains of its fortifications.

This whole area served as a base for the greater part of Wellington's army both during the months prior to the siege of Ciudad Rodrigo in January 1812 and the battle of Salamanca the following June; and his main lines of communication and supply passed through here during the winter of 1812–13 and before his advance on Vitoria.

During two successive winters, Wellington himself lived in a small granite house opposite the church at **Freineda**, not far south of Castelo Bom.

There was no room for all departments of headquarters in the same village. The officers in command of the artillery and the Royal Engineers put up in **Malhada-Sorda**, to the south, as did Judge-Advocate Larpent, and the medical department and the Commissary-General were quartered in Castelo Bom. The headquarters' press remained at Freineda. And here too Wellington kennelled his pack of hounds, for there was no want of foxes, and he would hunt two or three times a week. Less frequently a shoot was got up, game being abundant, although in fact Wellington was an indifferent shot. Those who preferred fly-fishing might try their luck with the trout teeming in the Agueda and Côa.

And thus passed the time. 'We never gamed nor do I remember to have seen a pack of cards at HQ', wrote one officer. Captain Thomas Henry Browne, who dined there occasionally, refers to Wellington only drinking the best French wines, sent in by guerrilla chiefs after they had captured a convoy. At other times a couple of mules would be dispatched as far afield as Coimbra to collect wine, cigars and such creature comforts, while at Christmas 1812 Wellington's guests shared two turkeys and some tins of mincemeat sent up from Lisbon.

The cheerfulness or gloom at table depended to a large extent on the news received from divisional commanders, or from England; Wellington himself was often the most playful of the party. When he wished the company to retire, he would call for coffee and leave the room a while later, when it was expected that his guests would likewise disperse to their respective quarters. 'He had a small portmanteau iron bed-stead, covered with Russian leather with one pillow of the same material'; but if he suspected any movement by the enemy 'he used to lie down on his bed-stead in his clothes, with his boots near him, ready to put on, & his cloak thrown around him. His horse, & that of his orderly dragoon were always ready sad-dled . . .'. Browne himself had to make do with a sort of hay-loft, and had difficulty keeping out the excessive cold, for, as he wrote:

The hail used to get under the tiles & fall on my bed as I slept. To remedy this as well as I could I borrowed tar-paulins from the Com-missary, & slung them over the spot . . . The Crevices in the walls I stopped with clay, & at last made a sort of fire place which was a great comfort.

According to Browne, Sir Robert Kennedy, the Commissary-General – who kept a pack of harriers and had excellent English horses – also kept the best table and dined off plate, but there was no lack of vituals at headquarters. At Freineda three women suttlers held sway, among whom was probably the formidable Antonia, 'a stout lusty person of rather a jolly countenance, dirty enough', who

always wore a massy gold necklace, to which a cross of the same material was attached & a pair of long pendant ear-rings. This Antonia was the greatest cheat of the whole set, & amassed a con-siderable fortune by her attendance at Head-Quarters, to which she was attached for . . . several years, her goods becoming worse & her prices more exhorbitant each succeeding campaign.

What impressed Commissary Schaumann was how quiet and unostentatious life was at headquarters, whether it was here or south-east across the frontier at **Fuenteguinaldo**. No one would have known that the Commander-in-Chief was so close, for there was

no throng of scented staff officers with plumed hats, orders and stars, no main guard, no crowd of contractors, actors, valets, cooks, mistresses, equipages, horses, dogs, forage and baggage wagons . . . Just a few aides-de-camp, who went about the streets alone and in their overcoats, a few guides, and a small staff guard; that was all!

But Schaumann, when referring to Fuenteguinaldo, could not help but remark on one very noticeable difference, that between

the friendly, hospitable Portuguese and the disobliging Spaniards! Everybody here is grave, monosyllabic, and gloomy; not a soul enquired whether I wanted anything to eat or drink.

Not far north of the highway lies **Almeida**, which for long remained one of the most powerfully defended strongholds on the frontier. The town itself has not much else to offer except its *pousada*, and its position. That there is still so much to see of the eighteenth-century fortifications is remarkable, considering its history. Twice in the late fourteenth century it had been captured during Spanish incursions, and it was here in 1387 that John of Gaunt and Nun' Alvares took leave of each other after their invasion of Castile.

In August 1704 it was a base of operations against the Spaniards, but in 1762 the garrison was forced to surrender when attacked by their neighbours. In February 1773 Richard Twiss was hospitably entertained here by Colonel Calder, governor in the absence of General Maclean, both being among the several British officers then in the Portuguese service.

Its Vaubanesque works, with their bomb-proof casemates, which had replaced the sixteenth-century fortifications, fell to the French in June 1808; but they were then obliged to evacuate it under the terms of the Convention of Sintra, and it was garrisoned by Portuguese, with Colonel William Cox in command. But when inspected by Captain William Granville Eliot of the Royal Regiment of Artillery and author of *A Treatise on the Defence of Portugal*, he could not see a dozen gun-carriages fit for service there, 'nor was there any wood in store for the construction of others. The embrasures were falling to decay, and the palisades of the covert-way mostly broken or carried away for fire-wood'. Notwithstanding these and many other defects which he took care to point out, he was of the opinion that with proper attention and some labour it still might be made strong enough to withstand a regular siege, and its defence sustained for some time.

It was from Almeida early in January 1809 that General Sir Alan

Cameron's contingent marched north via Torre de Moncorvo, Mirandela and Braganza to join Sir John Moore's army; but on learning that Moore was already in retreat, he sensibly retired on Lamego.

Although on 24 July 1810 General Craufurd's Light Division put up a spirited delaying action against the superior forces of Ney and Loison, Masséna's impetuous advance isolated the place. Immediately Almeida was invested, the French started digging parallels in the rocky ground, and at dawn on 26 July they began their bombardment. There are conflicting accounts of what happened at seven that evening, for there were no survivors in the immediate area of the immense explosion that devastated the town. It has been surmised that either a train of powder from a damaged barrel was ignited, or that a particularly heavy projectile pierced the strengthened main door of the building converted into the central magazine. Perhaps a charged bomb rolled into a subsiduary magazine and exploded, causing a chain reaction. Whatever the reason, the result was catastrophic. The castle and cathedral were torn apart and reduced to a heap of rubble. Being left with too little ammunition to carry on any protracted defence, Colonel Cox had no alternative but to capitulate.

With this thorn in his flesh fortuitously extracted, Masséna had little doubt that his march west towards Coimbra and the coast would be a walk-over: what could now stop him thrusting the skulking British leopard into the sea?

At **Vilar Torpim**, no distance north of Almeida, Colonel Leach, when in winter cantonments, apparently spent his evenings smoking cigars over Douro wine and dancing boleros, fandangos and waltzes with the good-looking daughter of an Israelite, in whose home he was billeted.

Further north still stands the fortified village of **Castelo Rodrigo**, and the nearby monastery of **Santa Maria de Aguiar**, with its Gothic church; while also in the vicinity are the partly reconstructed remains of a Roman temple known as the **Casarão da Torre**.

Turning south-west from Castelo Rodrigo, first passing below the heights of Marofa and across the gorge of the Côa, we approach **Pinhel**, where the former Bishop's palace (for it had been the seat of a bishopric until 1882) at one time housed the headquarters staff of Generals Graham and Picton. Above the town rises its castle, high up on the eastern wall of which are two gargoyles, which in an offensive posture relieve themselves in the direction of Spain.

At **Guarda** a battery of cannon-shaped gargoyles line the east wall of its fortress-like cathedral, and likewise point defiantly towards their neighbour. With the exception of that at Batalha, which may well have been its inspiration, the grey granite cathedral at Guarda is also the only church in Portugal with a clerestory *and* flying buttresses. The octagonal towers commanding its west front and the thick ribs of its vault emphasize its solidity; while the pair of twisted colonettes near the crossing and the keystone above are concessions to Manueline taste, for Boitic was working here between 1504 and 1517. The French stabled their cavalry in the nave, and the organ was 'sadly hacked about in a most wanton manner', but the four-tiered retable attributed to Jean de Rouen appears to be comparatively little damaged.

Due to its commanding site above the undulating wind-blown plateau, Guarda was fortified as a defense against Moorish incursions by Dom Sancho I as early as 1197, and castle ruins may be seen above the cathedral. Standing as it does at 1,000 metres, Guarda is also the highest town in Portugal and probably its most inclement, living up to its reputation as being *Fria, Feia, Forte, e Farta* – cold, well-supplied, strong, and ugly; although the latter epithet is not entirely fair.

From Guarda, the new highway descends in sweeping curves from the *meseta* to the formerly wild-boar-infested valley floor, dropping some 500 metres in six miles, and providing a splendid view across to a spur of the Serra da Estrela.

With the change of vegetation due to the difference in altitude, we appear to enter another country on approaching **Celerico**. Although an ancient site defending an important crossroads, and perhaps because on a customary invasion route, its surviving monuments are few.

Of more interest are those of walled **Trancosa**, to the north-east, where in 1283 Dom Dinis married Isabel of Aragón. The Portuguese routed a Spanish force near here in 1385, where two years later were concluded the lengthy negotiations whereby John of Gaunt, whose elder daughter Philippa had recently married Dom João I, agreed to allow Catherine of Lancaster, her sister, to be betrothed to the future Enrique III of Castile (then nine years old): in return – on receipt at Bayonne of a large sum in gold francs in compensation – he would surrender his own claims to the kingdoms of Castile and León.

It was at Trancosa in the 1580s that a local cobbler composed one of the first of many popular verses propagating the Messianic cult of Sebastianism, and only a few decades later the Inquisition were active among the 'New Christians' of the region, who seemed to have been particularly susceptible to the idea of the 'coming of the King'. Richard Twiss, in 1773, refers to having been entertained there by a New Christian, and drinking the finest red wine he had ever tasted, 'resembling Burgundy in colour and flavour, but superior in goodness'.

In March 1810 General Picton occupied the so-called Casa Real; and later in the same year General Beresford was given the title of Conde de Trancosa.

For the road from Celerico to Viseu, see Chapter 22. From Celerico, we bear south-west away from the Mondego to skirt the northern foothills of the Serra da Estrela, the Roman Herminius Major, traversing orchards and granite-propped vineyards to **Carrapichana**.

Close by is the ancient hilltop village of **Linhares**, formerly Lebiobriga, and the seat of a Visigothic bishopric. Narrow lanes flanked by fifteenth-century dwellings climb to the castle, remarkable for its finely chiselled masonry. It once commanded an older road winding along the valley side, and this may be followed still through **Melo**, with remains of a medieval palace, and fortified **Folgosinho**, to **Gouveia** (briefly Wellington's headquarters before retiring on Busaco), from which the main road can be regained with ease.

Beyond **Póvoa das Quartas**, its *pousada* (Santa Bárbara) providing a delightful view across the wooded Alva valley, we pass near **Oliveira do Hospital**, an attractively sited little market-town, and neighbouring **Bobadela**, once a Roman *municipium*, of which the gate-arch of its forum is the only obvious relic. Oliveira, which as its name implies belonged to the Hospitallers, retains in its church the tombs of the Ferreiros family and a carved equestrian figure similar to that in the museum at Coimbra.

São Pedro at **Lourosa**, to the left of the road, is one of the more remarkable churches in Portugal. Dating from AD 912, it is probably the work of Mozárabic masons. The *ajimece* windows, the characteristic Visigothic decoration in the entrance porch, and the broad horseshoe arches of the interior, will be noted. I remember well the elderly lady with the key, who after pointing out the baptismal stoup and confessional seat, touchingly insisted on presenting us with postcards as we had no coins on us at that moment. Such a gesture from one who could scarce afford it was something I never encountered in any similar situation in Spain.

Turnings are passed later for Penacova (see Chapter 21), and **Foz de**

Arouce, frequently mis-spelled Aronce in earlier descriptions. Some 500 of Masséna's rearguard were killed or drowned in the Ceira here when attempting to cross the river in their precipitate retreat from the Lines of Torres Vedras in the face of strong pressure from the Allies, whose losses were minimal. Commissary Schaumann saw its banks near the destroyed bridge

covered with dead bodies. A number of exhausted donkeys, horses and mules, which had not been able to wade across the large smooth stones of the roaring stream, and which the barbarians had made unfit for use by either hamstringing them or twisting their necks, were still writhing in the mud, half dead. Among them lay commissariat carts, dead soldiers, women and children, who had died either from want or cold, or through the explosion. Over the whole of this ghastly confusion of bodies, our cavalry now proceeded to march without mercy, until the whole was churned into a mess of blood and slush. Never during the whole of the war did I again see such a horrible sight.

Death and destruction, murder and fire, robbery and rape, lay everywhere in the tracks of the enemy. Every morning at dawn when we started out the burning villages, hamlets and woods, which illuminated the sky, told of the progress of the French . . . compelled to abandon upon the high road all the silver, gold, valuables, silks and velvets, costly ecclesiastical vestments, monstrances and crucifixes, which they had plundered . . . and as the Portuguese peasants cut the throats of all the Frenchmen they encountered, the Light Division became the heirs to all their abandoned treasure.

Even the most appalling scenes of the Thirty Years War, which Schaumann knew from historical descriptions, were 'nothing compared with the horrors, the misery and the devastation' that he saw on that road between Coimbra and the frontier.

It was towards the end of his retreat, having opened up communication with Almeida, that Masséna ordered his commanders to march south again, an absurd instruction in the circumstances, with which Marshal Ney (who had narrowly escaped capture near Foz de Arouce) insubordinately refused to comply, causing him to be relieved of his command and sent back to France in temporary disgrace.

The main road continues to wind along the narrow right bank of the Ceira to meet the Mondego shortly before entering Coimbra.

20

Coimbra – Conímbriga

'It was noise and narrow streets, and stink', complained Southey, for although **Coimbra** had all the appearance of a gloriously seated city when approaching it, the delusion ceased on entry. Professor Link, after passing an uncomfortable night there in 1797, warned travellers that 'in no large town throughout Portugal were the inns so bad, strangers being lodged in wretched apartments with miserable beds . . .'. My own reactions when settling for the less scruffy of the hotels I came across in Coimbra were not dissimilar.

And yet it is an interesting and animated place, as the only university town in Portugal – at least until the advent of the Republic – should be, even if I was unfortunate enough to see it when almost every stretch of wall was defaced by student graffiti and political posters, which hardly improved the townscape.

The Mondego, the Roman Munda, heavy with sediment, which must have silted over the foundations of the Roman bridge that most likely would have spanned it at this point, flows past the foot of the Alcáçova. This hill, on which stood their post of Aeminium, commanded the river crossing and the road from Lisbon to Braga – or Olisipo to Bracara, if you will.

It was not until AD 872, when the country as far south as the Mondego was wrested temporarily from the Moors by Alfonso III el Magno, king of the Asturias, that the place assumed its present name, borrowed from that of neighbouring Conímbriga. Sacked by Almanzor in 987, it remained in Moorish hands until 1064, when it was reconquered definitively by Fernando I of Castile, aided by the Cid, although it was briefly invested during an Almoravid incursion in 1116.

Coimbra was described in the mid-twelfth century by the Muslim geographer Idrisi as being

a small city, flourishing and well-populated, rich in vineyards

and orchards of apples, cherries, and plums, its fields very fer-
tile . . . and the inhabitants, who are the bravest of the Christians, possess many cattle great and small: the Mondego moves
many mills and bathes many vineyards and gardens.

During this confused period its citizens were mainly *Mozārabs*,
and when Paternus, one of their bishops, gained control of the
churches of Lamego and Viseu, it is said to have caused much
consternation in Braga. From 1139, when Afonso Henriques was
proclaimed King of Portugal, until 1385, Coimbra was considered
to be the administrative capital of the kingdom, having supplanted
Guimaraes, although in about 1250 Dom Afonso III had transferred
the main royal residence to Lisbon. The university, founded in
1308, was also moved there, not being re-established at Coimbra
until 1537.

Meanwhile, dominated by its bishops, the town stagnated, even
if it was the focus of an important school of sculptors, among them
João and Diogo Castilho, together with several of French origin
such as Nicolas Chanterène, Jean de Rouen, and Philippe Houdart.
But clerical influence remained powerful, and after 1567 Coimbra
was one of the three seats of the Inquisition in Portugal, and the
Holy Office was notably active there in the 1620s.

In many ways it remained isolated from Lisbon, largely due to
bad roads. When Catherine of Braganza, the dowager Queen of
England, and her retinue were making the overland part of the
journey back to Lisbon, it took ten days to cover the 130 miles
between Coimbra and the capital.

Wellington and Beresford passed through Coimbra in May 1809
very shortly before making their lightning attack on Oporto. In the
September of the following year, smarting from Busaco, Masséna
sacked the place, but the 4,000 wounded he left in its hospitals were
captured soon after by Portuguese militia commanded by Trant.

This contingent was strong enough to hold the north bank at the
Ponte de Santa Clara in March 1811, forcing Masséna's army to
cross the tributary Ceira at Foz de Arouce. According to Captain
Browne, when the British were able to enter Coimbra again, it
showed every appearance of having been completely ransacked,

and scarcely an inhabitant was found in it. Several of its beautiful
Churches had been converted into Stables for Cavalry, and were
filled with straw and dirt. The doors of the Vestries had been

forced open . . . Altars and Images were defaced, and the marks of pistol bullets shewed that they had been shot at, as a mark. Rich silk vestments, covered with gold or silver embroidery, were used as horse clothes . . . The splendid robes which the French had left . . . we gathered up respectfully, and cut them into waistcoats and dressing gowns. On our days of halt and washing, it was not an unusual sight, to see Officers, whilst their shirts were drying, pacing to and fro, in front of a bivouac formed by branches of trees, in the bedizened garments of Catholic Priests and Bishops.

The terrace of Santa Clara, high up on the south bank of the Mondego, provides the best general view of Coimbra. The convent was designed by João Turriano, a professor of mathematics at the university. In the lower choir is the original tomb, transferred here from Santa Clara-a-Velha, of Isabel of Aragón, who had married Dom Dinis in 1282, and whose saintly life is depicted on carved and polychromed panels. Her mortal remains were later placed in a silver shrine, although the display of her surviving garments appears to excite the sacristan more.

The adjacent cloister, inspired by the Great Cloister at Tomar, was erected for the poor Clares by Dom João V, who (as we know from his exploits at Odivelas) had a penchant for nuns; but his intramural activities here are not recorded.

Rifleman Simmons, who visited several convents in the town in December 1809, refers to these nuns in particular for hospitably handing out their home-made sweetmeats to British officers. (And a canon at Coimbra is said to have regularly entertained officers of the 29th Foot, accepting their rations and in return providing them with confections and desserts in addition to good wine.)

At a lower level, nearer the bridge, are the sad relics of Santa Clara-a-Velha (the older), its floor long ago silted up by the Mondego in flood, and little more than its fine rose-window survives to be appreciated. Like Santa Isabel, Inês de Castro (later translated to Alcobaça), had been buried here first. Her murder, the subject of numerous romances, is said to have taken place by a water-tank in the garden of the nearby eighteenth-century Quinta das Lágrimas (of tears).

Entering the old town through the Arco de Almedina, we pass close to the Casa de Sub-Ripas, a mansion believed to have been the scene of another murder, that of Maria Teles, who had secretly married João, the eldest son of Inês de Castro. It seems that Maria had excited the envy of Queen Leonor, her sister, who had little difficulty in persuading João that his wife was being unfaithful, meanwhile insinuating that if only he had been more patient, he might have married her own daughter. Precipitately, João hurried to Coimbra and stabbed the unfortunate lady, much to the queen's private satisfaction, who had no intention of having him as her son-in-law. João was then conveniently hounded from the country.

Adjacent is the Torre de Ante, with a small museum devoted to local manufactures, among which, as already remarked on by Major Dalrymple two centuries ago, is that of *palitos* or toothpicks, much white willow-wood whittling being done in the vicinity of Lorvão and Penacova. Just beyond is the restored Colégio Novo, its cloister designed by Filippo Terzi, and inspired by that at Tomar, which he had completed.

Few would deny that the fortress-like Sé Velha is one of the finest Romanesque churches in Portugal. Dom Sancho I was crowned in the newly completed cathedral, and in 1385 it was the scene of Dom João I's coronation. The massive square piers of the nave, once encrusted with *azulejos*, the bold triforium, the central lantern, and the elaborate Gothic retable of the Assumption by Oliver de Gand (Ghent) and Jean d'Ypres, are all impressive.

Skirting its Renaissance north portal and galleried apse, we pass below the delicately columned double-storeyed loggia of the former bishop's palace, now the Museu Machado de Castro, named after that sculptor, born at Coimbra in 1732. Near the entrance survives a Moorish tower, while the abutting church of São João de Almedina was probably founded on the site of a mosque.

The collections are important. Notable among sculptures is a mounted knight swinging his mace, and among paintings, an Assumption of the Magdalen – a rare subject. Numerous Roman and Visigothic artefacts are displayed in the *cryptoporticus*.

Close by is Romanesque São Salvador, and dominating the Largo da Feira, the seventeenth-century Sé Novo, the Jesuit cathedral. Beyond are the buildings of the Natural History Museum and Chemical Laboratory,[1] both designed by a certain Lieutenant-Colonel William Elsden, an architect *manqué* who had arrived in Portugal in about 1762, taught mathematics at the Military Academy, and according to Major Dalrymple, who met him here in 1774, was then second-in-command of the Corps of Engineers. Elsden also tried his hand at baroquizing the interior of the abbey at Alcobaça.[2]

Regrettably, much of the atmosphere of the old university quarter has evaporated with the wanton destruction of ancient buildings, replaced by vast characterless blocks under the aegis of Dr Salazar, who had been a student here. Sacheverell Sitwell condemned them as shaming in their blatant ugliness and with sculptures 'of insulting hideousness'; one wonders how ugly this quarter may have been at an earlier date. Captain Bragge, passing through Coimbra in January 1812, commented that

> The Town and Students are equally dirty and the numerous Convents and Colleges built with no more Architectural Taste than our Manufactories at Chard and elsewhere, and in every point of View the Town has more the appearance of a manufactory than a University.

The university had been re-established in the former royal palace, which stood around the present Patio das Escolas. A competent body of scholars were assembled by André Gouveia, and among those later invited to lecture was George Buchanan, a man 'of austere countenance, but mirrie, and quick in conference and awnswres to anie questioun'; but his presence provoked jealousy among other academics and influence was brought to bear on the Inquisition to imprison him in Lisbon for several months.

During the latter half of the sixteenth century its publishing activities flourished under the auspices of António de Mariz, the press having been set up in the cathedral cloisters. But the administration of the university slid into the hands of priests, who were only too happy to hand out 'doctorates' on payment of a fee to students who had never attended lectures. In 1772 Pombal cleansed these Augean stables by expelling the remaining Jesuits (whose Order had been suppressed in Portugal thirteen years earlier) and setting up a more liberal system; this was later held against him by some of the more obscurantist members, as might be expected.

Degrees were conferred in the Sala dos Capelas, its entrance embellished with sculptures by Claude de Laprade. Adjacent is the rector's residence, and the Sala do Exame Privado, hung with ponderous portraits of former incumbents, often the only memorial of their existence. In the west wing, beyond the Baroque clock-tower, is the Manueline portal of the university chapel, resplendent with seventeenth-century *azulejos*, painted ceiling, and red and gilt organ.

Even more impressive is the library, a very fine example of the João Quinto style, possibly designed by Laprade, although Manuel da Silva was responsible for much of its decoration. Sitwell has suggested that the king – whose portrait, framed by carved curtains parted by putti, dominates the far end of the room – who, although he had also initiated the library at Mafra, was certainly no bibliophile, commissioned it merely in rivalry to that of his brother-in-law, Karl VI, whose Hofbibliothek in Vienna was being built by J.B. Fischer von Erlach at the same time. Its three main sections are decorated in two shades of green and in orange, and its upper galleries sustained by tapering supports; the whole, with its chinoiserie japanning, is elaborately gilt. Notable too are the ebony tables, and the perspective ceiling paintings.

To the east of the university, and built on the site of its Roman predecessor, extends part of Filippo Terzi's aqueduct, known as the 'Arcos do Jardim', where it skirts the terraced botanical gardens, the hillside site of which was chosen by William Elsden. Further north is the Praça da República, flanked by the Parque de Santa Cruz.

The ascent continues to the Mosteiro de Celas, with its circular Manueline church and fourteenth-century cloister, and beyond to hilltop Santo António dos Olivais, but I would not consider their exploration essential.

The less energetic may descend the wide Avenida Sa de Bandeira. Later, on approaching Santa Cruz, one passes a curious domed fountain with subsiduary chapels standing in the Jardim da Manga, once the cloister of an ancient priory.

The west front of Santa Cruz has been spoilt by later additions, but it retains sculptures by Jean de Rouen, and by Chanterène, who also carved the corbelled pulpit and, although Diogo de Castilho was responsible for their general design, probably the recumbent figures on the tombs of Afonso Henriques and Dom Sancho I, his son, who were re-interred here in 1520. The paintings in the sacristy; Marco Pires' cloister (which was serving as a poultry-yard when visited by Southey), with its unusual weak-looking, vesica-shaped ribs; and the frieze of ships and castles above the Manueline stalls of the upper choir, should not be overlooked, nor the organ, a reminder that Heliodoro de Paiva, the composer of numerous masses and motets, was a canon here in the first half of the sixteenth century.

Few of the remaining churches of Coimbra are of any moment. However, the truncated apse of São Tiago, facing the Praça do

Comercio, is passed on traversing the narrow main street of the lower town to regain the Largo da Portagem and the Ponte Santa Clara.

Conímbriga, ten miles south-west near **Condeixa-a-Velha**, is the most extensive Roman settlement in Portugal so far excavated, and that only in part. The site straddles a tongue of land between two gorges, and around the perimeter of this promontory a wall was erected, with an outer rampart facing east, from which direction an aqueduct entered the town. The modern site museum is admirable.

Conímbriga was occupied from as early as 800 BC, and became a station on the road from Lisbon via Tomar to Braga. By the first century AD it was a *municipium*, and remained of importance until sacked by the Suevi in 468. (Coins from mints as far afield as Alexandria, Antioch, Byzantium and London have been found there.) Its Visigothic kings then transferred their residence to the more easily defended site of Aeminium (modern Coimbra), although it would appear that its bishops remained here until the penultimate decade of the sixth century.

Near the town gates are the remains of a large Roman villa, with mosaic pavements surrounding a large pool, the bronze fountain-jets of which have been replaced by replicas and now function again. Another villa stood within the gate, near the forum, while baths, temples and an amphitheatre have also been uncovered. The site continues to be excavated.

The excursion may be extended by driving north-west to **Montemor-o-Velho**, dominated by its hilltop royal castle, while within the *enceinte*, providing attractive views over the rice fields of the lower Mondego valley, is a church with Manueline columns. The village was the birthplace of Jorge de Montemayor, the poet and pastoral novelist of Jewish descent, whose influential *Los siete libros de la Diana* was published in Valencia *c.* 1559. Nossa Senhora dos Anjos contains the tomb of Diogo de Azambuja, the navigator, who in the 1480s established the settlement of São Jorge da Mina on the Gold Coast. Another native was Fernão Mendes Pinto, who Aubrey Bell refers to as 'this prince of travellers and adventurers', and whose *Peregrinaçam* was published posthumously in 1614.

It was near neighbouring **Figueira da Foz**, then a small port at the mouth of the Mondego (its fort already occupied by a group of students from Coimbra who had formed the 'Academic Volunteers', which played a part in covering the disembarkation), that

Wellington's expeditionary force landed in the pounding surf during the first week of August 1808 (see Chapter 15). It has a museum of some quality.

If returning towards Coimbra, make a short detour north of **Tentúgal** to the church of **São Marcos**, a relic of a mid-fifteenth-century Hieronymite convent, which contains a wealth of sculptural monuments. Among them is the tomb of Fernão Teles de Meneses, carved by Diogo Pires the Elder, its Gothic curtained canopy held aside by hairy men. Among other features of interest are the two Manueline tombs of members of the Da Silva family, and the retable by Chanterène, in spite of its having been tastelessly retouched.

To the east rises the 'damned long hill' of Busaco.

NOTES

1. According to Dalrymple, this contained 'an excellent collection of instruments for experimental philosophy', recently arrived from England; but only a few years later another traveller remarked on seeing astronomical instruments covered with rust and dirt!
2. At an earlier period there had been a small English Factory at Coimbra, and five English families, including that of a physician, were still in residence there in the 1770s.

21

Busaco

Busaco is approached with ease from Coimbra by following the N1 to **Mealhada**, there climbing through the old spa of **Luso**, its bottled waters gushing freely from its fountains, to reach the Porta das Ameias, the battlemented gate of the walled Mata do Buçaco.

This State forest lies near the northern extremity of the Serra do Buçaco, and preserves a remarkable number of magnificent trees, both native and exotic, including the rare Mexican cedar (*Cupressus lusitanica*), extinct in its original habitat.

An edict dated 1622 prohibited women from entering this precinct, which would seem to confirm that the Discalced Carmelites, who were not presented formally with the estate by the Archbishop of Braga until four years later, had already taken possession; and it was they who in the following decades indulged in extensive planting. If it was not for their entreaties, the forest would have been set alight by the pursuers of Castelo-Melhor, Dom Afonso VI's fallen minister, who fleeing from Lisbon, had hidden there, later making his escape to England. Afforestation proceeded spasmodically during the next century and a half, although the east slope of the ridge was comparatively bare in 1810, when Wellington's great defensive battle took place on that 'damned long hill'; and it was still much more open earlier this century than it is now.

The forest road winds through the trees towards the Palace Hotel, which now engulfs the former conventual dependencies. This incongruous pseudo-Manueline confection was designed by Luigi Manini, a scene-painter at the São Carlos opera-house in Lisbon, as a summer palace for the royal family, which does not say much for their taste in accepting it. With the demise of the monarchy only three years after its completion, it was converted into the present luxurious establishment, which in some respects appears to have little changed since then. To be fair, the plumbing has been modernized, and the cellar is said by those who can afford them to contain some remarkable vintages. They may have offered some comfort to General Spinola, who during a crucial stage of his presidency made his retreat here, on 10 August 1974 landing by helicopter on the lawn; but he resigned not long after.

On its north façade is the black and white pebble-encrusted entrance to the remnant of the former convent, with its diminutive chapel and gloomy cork-lined cells, which with neighbouring hermitages were requisitioned by Wellington's staff on 21 September 1810. Wellington himself was not too pleased with the room placed at his disposal, as it had only one door, so he chose another more secure, with two, which was then sluiced out and dried by lighting a cheering fire. The abbot was not disturbed, nobody wanting his cell, for 'it was found full of lumber, rags, and old iron', while the monks dossed down in the church and sacristy and any unoccupied corner they could find. Some narratives state that Wellington passed the night immediately before the battle in the open among his troops, wrapped in his cloak, which accords with his character.

Near the Queen's Gate is a small military museum, a commemorative obelisk, and a viewpoint looking out over the area through which Masséna's army approached the hog's-back hill from **Mortágua**.

Wellington had taken up a position on the ridge just west of its crest, along which some sixty guns were concealed; but he deliberately left a thin line of sentries to be seen by the enemy. His main force consisted of some 49,000 men. This included 24,500 Portuguese troops, who although well trained by Beresford and his officers, were largely untried recruits. These brigades were therefore attached to the British divisions and distributed along the reverse slope. As William Tomkinson noted at the time, 'Every one expected and wished for a general attack at daylight. The army is in most beautiful order, and the Portuguese as fine-looking men and as steady under arms as any in the world'; and Commissary Schaumann later wrote confirming that 'They behaved just like the English troops, and, indeed, fought with such valour that the French believed them to be Englishmen disguised in Portuguese uniforms'.

A month had passed since Almeida had been forced to surrender, and meanwhile Wellington had concentrated his dispersed forces on what was a formidable defensive position to await the relentless but arduous French advance. As he stated in his *Dispatches*: 'There are many bad roads in Portugal, but the enemy has taken decidedly

the worst in the whole Kingdom'. The breaking up of several other
cross-country tracks running west had been part of his deliberate
plan, for Masséna would be thus deflected directly towards the
Serra da Buçaco.

Craufurd's Light Division straddled this road as it snaked up to
the summit of the ridge, while Picton's Third Division was positioned across another track ascending further south. Between them
was Brent Spencer's First Division, while two others, commanded
respectively by Leith and Hill, extended along the ridge to the
south. The left wing was defended by Lowry Cole. Schaumann was
evidently much impressed by Wellington's display of

> extraordinary circumspection, calm, coolness and presence of
> mind. His orders were communicated in a loud voice, and were
> short and precise . . . He wears no befeathered hat, no gold lace,
> no stars, no orders – simply a plain low hat, a white collar, a grey
> overcoat, and a light sword.

The French army, consisting of three Corps, commanded by
Junot, Ney and Reynier, totalled 66,000 men. On arrival, they dispersed over the valley floor, where the glow of numerous bivouac
fires gave away their positions as soon as night fell. The Allies
remained in darkness.

In the early morning mist of 27 September, undissuaded by the
saner counsel of his subordinates, Masséna ordered his dense columns up the steep flank and lateral spurs in a frontal attack. Not
surprisingly, as at Vimeiro, they were hurled back in confusion
repeatedly, with a loss of at least 4,600 men, compared with less
than 1,200 on the part of the Allies.

It was not until, belatedly, the French cavalry had worked their
way laboriously round the northern extremity of the ridge that
Wellington, his flank in danger of being turned, ordered his forces
to retire leisurely through Coimbra towards the prepared defensive
lines north of Lisbon.

As a matter of course, Coimbra was sacked by Masséna as he
drove his opponent south 'in full retreat' after what is described
even now by chauvinistic pens as 'a great victory'.

Follow the road from the obelisk to the Cruz Alta, providing a
view over the coastal plain, with the pounding Atlantic visible
beyond a line of dunes in the distance. A good forest road, which
follows Wellington's line of lateral communication during the

battle, leads south along the main ridge to Penacova. (This later crosses a new main road, which will circle west to meet the N1 north of Coimbra.)

Penacova itself is an ancient and picturesque place perched high above the Mondego, descending from which one skirts the river's right bank on the approach to Coimbra. This riverside road passes close to the huge early-eighteenth-century church of Santa Maria at **Lorvão**, notable for its stalls of exotic woods and the repoussé silver tombs designed by Manuel Carneiro da Silva in 1713 to hold the remains of Teresa and Sancha,[1] two daughters of Dom Sancho I, both of whom had been abbesses of the convent founded there in the twelfth century. It was here that the remarkable illuminated manuscript of *The Apocalypse of Lorvão* originated, dated 1189, and now preserved in the Torre de Tombo at Lisbon.

NOTES

1. Their sister Mafalda, who died in 1256, is buried in the Cistercian convent of Santa Maria at **Arouca**, some fifty miles due north as the crow flies, which may be visited by the indefatigable ecclesiologist prepared to make the expedition; but one may well be disappointed by Carlos Gimac's early-eighteenth-century rebuilding. The jolting *pavé* road leads north-west through the hills via **Vale de Cambra** from **Oliveira de Azeméis** (on the N1 between Coimbra and Oporto); the road on to **Castelo de Paiva**, perched high above the Douro, winds and climbs through eucalyptus forests. Both approaches are bad, and there are other tracks which promise even rougher rides.

   Mafalda, aged twenty-one, retired there after the annulment of her marriage in 1215 to the twelve-year-old Enrique I of Castile (who died accidentally in 1217). A later inmate was Clara Warre, sister of General Sir William Warre, who, together with Lord Beresford, rode over to visit her during a lull in the Peninsular War.

22

Viseu – Aveiro – the Beira Littoral

A new highway runs west from Celorico roughly parallel to the sinuous older road. It follows more closely the natural profile of the terrain and where it runs along the spine of ridges, as it does quite frequently, provides several extensive viewpoints on the approach to Viseu.

Now the flourishing agricultural centre of its district, also reputed for its Dao wines, **Viseu** is an episcopal city of ancient origin, although there is no historical evidence that Viriatus made his last stand there against the Romans in 139 BC. Nevertheless, a fortified Roman camp near the river Pavia, which could be diverted to flood its defensive ditch, and defined by a line of trees, is still referred to as the 'Cava de Viriato'. Later known as Interanniensia, Viseu became the focus of several Roman roads, although little can be seen of Roman remains. There is doubt, too, whether Don Rodrigo, 'the Last of the Goths', was buried in São Miguel do Fetal here in AD 711, as has been claimed.

In 1028 Alfonso V of León was killed when besieging the place during the Reconquest, but another three decades passed before it fell to Fernando I. Philippa of Lancaster's eldest son, Dom Duarte (Edward, named after his grandfather, Edward III) was born here, although the title of Duke of Viseu was given later to Henrique, a younger brother.

In the early months of 1810 it was a British headquarters, with 'cold rooms, hard beds, bad fare, but good civility and respect from all classes, and a most inveterate hatred of the French', as General Picton cheerfully complained. The Allies then retired at their leisure in the face of Masséna's advance towards the ridge of Busaco. To reach Viseu they had, in Masséna's own words, already marched 'across a desert; not a soul to be seen anywhere; everything is abandoned'.

The older town lies huddled below a rock outcrop dominated by

150

its early-sixteenth-century cathedral, which faces the more pictur-esque twin-towered façade of the Misericórdia, Tristram Hillier's painting of which served as the frontispiece to Sacheverell Sitwell's *Portugal and Madeira*. When Sitwell visited Viseu, he found the cathedral 'undergoing furious and noisy restoration . . . an insensate example of how the Portuguese destroy their ancient monuments', but at least the interior, largely rid of the clutter of piety, now displays to advantage its fine vault, the ribs of which are carved to represent knotted cables, a characteristic Manueline conceit.

The present building replaced the Romanesque cathedral, which had arisen on the site of a mosque. Its uninspired west front is a mid-seventeenth-century reconstruction by Juan Moreno, a Span-iard, who also added the towers. Notable are its choir-stalls, and the *azulejos* in the north chapel. The surviving paintings from Vasco Fernandes' retable, replaced by those of Santos Pacheco, are now preserved in the adjacent museum. Off the upper cloister, display-ing attractive late-seventeenth-century *albarrada azulejos*, opens the chapter-house, containing the cathedral treasure, where among the usual cult objects is a handsome bishop's sunshade, a compara-tively rare survival.

The museum, named after 'Grão Vasco', who Viseu claims as her own, is in the former Bishop's palace. While undoubtedly his paintings are its most important – among them *The Pentecost*, in which the cathedral ribs are depicted – also of quality are those attributed to Gaspar Vaz, and a series of scenes from the life of Christ, of the School of Viseu of about 1520, in which that of the *Adoration of the Magi* shows a Brazilian Indian in place of Balthazar, the African Negro of tradition.

Descending behind the cathedral apse, we reach the thronged Rua Direita, traversing the older town. At its north end stands São Bento, with good *azulejos*, although these may be seen in several other churches, among them the Carmo, and – just south of the central square – São Francisco, with its octagonal chancel.

On regaining the new highway – a distinct improvement on the contorted older road which crept along the valley side parallel to the railway and through **Vouzela** – we round a spur of the Serra do Caramulo, high above the valley of the Vouga, beyond which rises the Serras da Arada and, further west, da Gralheira.

The Misericórdia at Vouzela has been variously described: by the Selective Travellers as 'worth the visitor's while' to enter, by Sitwell as 'creepily unpleasant . . . with horrid portraits of early-nineteenth-century benefactors, fly-blown objects, and mange and ringworm in all around'. I, for one, would trust the latter description over the habitually cloying gush of the former. The police-station has a Baroque façade, but I was unable to see much else of the town, for it was virtually impossible to circulate, all its streets having been taken up to introduce drainage.

Indeed, there was little alternative but to make a long detour, working our way laboriously along the higher slopes of the wooded valley before climbing down to cross the Vouga before it reaches the coastal plain.

The transverse highway makes a rapid descent to this littoral from its ridge-top course to approach Aveiro, first skirting an insatiable cellulose factory, which pollutes the atmosphere for miles around with its fetid stench. This is fed by the ubiquitous eucalyptus, which have been chosen too frequently to reafforest large areas, to the country's detriment but the paper producers' profit.

Predictably referred to by those who must describe any water-logged town as the 'Venice of' wherever it may be, **Aveiro** lies on the edge of dull mud-flats adjoining the bank of the marshy lagoon or Ría de Aveiro, into which flow the Vouga and several other tributary streams. It does a considerable trade in salt, obtained by evaporation, and there are shipyards in the vicinity.

In the earlier sixteenth century it prospered as a fishing-port with the exploitation of the cod-banks of Newfoundland. The catch used to be taken into the interior in creels carried on the heads of short-skirted, big-boned fishwives, still occasionally seen striding along bare-footed. Many of them came from neighbouring **Ovar**, and the itinerant fish vendors in Lisbon are still known as '*varinas*'. Ovar lies at the north end of these sombre broads, but the district is no longer the wilderness described at the turn of the last century as 'so perfect and so destitute of any trace of civilization, that no part of Siberia or Africa could exhibit greater solitude'.

In 1575, a year of great drought, a violent storm cast a sand-bar across the mouth of the Vouga, which, overflowing its banks during winter floods, inundated the low-lying littoral. The lakes it formed became fever-breeding swamps, causing the local population to fall by almost two-thirds, and it was not until 1808 that a canal was cut through this bar to drain them.

In May the following year, the solitude of the lagoon was disturbed by a flotilla of flat-bottomed boats sailing north and transporting – a brigade at a time – General Hill's division. It was by this amphibious operation that he outflanked the French retreating on Oporto, the capture of which is described in Chapter 26.

From the Praça Humberto Delgado at Aveiro, in fact a widened bridge over the central canal, here spanned by several hump-backed bridges – giving it a slightly Dutch air – we may make our way to São Domingos, described by J.M. Neale as 'a squalid and tawdry room', later raised to cathedral rank and monstrously modernized in more recent years.

Opposite is the former Convento de Jesus, now the regional museum, in which the portrait of Dom Afonso V's daughter, Santa Joana, is attributed to Nuno Gonçalves. The richly decorated chapel devoted to this princess, who spent her last fourteen years here, dying in 1489, displays a charming series of naïve paintings describing her life from the time she left her father's palace. Less attractive is her tomb, a confection of marble marquetry by João Antunes, completed eighteen years after Joana's unaccountable beatification in 1693. It is recorded that her capacity to suffer the lice bred in her chemise was greatly admired by her hagiographer. The chinoiserie panelling and the ceiling of the upper choir, the portable organs, the *azulejos* in the refectory, and the sixteenth-century Albuquerque tomb in the cloister, are all notable.

North of the railway-station is the octagonal chapel of Senhor das Barrocas, its design attributed to Antunes, containing work by Claude de Laprade.

The same sculptor's dramatic tomb of Manuel de Moura Manuel, Bishop of Miranda do Douro, may be seen in Nossa Senhora da Penha at **Vista Alegre**, some three miles south, beyond Ilhavo.

The museum at **Ilhavo** displays an interesting collection of models of local fishing-boats and the *moliceiros* or seaweed-harvesting vessels which, like water-beetles, are frequently seen skimming the placid surface of the lagoon.[1]

The extensive deposits of china clay at Vista Alegre made it a sensible site on which to establish a porcelain manufactory, which still flourishes. It was founded in 1824 by José Ferreira Pinto Basto, whose wife Bárbara Inocência Allen was of English descent. Formerly it manufactured glass objects as well, and it is said that its fragile wares were carried to Oporto and Lisbon on the backs of camels, these creatures being the smoothest form of transport on the rough Lusitanian roads.

If driving north to Oporto, it is worth making the short detour to

Vila da Feira to visit the well-preserved castle of Santa Maria, pictur-esquely placed on the summit of a wooded hill north-east of Ovar and easily approached from the motorway. The noble fifteenth-century keep, with its four cone-capped towers and impressively vaulted hall, was reconstructed on much earlier foundations cover-ing the site of a pre-Roman sanctuary, while the barbican dates from the thirteenth and fourteenth centuries.

NOTES

1. The Pousada da Ria, on the far side of the Aveiro's lagoon, approached from the north via **Murtosa**, provides almost lacustrine accommoda-tion; but beware the strong undertow of the breakers on the nearby Atlantic beaches.

23

The Upper Douro valley:
from Miranda to Vila Nova de Foz Côa,
and on to Lamego

Miranda do Douro lies out on a limb at the north-eastern extremity of Portugal. I found it an agreeable little town, due perhaps to the comfort of the Pousada de Santa Catarina after a tiring cross-country drive from Braganza. Not all travellers have been so lucky. Rodney Gallop, who visited Miranda sixty years ago, refers to it as one of those places where, in Murray's subtle phrase, one may 'pass the night but not sleep', and in parody of Hilaire Belloc, asked himself 'Do you remember the inn at Miranda?' Regrettably, a form of 'tourist blight' is now noticeable in the rash of shops built there to sell trinkets to Spanish trippers.

Gallop also commented on the Leonese patois known as Mirandés spoken in this sequestered region. The women had then no special costume 'except perhaps the black stockings which seduced maidens used to be compelled to wear, although apparently, this occasioned them no difficulty in finding a husband'. Among less edifying customs he came across was that of burying hens up to their necks in the earth and stoning them to death, which only lately has been successfully discouraged by the authorities.

Miranda may be approached with ease from Zamora, from which the road first climbs down into the boulder-strewn valley of the Esla, and then cuts across a meander of the Duero (as the Douro is spelt in Spain), before again descending into its gorge, here forming the frontier. The road enters Portugal by passing along the brow of a huge dam, one of several harnessing that foaming torrent. Since its construction, Miranda is no longer the isolated fastness it was, but apart from the huge reservoirs formed by the Douro's Spanish tributaries, the Tormes to the south, and the Esla, this borderland cannot have changed very much over the centuries.

The fortress itself had blown up during a Spanish attack in 1762, killing 400, but the walled '*castanilla*' of Miranda retains many dwellings dating back to the sixteenth century or earlier, which survived the blast, as did the cathedral. Little remains of the bishop's palace; and of its dependencies, only an arcade of an unfinished cloister.

Miranda had been a bishopric since the mid-sixteenth century, and remained so until 1782, when this was transferred to Braganza. The cathedral itself, of basilican plan, with three aisles of equal height, and attributed to both Gonçalo do Torralva and Miguel de Arruda, presents an austere west front, but contains several features of interest, including the main *retábulo*, constructed at Valladolid and transported here piecemeal; and also much of the *talha*. More frequently and reverently pointed out by the peasants – and indeed it is a curiosity – is the local cult figure, a puppet-like image wearing an opera-hat and a white bow-tie, known as the 'Menino Jesus da Cartolinha'.

Late in May 1813 Miranda played its part in one of the more spectacular sequences of events of the Peninsular War. It was Wellington's intention to mislead the French into thinking that the next Allied offensive would be an advance into Spain from their cantonments near Guarda, from which he would march directly east across the *meseta* and skirt the north flank of the Guadarrama range, where Joseph Bonaparte's army awaited them. In his stratagem, planned in detail during preceding months, Wellington was entirely successful.

Anglo-Portuguese troops totalling some 64,000 men had been concentrating in the Trás-os-Montes around Miranda and Braganza, with General Sir Thomas Graham in command. Pontoons had been shifted secretly from the Tagus near Vila Velha to the Duoro well inside Portugal; and to save precious time they had been placed on horse-drawn carriages, using axles and wheels borrowed from the artillery, rather than relying on ox-transport, enabling the complex exercise to be completed within four weeks.

In outline, the following movements took place immediately after 20 May, when Wellington and his headquarters staff, together with the Light Division, three cavalry brigades, General Sir Rowland Hill's Corps and some Spaniards – about 30,000 men – moved forward from the frontier near Ciudad Rodrigo towards Salamanca, without in any way attempting to conceal the direction of their march. Salamanca was taken on the 26th, and the French retired north-east, assuming that the entire Allied army was facing them.

Before dawn on the 28th, Wellington himself set off to ride some fifty miles north-west to reach the gorge of the Douro opposite Miranda, where he was slung across the swirling rapids in a 'kind of hammock' suspended by ropes. Next day he galloped north-east, joining Graham at Carbajales to inspect the bulk of his assembled forces.

General Daricau's cavalry, stationed at Zamora, had made a sweep to the west of the Esla less than ten days earlier and had reported back that all was well: there was no sign of the Allies, and no reason to suspect any attack from that quarter.

However, although the Esla was swollen by melting snow, by 31 May the whole Anglo-Portuguese army had advanced and – the infantry using the pontoons – had crossed already. Once the French realized that they had been out-manoeuvred by this huge out-flanking thrust, they had no alternative but to retreat rapidly towards Burgos. Hill's vanguard joined up with Graham at Toro on 3 June. Wellington's entire army was now north of the Douro, and during the next eighteen days the same manoeuvre was repeated regularly, each time turning the French right flank and forcing them back towards Vitoria, where on 21 June they suffered their most decisive defeat of the war.

But returning to Portugal, we must picture the astonishing sight described by Private William Wheeler, who, on 24 May, while encamped on the plains of Miranda, was carrying on a conversation with a group of Spaniards from a neighbouring village. They were in full view of his division, but its tents were not yet pitched. On hearing the bugle sound to 'stand by', Wheeler managed to draw the Spaniards' attention to a point in the opposite direction until the bugle was heard again. One can imagine their surprise when he then swung round and pointed to where, a minute before, only soldiers stood, for

> now the whole camp was studded with several hundred bell tents as white as snow and as regularly placed as if it had been the work of much labour and time. To a people so naturally superstitious as the Spaniards are it must appear like magic. I am inclined to think they looked on it in no other light for they expressed their astonishment in a volley of 'Caravos' [*carajos*], and then devoutly

crossed themselves exclaiming 'Jesu Maria – these English are the Devil'.

It is very likely that some of this equipment was lost by Wellington's cavalry when crossing the Esla. Certainly that river was blamed for any subsequently mislaid by the troopers, and the invariable excuse given at later inspections caused one commanding officer to exclaim: 'Bless me! That Esla must be choked up with camp equipage . . .'.

The road south-west from Miranda rides high above the Douro gorge, from which byroads descend to its downstream dams, to approach **Mogadouro**, another old frontier town, beyond which we climb over hills to a junction for **Torre de Moncorvo** and an alternative but less interesting route to **Vila Nova de Foz Côa**. The improved road bears due west along a ridge of the Serra do Reboredo, providing several wide views.

The left fork here leads to curiously-named **Freixo de Espada à Cinta**, or 'ash-tree of the girt sword', most probably because Dom Dinis, when founding the town, made the gesture of buckling his sword to such a tree. The tall heptagonal *torre de menagem* and stretches of surviving wall are evidence of its former importance. Close by is the tower of the Misericórdia, and the Manueline Igreja Matriz, although in part it dates back to the thirteenth century. Sixteen paintings attributed to 'Grão Vasco' embellish its *retábulo*, among other features of interest.

At Freixo we enter the region of demarcated 'port wine' vineyards of the Upper Douro, which extend back for some distance above both banks of its deep gorge. We regain the torrent as it swings west away from Spain and below a forest of almond trees and cross it at **Barco de Alva**, where the river is joined by the tributary Agueda, but several long stretches of its serpentine course are roadless, although from Barco de Alva the south bank of the Douro is skirted by a single-track railway, crossing to the north below São João da Pesqueira. It is only from Pinhao, some distance downstream, that one of its banks is followed by a road.

To reach **Pinhao**, a detour must be made by climbing steeply south near a monument at Mata de Lobos recording the Portuguese defeat of a Spanish incursion led by the Duque de Osuna in July 1664. At **Figueira de Castelo Rodrigo** turn north-west towards **Almendra**, with its large Baroque mansion and fortified church, and the ruined castle of **Castelo Melhor** not far beyond. The gorge of the Côa is crossed not far short of the main transverse road.

The church at neighbouring Vila Nova de Foz Côa, with a good Manueline portal, is notable for the cant of its pillars, its stone pulpit, well-carved altar and painted ceiling.

A cross-country road winds over the hills close to fortified **Numão** to approach **São João de Pesqueira**, a large viniferous village, surrounded by port *quintas*, lying on a plateau above the steep, schistose, terraced slopes dominating the Cachão de Valeira. Captain Thomas Henry Browne refers to barns here being converted into theatres, where to while away the long winter evenings of 1811–12, 'performances of the most ludicrous description' were given by members of the two divisions cantoned in the neighbourhood.

Until 1792 this was the highest point of navigation by the picturesque lanteen-sailed *barcos rebelos*, which formerly carried the wine barrels down to Oporto. The river-bed was choked by granite slabs, until these were dynamited, but rapids remained. It was here also, when the Douro was in spate, that Baron Forrester was drowned in May 1861, his vessel either capsizing or splitting on striking a rock.

Joseph James Forrester, who had joined his uncle's firm in 1831, was then the doyen of the 'pure wine' school, and the author of influential books on port. He was also a fine cartographer and profilic watercolourist.[1] After lunching at the neighbouring Quinta de Vargellas, he embarked with Baroness Fladgate and Dona António Adelaide Ferreira, both of whom survived the accident, being bouyed by their crinolines and washed up on a beach further downstream; but Forrester's body was never found, although his son William was told later that it had been, less the leather money-belt laden with gold sovereigns to pay wages; but the real truth will never be known.

Few Englishmen ventured into these wild regions of the Alto Douro until about 1700, when Thomas Woodmass, a young Yorkshireman, was curious enough to explore it. Others, among them Peter Bearsley, were also investigating the possibilities of buying and exporting the produce of unusual strength that could be found in the cellars of isolated monasteries, and certain peasants did business with the shippers; but for some time the latter remained secretive concerning the precise whereabouts of these vineyards. Trade in the wines flourished, even if in earlier days it was often sophisticated when not actually adulterated; to such an extent that the future Marquês de Pombal intervened in 1756 to found the 'Companhia Geral da Agricultura dos Vinhos do Alto Douro',

which did much to correct abuses. Not surprisingly, a long battle
ensued between the Portuguese company and the British shippers,
who considered any enquiry into their methods to be a gross
interference.

The Port Wine Institute, which superseded the Companhia
Geral, has its headquarters at **Peso da Régua**, on the north bank of
the Douro further downstream, and the westernmost town in the
demarcated area.[2] Not far distant from it, the Quinta do Salgueiral,
acquired in 1744 by the Bearsley family – later to become the company of Taylor, Fladgate and Yeatman – is probably the oldest
British-owned property on the Douro.

From Peso de Régua, both banks of the Douro are followed by
tortuous roads leading west and climbing high above the swirling
stream and away from the port-wine vineyards through those producing *vinhos verdes*, but the drive can become monotonous. Near
Entre-os-Rios we cross to the right bank, and traverse progressively
more inhabited districts by a wretched road, as Oporto itself is
neared.

It was at Peso da Régua, in July 1811, that the greater part of
Wellington's battering train of heavy guns and their ammunition
was unloaded after being brought upstream from Oporto in
advance of his projected siege of Ciudad Rodrigo. This had required
the assembly of 160 vessels and, under the supervision of Major
Alexander Dixon, the guns were transferred to over 1,000 creaking
carts, which were then dragged up what was described by Somers
Cocks as 'a superb cabrazada' or goat-track, for the road even now
zigzags steeply up the almost precipitous bank to approach Lamego.
From there the siege equipment was hauled laboriously south-east
to **Vila da Ponte**, near **Sernancelhe**, just off the road to Trancosa (see
Chapter 19).

At an earlier stage in the war, in May 1809, Beresford's troops
had met up at Lamego with the Portuguese under General Silveira,
before moving on Amarante. During the winter of 1811–12 it was
one of the principal supply depots for Wellington's army in cantonments further east.

Lamego has changed since John Mason Neale described it in the
1850s as 'a very dirty, not particularly picturesque, and somewhat
uninteresting city'; but, as he refers also to an 'execrable' *estalagem*
providing 'scanty fare', this may well have affected more than usual
his habitual jaundiced opinion (although I can, from my own

experience, sympathize with him as to the affect an inhospitable hostelry can have on one's judgement of a place). I have more sympathy with Lord Porchester, who in 1827 found Lamego 'full of picturesque beauties and old remains of art', even if one of the remains he was hoping to see, an ancient church, had been razed to the ground by its proprietor not long before!

Lamego's history, since Fernando I eventually recovered it from the Moors in 1057, is not of great interest, although it was an episcopal city. In spite of the opposition of a doctor named Pedro Furtado – who cured 'the mother of the sons of the Archbishop of Lisbon' – the Inquisition was established here, active in hounding the New Christians of the district, of whom Furtado was doubtless one.

The cathedral, of which a Romanesque belfry survives, was rebuilt in the Gothic taste in the early sixteenth century, and even the cloister with its belvedere, completed in 1557, although mainly Renaissance, retains Gothic details. The interior preserves two good organs, and some damaged frescos by Nicolau Nasoni, dating from the late 1730s, before he devoted himself almost exclusively to architecture; but a silver altar-frontal completed in 1768 by Master MFG deserves inspection. The paintings by 'Grão Vasco', which formed the main *retábulo*, are in the adjacent bishop's palace, now the museum, together with a number of remarkable Flemish tapestries of the Temple of Latona, the Story of Oedipus, etcetera. A chapel saved from the demolition of the Convento das Chagas earlier this century has been incorporated in the building.

There are several other mansions and churches close by, while west of the main avenue, and within Lamego's medieval *enceinte*, rise relics of its thirteenth-century castle.

Conspicuous on the summit of a hill immediately to the south is Nossa Senhora dos Remédios, reached by a double flight of almost 700 steps, which invite comparison with those of Bom Jesus near Braga constructed several decades earlier. Fortunately, it may be approached with ease by car, by turning off the Viseu road. The pilgrimage church was built in the 1750s by an unknown architect, but its towers are a nineteenth-century addition. The octagonal granite platform of the upper terrace, providing a remarkable view, is surrounded by dramatically placed but inelegant statues, obelisks and other Baroque embellishments; while on lower landings are pyramidal-roofed pavilions and fountains.

Also of interest in the vicinity of Lamego is **São João de Tarouca**, some six miles south, where the church of the Cistercian monastery contains the tomb of Pedro, Count of Barcelos (*circa* 1280–1354), a bastard of Dom Dinis and compiler of the *Livro das Linhagens*, the *Burke's Peerage* of the time. It also displays a painting of Saint Peter, ascribed to both Gaspar Vaz and Cristovão de Figueiredo, which is similar to that to be seen at Viseu.

Less easy to find is **São Pedro de Balsemão**, not far north of Lamego, but enquire first at the local *posto de turismo* for precise directions and if it is open or not. This seventh-century Visigothic basilica was remodelled in 1643, but several stones with Roman inscriptions have been embedded in its walls and it also preserves the tomb of Afonso Pires, a mid-fourteenth-century bishop of Oporto.

The road ascending towards Nossa Senhora dos Remédios continues south-west across the hills to Viseu, with the Serra de Montemuro rising to the west, via **Castro Daire**, on the romantic gorge of the river Paiva. It later passes near a well-preserved stretch of Roman road. Viseu itself is described in Chapter 22.

NOTES

1. Born at Hull in 1809, Forrester received his Portuguese title after making the first detailed map of the Douro, together with *Papers relating to the Improvement of the Navigation of the River Douro* (1844). In the same year his pamphlet entitled *A Word or Two on Port-wine* was published anonymously, followed in 1845 by *Observations on the Attempts lately made to reform the Abuses practised in Portugal in the Making and Treatment of Port Wines*, and the *J.S. Oliveira Prize Essay on Portugal* (1853).

2. The Institute sets out to supervise and regulate the port wine trade, imposing quality control and issuing certificates of origin, etc. It is not my intention to write very much on the wide subject, covered in detail in several authoritative books (see Bibliography), although naturally it is to a certain extent referred to in the chapter on Oporto itself.

24

Trás-os-Montes:
Braganza to Oporto via
Vila Real and Amarante

The *enceinte* of Celtic Brigantia, standing on a height above
Braganza – or correctly, Bragança – the ancient capital of the former province of Trás-os-Montes, is still dominated by its castle keep
erected by Dom Sancho I in 1187, which withstood a siege by
Alfonso IX of León a dozen years later. John of Gaunt, Duke of
Lancaster, and Dom João I passed through Braganza in March 1387
prior to the Anglo-Portuguese attack on León, and it was probably
in the neighbouring village of **São Julião de Palácios**, that the
former confirmed the abrogation of any rights which he and his wife
might have to the throne of Portugal (his daughter Philippa having
married Dom João not long before).

Dom João had made his headquarters at São Julião after the
then arduous journey from Oporto, and Lancaster would have followed the latter part of the same road, for the direct cross-country
track leading from Chaves, with its flooded fords, was impassable
for his retinue and army, which on entering Portugal from Orense
via Verín would have marched almost certainly from Chaves to
Mirandela. Even in the eighteenth century this was the usual detour
during winter months.

The title of Duke of Braganza was created by Dom Afonso V in
1442 for one of Dom João's natural progeny, also named Afonso.
Any entitlement to the succession they may have claimed were
ignored by Philip II of Spain in 1580, and it was not until 1640 that
the eighth duke was elected to the Portuguese throne in the person
of Dom João IV.

The surname of Charles II's queen, Catherine, may still conjure
up a rather different image of what some have assumed, incorrectly,

to have been her home town (the family preferred their seat at Vila
Viçosa), and they may be disappointed if expecting too much.

In 1770 the seat of the bishop was transferred here from Miranda
do Douro, and mid-sixteenth-century São João Baptista – with
painted panels in its sacristy and a gutted organ-case – was elevated
to cathedral status.

I know not whether the municipality have yet won their running
battle against the intransigent ecclesiastics of Braganza with regard
to the right of admission to her churches, several of which I found
locked tight when attempting to explore them; perhaps their guardians have relented by now. São Bento is said to contain a *Mudéjar*
ceiling, a painted barrel-vault, and a sumptuous *retábulo*; while
São Vicente, originally Romanesque, according to tradition, was
where the future Dom Pedro I clandestinely married Inês de Castro
in 1354.

Of some interest is the Museu do Abade de Bacal, installed in the
former bishop's palace, containing three bishop's litters and the
local archaeological collection, some of the more curious *stelae* from
which have been embedded in a wall of its garden. Among the
ethnographical artefacts is a section devoted to the *Pauliteiros* or
ritual stick-dancers of the region, which Rodney Gallop had seen in
action there some sixty years ago.

A cobbled lane ascends to the gate of the walled upper town,
containing the *domus municipalis*, a rare survival of Romanesque
civic architecture, even if over-restored and incongruously tiled.

The road bears south-west past **Castro de Avelas**, a place of very
ancient foundation. It has a ruined twelfth-century church of a
Benedictine monastery, the brick-built blind arcading of which is
the only example of this style extant in Portugal, although frequently seen much further east, notably at Sahagún in León.

The new highway under construction is a distinct improvement
on the old, and is part of a project to make this north-east corner of
the country less remote, and to provide direct access to Oporto from
the Leonese *meseta*. It rarely follows the line of the older road,
which I well remember, for it was crossed by the railway at least five
times within a dozen miles and, as luck would have it, when we
drove along it a train was chugging past, each time approaching the
next level-crossing only seconds before we did!

From **Mirandela**, where the Tua is spanned by a long medieval
bridge of Roman foundation, and which is dominated by a late-
seventeenth-century palace of the Távora family, the southern

slope of the Serra do Vilarelho is skirted to enter the small town of Murça, on the northerly boundary of the port wine demarcated region. Its chief monument is a roughly sculpted boar, the 'Porca de Murça', of pre-Roman date, and probably from the same litter as the so-called 'Toros' de Guisando, which proliferate south of the Sierra de Gredos in Spain. The epithet 'Porca de Murça' also implies a political turncoat.

We continue to wind over the hills some distance north of Sabrosa, birthplace of Fernão de Magalhães, known to the English as Ferdinand Magellan. After a controversy with the Portuguese Court, he had offered his services to Spain, where from Sanlúcar de Barrameda, near Cadiz, his fleet of five ships set out in 1519 on their voyage of circumnavigation. Magellan himself was killed in the Philippines, but one vessel, commanded by Juan Sebastián Elcano, a Basque, survived the journey, limping home in 1522.

On approaching the outskirts of Vila Real, we pass near the finialed façade of the Baroque **Solar de Mateus**, built by Nicolau Nasoni in the early 1740s for António José Botelho Mourão. In recent decades a view of the mansion has embellished the labels of an extensively marketed rosé wine, its *pétillance* produced by carbon dioxode gas and not from natural effervescence as in the *vinhos verdes*. Nevertheless, it appears to have titillated the jaded palate of the late Sacheverell Sitwell, whose favourable opinion, published some forty years ago, is not shared by many connoisseurs, one of whom has referred even to the 'oïdium mateum'; but then, as David Francis discreetly remarked, Sitwell was a man of eclectic tastes! When I saw it first – several years ago – the fabric of the building was in a sorry state of disrepair, with at least two of its exterior walls being shored up by wooden beams: thankfully, it has been restored since. Whether the manufacturers of the wine in any way subsidized this work – for there is no connection between them and the edifice, whose image has been so profitably turned to account – I would not surmise.

Royal rights were granted to **Vila Real** by Dom Afonso III in 1272; and it was here in 1482 that Diogo Cão, the first navigator to reach the mouth of the Congo, was born. In February 1832 the reactionary Count of Amarante established the headquarters of his insurrectionary movement here before making the military *pronunciamento* at Vila Franca de Xira that May in defiance of the liberal government of the time. Known as the 'Vilafrançada', it petered out soon after.

Vila Real, although the largest town in the Trás-os-Montes and an important hub of communication, is of comparatively slight interest, even if Gothic São Domingos has been raised to cathedral rank. São Pedro contains good Baroque carving, but the Clérigos is notable for little else than its unusually narrow façade confined by the junction of two streets.

A section of the new highway crosses the Alto do Espinho, with the Marão rising to the south, before climbing down into the valley at **Amarante**, a straggling old town on the Tâmega, there spanned by a handsome three-arched, obelisk-embellished bridge of 1790, among others.

In mid-April 1809 General Silveira's contingent held the left bank here, frustrating General Loison's attempt to cross with a much superior force; but on 2 May the Portuguese were surprised and forced to retire on Lamego, which Beresford's Corps had just entered. Rallied by his presence, they advanced again on Amarante, in the face of which Loison jettisoned his wheeled transport and artillery and scrambled in confusion over the rugged hills to the north-west towards Guimarães. Here, two days later, he joined up with Soult, retreating equally precipitately after his discomfiture at Oporto. Beresford then counter-marched to the Douro before pressing on towards Chaves to cut off any French who might attempt retreating east.

Well viewed from the bridge is the picturesque church and convent dedicated to São Gonçalo, its dependencies containing two Renaissance cloisters. Gonçalo, a vigorous fellow by all accounts, is said to have reconstructed the earlier Romanesque bridge with his own hands, and in 1561 was beatified for his labours; but this particular erection collapsed in 1763. The church preserves his tomb and some richly carved and gilt woodwork, although the organ-case itself is gutted. The tomb retained such potent properties that husband hunters past their first youth had merely to rub their bare flesh against it to be granted a spouse within the year; and to make doubly sure, at the biannual festivals in his honour, phallic-shaped cakes called '*testículos*' de São Gonçalo were baked and nibbled, which they still are, and continue to have a ready sale.

At a higher level stands cylindrical São Domingos, an eighteenth-century edifice said to contain a fine organ-case and Rococo *talha*; while further up the hill rises São Pedro.

Although the new highway will drive south-west, bypassing Amarante, one may follow the older main road circling to the north-west, from which a turning climbs down steeply to **Travanca**, where the twelfth-century church of the monastery of São Salvador retains two good Romanesque portals and a separate tower of some interest.

Regaining the ridge, the adventurous may descend again on a road marked to **Marco de Canaveses**, later bearing right to **Vila Boas de Quires**, near which is the remarkable Baroque façade of the so-called 'Casa das Obras'; this is all that exists, for the rest of the building was never completed.

The main road continues through **Penafiel**, retaining a number of old granite houses, later traversing increasingly populated districts on approaching Oporto. But first, the worthwhile detour should be made from just beyond Penafiel to **Paço de Sousa**, where, adjacent to two charming *quintas* is the very fine twelfth-century monastic church of São Salvador, containing among other features the tomb of Egas Moniz, a counsellor of Afonso Henriques, whose legendary exploits are carved on it in high relief.

25

Chaves to Braga

With its canting device of keys (*chaves*) the fortress town of **Chaves** was long the key to this entrance into Portugal from Spanish Verín via the upper valley of the Tâmega. Its Vaubanesque fortifications were unable to resist either General O'Reilly's Spanish army in 1762 or the advance of the French early in 1809, although the place was recaptured later by Silveira's Portuguese. It was here that Beresford, after countermarching from Amarante, cut off the French retreating from Oporto, some twelve hundred men being captured as they attempted to grope their way across the inhospitable mountains into Galicia.

The hot springs of Aquae Flaviae, and its strategic position on the road from Braga to Castro de Avelás (near Braganza) and on to Astorga or Salamanca – here crossing the Tâmega on an impressive sixteen-arched Roman bridge – caused Chaves to grow in importance. Its Suevic occupation was described in annals compiled by Bishop Hydatius in 456. Its more recent history is of slight interest. As with Braganza and Braga, it was an outpost of reaction, and in 1912 the town was held briefly by a monarchist faction rising against the infant Republic, but to little effect.

It was here, in the Igreja Matriz – rebuilt in the sixteenth century but retaining Romanesque features – that Afonso de Braganza, natural son of Dom João I and first of the ducal dynasty, was initially buried, in 1461. Among other monuments are the late-seventeenth-century Misericórdia, and the imposing *torre de menagem*, commanding the bridgehead and now housing archaeological collections; while near the south end of the bridge stands the Igreja da Madalena, with its octagonal nave.

The detour should be made to **Outeiro Seco**, a short distance north of Chaves, where Romanesque Nossa Senhora da Azinheira preserves characteristic exterior corbels.

Traversing the bald hills of the Terras do Barroso, the original home of the liquid-eyed, lyre-horned oxen now ubiquitous in the Minho, we skirt the huge Alto Rabagão reservoir, north of which, in the upper Cávado valley, lies **Montalegre**, a walled hill-town with a restored castle. It was here that Wellington spent the night of 18 May 1809, having decided to give up his relentless pursuit of Soult's shattered army retreating from Oporto. The French were able to keep just ahead of the British only by hamstringing all their lame mounts or mules and jettisoning their baggage and artillery.

Scattering a body of poorly armed *ordenança* attempting to hold the bridge spanning the Cávado at **Salamonde** (now the site of a dam), they had continued their headlong flight by surging across another bridge, which, fortuitously and contrary to orders, had not been destroyed by the local peasants, as it remained their only means of communication over the river in flood.

According to Major Charles Cocks, on reaching Montalegre the French had murdered the Portuguese guides they had forced to accompany them, lest they should be of any use to their pursuers. Then, finding the road east had been cut by Beresford, their only recourse was the scramble helter-skelter over the rugged frontier range towards Orense, leaving a trail of wreckage in their wake. Commissary Schaumann, surveying the site on which they had very briefly bivouacked, recorded that

All the furniture and even the crockery had been taken from the houses of a neighbouring vilage, and had been brought into the field. The beds and the mattresses lay in rows in the mud. The drawers from the various articles of furniture had been used as mangers. Wardrobes had been transformed into bedsteads and roofs for the huts; all the crockery and glass lay in fragments on the ground. The chairs, staircases and window frames had been used partly as fuel for the kitchen fires, and partly to feed huge bonfires which had been lighted when the French had withdrawn. The unfortunate inhabitants stood all around lamenting their plight. All the crosses and statues of the saints on the road had been thrown from their pedestals, and the alms-boxes in front of them broken open and plundered, while all the altars and chapels had been ruined and polluted. In the churches even the graves had not been spared, and the sanctuaries had been rifled. Altar candlesticks, and arms and legs of apostles and saints, torn vestments, chalices, prayer books, and the like, mixed up with straw and filth, lay all about them. In one chapel were a number of French prisoners with an English guard over them. I saw one well-dressed Portuguese at the head of a band of peasants offering the English sergeant ten gold florins to give the prisoners up. The cruelties perpetrated at this period by the Portuguese hill-folk against the French soldiers who fell into their hands are indescribable. In addition to nailing them up alive on barn doors, they had also stripped many of them, emasculated them, and then placed their amputated members in the victims' mouths – a ghastly sight!

Wellington's exhausted regiments turned south. Once regrouped and re-equipped, they marched across country by easy stages to Castelo Branco and into Spain on the first phase of what was to be the Talavera campaign.

Continuing west, we follow the lofty left bank of the Cávado, with views across to the Serra do Gêres, now partly a nature reserve.

Beyond the Pousada de São Bento a byroad descends to the valley floor and climbs towards the frontier Portela do Homen, where an unexplained concentration of Roman miliary columns stands close to a stretch of Roman road.

The main road passes north of **Póvoa de Lanhoso**, with the well-preserved relics of a twelfth-century castle, partly dismantled, and the neighbouring church of a Benedictine monastery at **Font' Arcada**. It is likely that this village gave its name to a reactionary insurrection against Costa Cabral's government in April 1846, which all started because a local peasant woman, personified by 'Maria da Fonte', together with the municipality, insisted on continuing the insanitary custom of burial beneath the floors of churches rather than in consecrated ground away from village centres. Perhaps this was partly due to a wish to be interred in the most sanctified ground available – as in Ireland to this day, where for private reasons or hereditary right some persons still insist on burial within a monastic precinct, even if in ruins and with only Heaven above to protect them.

At **Taide**, a short distance south, is the sanctuary of Nossa Senhora do Porto de Ave, above which rise garden terraces embellished with statues and chapels in the style of Bom Jesus (see below).

From Póvoa itself, the byroad to **Sobreposta** may be followed, not far south of which lie the extensive remains of the **Citânia de Briteiros**, probably settled between 300 and 200 BC and abandoned by AD 300. It is said to be the last stronghold of the northern Celtiberians against the invading Romans. I doubt whether the gentle old guardian I met there is still in evidence, who by all appearances was a direct descendant of his Celtiberian forefathers. As we left the site, he was sitting alone, gazing at the setting sun and singing plaintively to himself: it was one of those rare and elusive experiences difficult to define or to recreate, but which will not be forgotten.

Here, straddling the slope of the boulder-strewn hill, are the ruined walls of over 150 stone huts, separated from each other by paved causeways, some skirted by stone conduits. Several dwellings have more than one compartment, a few are rectangular, while one larger than the rest was doubtless a meeting-house. The site is surrounded by terraces and trivallate fortifications, in part re-erected. Near the summit are sarcophagus-like remains, and two habitations reconstructed by Francisco Martins Sarmento, who from 1875 had excavated the site. Most of the artefacts discovered, including ornamental lintels, may be seen in the museum at Guimarães named after him. Coins of sixty-four different denominations, most of them minted in silver or bronze, have been found within the *enceinte*, dating from 149 BC to the era of Constantine the Great. Some had been struck at Evora and Mérida, but most were from mints scattered throughout the Iberian Peninsula.

On another expedition, I sought out the **Citânia de Sanfins**, south-west of Guimarães, between **Roriz**, with its charming Romanesque church, and **Paços de Ferreira**. It was on a misty January morning, and visibility was bad, but the atmosphere, although very different to that of Briteiros, was equally powerful. I would recommend that both sites should be visited, together with the site museum close to the village of Paços de Ferreira. Of particular interest at Sanfins are the public baths.

On returning to Sobrepostas, turn left for **Bom Jesus**, where the umbrageous esplanade adjacent to the late-eighteenth-century church, replacing an earlier sanctuary, provides an extensive view over the city of Braga. From here, a monumental flight of steps descends the steep slope of Monte Espinho. Its upper section, devoted to the Three Virtues, is flanked by chapels; at lower levels, each landing is embellished with flamboyant Baroque statuary and grotesque wall-fountains symbolizing the Five Senses.

This grandiose folly, designed in the 1720s by the then archbishop of Braga, was praised by Alexander Jardine,[1] more often than not critical of the extravagance of the Catholic Church, who remarked that it

> must have been attended with great labour and expense. Where despotism has left no other power but the church that is capable of great works, the public are obliged to her when she chuses to employ a numerous poor, though in useless labour: and still more, when she employs them in works of taste.

The conceit proved infectious, for within a few years several similar staircases or 'escadórios' were being constructed, among them those at Lamego and, on a smaller scale, at Tibães.

For Braga itself, see Chapter 27.

NOTES

1. Jardine, the author of the discursive *Letters from Barbary* (1788), was the British consul at La Coruña from 1779 to 1795. He died in Portugal in 1799, probably at Oporto.

26

Oporto

The blustery Pena Ventosa, a crag commanding the north bank of the Douro at **Oporto**, was undoubtedly in Lusitanian occupation, but it is still in dispute whether it was this site which was adopted as a Roman *castrum* by Decimus Junius Brutus, or another on the far bank. Called Cale, the settlement is mentioned in the *Antonine Itinerary* as lying on the main highway from Olisipo to Bracara Augusta, and defending the ferry crossing the Durius here.

The name Portucale is first mentioned in AD 456 in the *Chronicle* of Bishop Hydatius of Chaves, but this appears to have applied to the site of Miragaia, near the present Custom House. The Burgo do Porto grew up around the sixth century church built on the Pena Ventosa by the Suevi, razed by the Moors some 200 years later.

Although a certain Vimara Peres captured the town in 868 and later held much of the line of the Douro, it was not until 982 that the river-port was reoccupied definitively by the Christians and rebuilt, becoming the capital of the country of Portucalia and of the so-called Terras de Santa Maria, an area of newly won territory stretching south towards Vila da Feira.

Count Henry of Burgundy and Dona Teresa (the illegitimate daughter of Alfonso VI of Castile and León), the parents of Afonso Henriques, founded a cathedral in the twelfth century. And the port was granted several privileges; but a decree, which ostensibly remained in force until 1505, stated that no nobleman 'or powerful person' might own property or stay for more than three days within its walls.

In 1107 a fleet of Scandinavian crusaders commanded by Sigurd, sailed in from Bergen *en route* to the Holy Land, for it was a convenient port of call. Forty years later another expeditionary force disembarked there – this time of English or Anglo-Normans bound for the Second Crusade – apparently preceded by their reputation for being 'plunderers, drunkards and rapists, men not seasoned with the honey of Piety'.

After listening patiently to Bishop Pedro Pitoes' proposal that they
continue south to reinforce Afonso Henriques' army about to recon-
quer Lisbon, and no doubt fortified with good wine and the promise
of limitless loot, opportunely – but not until ten days later – they
lurched back to their ships to follow up what sounded like a far more
profitable enterprise, for apart from providing them with the usual
dissipations of a port, the place did not appear to offer very much else.
As a precaution they took as hostages both the bishop and João
Peculiar – for that was the name of the Archbishop of Braga – who
between them should have been sufficient collateral.

The *Portuenses* themselves were an obstreperous lot. In 1209,
having been incensed by Bishop Martinho, they penned him up in his
palace for five months, but perhaps the Dominican monastery established there in 1237 later played its part in making them more sub-
missive to the dictates of the Church.

By the 1370s a boundary wall was completed, a stretch of which
may still be seen near Santa Clara, its northern limit running from
the Praça da Batalha to the Jardim de João Chagas, and the town
expanded within its circuit. Meanwhile the cathedral was reconstructed, and it was in this church just before Easter 1387 that
Dom João I and John of Gaunt's twenty-eight-year-old daughter
Philippa were married with all customary pomp and raucous celebra-
tion. Fernão Lopes reported that ahead of their procession went 'so
many pipes, trumpets and other instruments, that nothing else could
be heard', and behind them came noblewomen and citizens' daughters, singing; but the crush was so great in the small space between the
palace and church that it was well nigh impossible to marshal the
crowds.

And no doubt the wine flowed, but whether this was produced
from vines said to have been brought from Henry of Burgundy's
native country to Portugal, is doubtful. A claret type wine was cultivated near the river Lima, but although from this time the life of *o
Porto*, the Port, or Oporto, as it was named by the mercantile English,
became progressively and inextricably involved with them, English
interests in the wine now known as port did not mature for another
three centuries.

In 1394 Philippa's fourth son, Dom Henrique, 'the Navigator',
was born here, according to tradition in a palace flanking the Rua da
Alfândega Velha. In 1415, when Dom João I's fleet was preparing
for the Ceuta expedition, it is said that the citizens dispatched their
best meat, suitably salted, to the ships, reserving merely the offal for

themselves, earning them the ungrateful nickname of *tripeiros* or tripe-eaters. They rightly retaliated by calling the inhabitants of Lisbon *alfacinhas*, lettuce-nibblers.

Only one *auto-da-fé* was celebrated in Oporto, in 1543, for the Inquisition was established there only briefly. Nevertheless in 1618 several descendants of Castilian *Conversos*, who had been allowed to settle there, were arrested on suspicion of being backsliding *Marranos*.

Its citizens remained an independent lot, frequently resisting what they considered impositions from the capital. After a tax had been laid on linen and woollen goods, the women of Oporto attacked the minister responsible in what was then known as the 'Revolta das Macaracos', or spindles; and in 1661 more anti-tax rioting occurred.

In 1680 the firm of Quarles Harris was founded in Oporto, and in that same year Sir Robert Southwell, writing from Lisbon, was promising to send Lord Arlington in London some 'white Oporto wine' after the vintage; but although another company, Kopke, dating back to 1638, was engaged in the wine trade there, again it is unlikely that the wine these establishments were exporting was what we now know as port. Indeed, the first British merchants in Oporto were trading in other commodities, the centre of wine exporting then being Viana do Castelo. It was not for another decade that wines were sent down the Douro from Lamego, being shipped from Oporto by the two sons of a Liverpool or Yorkshire merchant. Peter Bearsley, the son of Job Bearsley of Viana, was one of the first wine shippers to move to Oporto, where in 1704 he was visited by Thomas Woodmass of Kettering, who found lodgings with Mr Page in the Rua Nova.

By this time the small English and Scottish community was well established under their consul, John Lee. Messrs Hunt, Roope and Company had had premises at both Viana and Oporto for some fifty years, shipping *bacalhau* (salted cod) from Newfoundland, and wheat and wool from England; and in exchange exporting wine, cork, fruit and other goods; but this bartering of cod and cloth for wine had been going on since the fifteenth century or earlier.

The expatriates had their problems, particularly in their relations with the Catholic Church, although generally they kept what would now be termed a low profile in this respect. In 1682 the Revd Samuel Barton was informed that he must leave the country, as only one Anglican chaplain was allowed: at the Lisbon Embassy. It was thought that this decision by the ecclesiastical authorities may have been instigated by four or five merchants who had turned Catholic (including Pickering and Wrothsly of Houblon's London-based firm), abetted by the Jesuits and the English Seminary at Lisbon.

Barton was discreetly replaced by Edward Hinde, who remained there two years. His letters to his friend the Bishop of Ely well describe the nauseating excesses to which the Papists went during Lent, doing penance by crawling round on their hands and knees, lashing their backs until they were 'as raw as a piece of beef and as bloody as butchers'. They would even go to the length of excommunicating such inanimate objects as the sand bar at the river mouth when a ship was lost there; to exorcise the devils lurking there, the bishop sailed down river at the head of a procession of boats, the foremost carrying an image of Christ and firing small guns, the banks lined with people thumping their chests, and so on.

Any Protestant who was so unfortunate as to die at Oporto had to be buried secretly at low tide: no service was allowed and no records were to be kept, at least officially. (This Peninsular practice is confirmed by Richard Ford, who observed that until 1830, when a Protestant burial ground had been permitted at Malaga, 'heretical carcases . . . used to be buried in the sea sands like dead dogs, and beyond the low water-mark; and even this concession offended orthodox fishermen, who feared that the soles might become infected'.) Southey, whose uncle had been chaplain at Oporto, maintained that until the 1780s no clergyman would ever be seen to officiate at a funeral, such were the prejudices of the natives. The body was still buried in a common grave on the river bank, without any monument, although by then the consul was allowed to read a form of service. According to Southey, some thought this was beneath their dignity, and the vice-consul was appointed, who deputed it again, and on one occasion

> it devolved upon a watch-maker. This poor fellow drank very hard, and one evening at the grave he mumbled at the service, and turned his book first this way and then the other, till a bystander had the curiosity to look over him, and found instead of a prayer book he had brought the History of the Late War!

Woodmass noted that the shippers kept very much to themselves, even employing English-speaking Negro servants, some from Carolina, so that they could avoid the vexation of having to converse in Portuguese with their cooks. These viticulturalists were even said to compel the up-country peasants to sacrifice the honour of their daughters if they wanted to sell their wine, for 'they . . . only bought from growers who allowed their daughters to dance with them' (which J.B. Trend has suggested was merely making political capital out of old-time vintage customs).

When visiting Oporto one Christmas in the 1780s, Major James Ferrier, writing under the pseudonym of 'Captain Arthur Costigan', found the English merchants

> a worthy, friendly and hospitable set of Gentlemen, as attentive to their counting-rooms and business every day before dinner, as they are to their dressing, cards and other amusements in the evening; many of them have been twenty or thirty years resident in the country, yet know but a few words of the language.

When they chose to take a day off, making up a party of pleasure with the ladies, they would set out to some place to which a good dinner had been sent beforehand, and there would

> dance, eat and drink heartily, play at cards, and then return in the evening, without any manner of communication with the inhabitants . . . neither have they any time, even if they had the inclination, to study the country they live in, any little moment they have to spare being towards the evening, and then the cards, the eternal cards are constantly at hand to swallow it up.

This trait had already been dignified by the foundation in 1727 of a British Association, in which the older, established members attempted to exclude the newly-arrived merchants, many of whom they considered mere counter-jumpers.

The Lisbon earthquake did not affect Oporto physically, where building had flourished, notably between the years 1730 and 1763, when the Clérigos was completed by Nicolau Nasoni.[1] In 1770 work had started on a new hospital, dedicated to St Anthony, following the designs of John Carr of York, although when seen by Alexander Jardine nine years later, it was still far from finished; and, as he astutely observed – echoing the opinion of Major Dalrymple who had visited the site in September 1774 – there was doubt whether it would be completed 'in less than an hundred years; and perhaps never': and both were right.

Nevertheless, Jardine considered that the town had been 'much improved and beautified' by João da Almada, the governor, partly 'with the assistance and advice of our good consul'.

This would have been John Whitehead, whose advice Jardine no doubt had sought on his own behalf also, for he was about to take up the post of consul at La Coruña, one which he was to hold until 1795, when the outbreak of war caused him to move from Spain to Portugal – perhaps Oporto – where he died four years later.

Whitehead, born near Manchester in 1726, was a remarkable man in many respects. He was consul to the Oporto Factory from 1756 until his death in 1802. One of the first problems he had to contend with was the establishment by Pombal of the Portuguese 'General Company of Agriculture of the Wines of the Upper Douro', which was to have serious repercussions on what was until then virtually a British monopoly. In the following year the so-called 'Tipplers' Riot' broke out in Oporto, said by Pombal to have been instigated by the English, which was put down by that enlightened if dictatorial minister with some ferocity.[2] In fact these riots had been caused by an additional measure instituted by Pombal to restrict the number of taverns in Oporto, and it was remarked at the time by a French merchant whose parents lived there, that the riots were not serious, but – as has been frequently the case in similar situations – the commander of the local militia magnified the commotion in order to increase his own importance and to justify his severity.

Although many members of the Factory no doubt sympathized with the rioters, and one of the accused happened to be the servant of an Englishman, there was no known connection, and it is more likely that the fuss had been stirred up by the Jesuits, who had every reason to hate Pombal, and would use any lever at hand to try and unseat him.

Nevertheless, with the advent of such strong competition, the English Factory did suffer, Whitehead reporting in 1764 that there had been a decline in business, and it is possible that a few shippers even returned home, although Richard Twiss, visiting Oporto in February 1773, reckoned that there were still about thirty British families there.

As there was no tolerable inn, Twiss lodged at an English house on the quay, even if this entailed climbing steep lanes or hiring a litter or sedan whenever he went out. Usually the litter was suspended between two horses or mules, although Major Dalrymple had noticed that some of the Factory ladies had prevailed on the few *Gallegos* in Oporto to carry their chairs, as the *Portuenses* declined to do the work of beasts.

The English merchants assembled daily in the Rua Nova dos

Inglezes (now the Rua do Infante Dom Henrique) to transact business, protected from the sun by sail-cloths hung from the houses
opposite; and presumably, when it rained, which was not infrequent,
they sought the shelter of one of the three houses they owned in the
street. Whether one of these was used then as the 'Factory House' is
uncertain. Twiss attended an assembly there, at which were some
twenty English ladies; while Dalrymple apparently 'feasted most
voluptuously with the consul and factory, who were remarkably civil
and attentive; the only thing I disliked about them', he felt bound to
add, 'was their supercilious treatment of the Portuguese, from whom
they derive their wealth and opulence'. He also commented on the
fact that the members

> complained heavily of the exclusive privilege of the wine trade,
> granted to the Portuguese company, which, from all I could find,
> appeared rather a disadvantage to the factory, than to Great
> Britain; for, from the principle that a rivalship in commerce is of
> advantage to the consumer, the London market has been supplied
> with better wine since the establishment of this company, and the
> commodities of England are still exported as before. The shops are
> filled with baizes and coarse cloths, and every person I met, was
> clad with some of the manufactures of Britain. This [Pombal's]
> wine monopoly affects the people of the country very severely: a
> man possessed of a vineyard in the wine country, is obliged, if
> required, to sell its produce to the company, and repurchase it
> from the monopolizers at an advanced price . . .
>
> It is surprising, that any nation that has the least pretence to
> refinement, should so long persist in drinking such an infernal
> liquor as the wine sent from this place to the English market; in its
> genuine state it is agreeable; but to please the palate of my boreal
> friends, such a quantity of spirit is incorporated with it, that it is
> rendered poisonous and destructive to those who use it.

Major Dalrymple waited on the Commandant, in company with
Consul Whitehead, and drank tea with his lady. Although Whitehead was far more communicative with the Portuguese than most
Englishmen, 'Captain Costigan' thought him a somewhat eccentric
bachelor, who lived in a large mansion attended only by

> a withered old Portuguese beldam, past eighty, who makes his
> bed, lights his fire, and sends him his breakfast, and a young

Galician boy, who cleans his shoes, and brings him a powdered wig
once or twice every day from the nearest barber's shop.

The consul was also a great bibliophile, amateur architect, astronomer and mathematician, who with his passion for the sciences had
erected a lightning conductor on his residence, which caused some
consternation, and even a visit from commissaries of the Inquisition.
Fortunately they were not entirely unintelligent men, and appeared
satisfied by his explanation.

While John Croft was treasurer to the Factory, it was agreed that
the three houses belonging to them should be demolished and
replaced by a more spacious structure, a proper Factory House, which
would provide all the essential amenities for such an august assembly
of merchants. Naturally, it would contain accommodation for Mr
Whitehead, who, probably advised by John Carr, had provided the
plans for an unostentatious Classical edifice.

This was run up between the years of 1787 and 1790. Most members were pleased with the result: its granite solidity reflected their
own character, although Dr John Wright, who had quarrelled with
the Factory, considered it both inconvenient and pretentious. Con-
suls were still allowed to use the place as an office until the mid-1830s,
when part of the space was converted into a library.[3]

Whitehead was succeeded as Consul by his nephew, William
Warre, who had inherited many of his uncle's interests, and it must
be Warre or his father, another William, who is referred to by Professor Link as one of several merchants possessing 'both knowledge and
the love of science'.[4]

In June 1808, while Lisbon was occupied by the French under
Junot, Oporto defiantly proclaimed the Prince Regent. A provisional
junta was set up under its patriotic and bellicose bishop, and a Loyal
Lusitanian Legion was raised there by Sir Robert Wilson. In the previous October, before their property was sequestered, following the
demands of a French ultimatum, several members of the Factory,
together with their families, valuables and select wines, sailed for
England in a fleet of sixty vessels, leaving Joseph Camo, an American
citizen and partner in one of the shipping firms, to protect their
interests.

Late in March 1809, two months after the battle at La Coruña,
Soult's army, after fighting their way through Galicia, stormed and
occupied Oporto. Panic-striken, many citizens in attempting to
escape had surged down to the bridge of boats strung across the

Douro, but it gave way under the press and hundreds were drowned.

On 12 May Wellington was to carry out one of the more daring and spectacular offensive actions of his career, which took Soult almost entirely by surprise. Although expecting an attack from the sea, the experienced commander had taken the precaution of withdrawing all craft from the south bank of the Douro and placing them under guard. General Franceschi's troops, who were further south, had retired on Oporto under pressure from Hill, who was marching north from Ovar. But Soult had neglected to leave outposts on that far bank, dominated, as it still is, by the Serra Convent.

At that time this area was masked by woods, enabling Wellington and his staff to approach unnoticed. He observed from the convent that at no great distance upstream stood what appeared to be a seminary, still under construction but already surrounded by a walled enclosure, a defensible site to which troops might be ferried without being spotted by the French, for there was a high-banked bend in the river here, if only he had boats to hand.

Providentially, one skiff had crossed unseen during the night, which was commandeered immediately. Within a short time several barges had been collected and sufficient men passed across to make a foothold before Soult realized that the Allies were already in force in a position from which they could only be dislodged with difficulty. Rapidly assembled, the French hastened to the eastern suburbs, leaving unguarded all the lighters and other vessels tethered to the north bank. Within minutes these too had been rowed over, and more British units, now supported by artillery firing from near the Serra Convent, were being ferried across the Douro comparatively undisturbed.

Meanwhile, another bridgehead had been made further south-east at Avintes, and light dragoons were approaching Soult from the rear. There was little he could do to stem the tide. Any attempt to make an orderly withdrawal was out of the question. Thoroughly demoralized, his army was soon streaming east in full retreat, Soult himself hospitably leaving his dinner in the Palácio das Carrancas to be eaten by Wellington and his staff before they set off in pursuit.

In this action the Allied losses were 123 in all: those of the French were double, not taking into account those made prisoner, together with some 1,500 left in the Oporto hospital, some seventy guns, and quantities of valuable equipment.

The Factory House, requisitioned by the French, had served as a coffee-house, run by the enterprising Senhor de Queiroa, and

although British officers had the run of the place during the inter-
vening period, it was not until late in 1811 that it regained its original
appearance. Writing in December 1808, Lady Holland had described
part of the building – 'spacious, clean, and possessing the comforts
of fireplaces' – as providing accommodation for English travellers,
into which she and Lord Holland had gratefully moved from their
'wretched posada'.

But once the tide of war had turned, no longer was there room at
that inn for outsiders; and it would appear that it needed very considerable refurbishment, for in 1815 it was referred to as being unfit to
house George Canning, should he visit Oporto, which in the event he
chose not to.

Some of the 'elder statesmen', on returning to the city, and finding that other English merchants dealing largely in woollen and cotton goods had assumed they could expect the same privileges as the
wine shippers, disputed their right to membership. There were also
squabbles concerning the appointment of chaplain.

By 1817 the community was allowed to erect a chapel in the cemetery site previously acquired by Consul Whitehead, on condition
that it had no external ecclesiastical appearance. But it was not until
1843 that this was consecrated – by the Bishop of Gibraltar – on
which occasion, with great condescension and for the first time, ladies
were invited to dine at the Factory House. Several travellers, while
recording their appreciation of hospitality received, had remarked on
the self-congratulatory exclusiveness of some members. Before any
function to which persons of their own class and Portuguese families
of consequence were invited, the guest list was scrutinized by the
committee, who in 1819 decided that 'No Portuguese officer under
the rank of Field-officer can be invited'. However, over the decades
this keeping up of distinctions became progressively relaxed.

The chaplain from 1825 until 1871 was the Revd Edward Whiteley
(1795–1876?), and he appears to have been, like Whitehead, a worthy character, although not every visitor to the Factory Church
approved of his tender conscience. The Revd Kinsey, chaplain to Lord
Auckland, when visiting Oporto in 1827, had complained:

the peculiar text of the sermon at once awakened our suspicions of
what the nature of the discourse was to be, when we heard it vehe-
mently affirmed that the greater part of the congregation . . . were
under the sentence of eternal reprobation and that nothing could
save them.

Their animosity would appear to be mutual, for Whiteley, when referring later to Kinsey's own book, *Portugal Illustrated*, could not forbear to remark that it

> would be valuable if its contents were as attractive as are its paper, print, and embellishments; but the very short time the author was in Portugal, and the few portions of the country which he actually visited, scarcely afforded him the means of writing his very large volume, either with authority or with accuracy.

The normally censorious Revd John Mason Neale (1818–66), compiler of Murray's *Handbook to Portugal*, described Whiteley as being 'probably better acquainted with the scenery of the north of Portugal than any other person now living, and whose Courtesy in communicating his information to tourists is beyond all praise'. Neale, a 'Puseyite' clergyman, had visited Madeira for the sake of his health in 1843. A decade later he approached the publisher John Murray, offering his services in the possible future publication of a guide to Portugal. He had noticed that Murray had already published a brief description (by an author who wisely chose to remain anonymous), entitled *Hints to travellers in Portugal in search of the beautiful and grand*, which, although it had received an enthusiastic review in the *Athenaeum* in September 1852, was in his opinion of slight worth; indeed he feared no one could derive much information from it, for 'the whole of the South is omitted, not a direction is given as to the way of travelling, except that one statement as to the existence of mules is made . . . and some strange mistakes here and there occur'. Neale went on to inform Murray that it was his intention to make a six to eight week tour of Portugal the following spring and in the event, he was commissioned for a fee of 100 guineas (£25 on account) to compile such a guide, which would accompany others in that growing series. John Murray III had personally compiled a *Handbook for France*, published in 1843.

After traversing Old Castile with three travelling companions, Neale entered Portugal at Miranda do Douro on 20 May 1853. He made a second tour the following spring, on that occasion accompanied by the Revd Joseph Oldknow, whose own account of the expedition, *A month in Portugal*, was hardly noticed by reviewers when published in 1855.

Although Neale met the Revd Whiteley in Oporto, it is quite likely that he was unaware that the chaplain was the author of *Hints to travellers*, a work of which it would appear he was not too proud. Whiteley had written to Murray in June 1852: 'Be pleased to bear in mind that I do not wish my name to appear in the Title, nor that it should at present be known who wrote the little work. I shall be happy to render you any assistance in compiling a Hand-Book for Portugal'. Understandably, the kind offer was not taken up. Nevertheless, his obvious enthusiasm and local knowledge must have impressed Neale to the extent of requesting Murray to send proofs of his own compilation to Whiteley for correction. I have been unable to verify that this was done.[5]

The *Handbook* was published in October 1855, and a second and identical edition came out the following year.[6] Travellers intending to visit Portugal would hardly find Neale's introductory paragraphs encouraging, for he starts by describing roads as scarcely existing; inns remained

in the primitive barbarity which was characteristic when there were convents to shelter the tourist; the labour of a journey, especially through the wilder parts, is scarcely to be conceived but by those who have experienced it; and any one who has, will easily comprehend how it is that the word travel signifies both a toil and a journey.

It is not surprising that its appearance made little impact. In no way could it be compared with Richard Ford's authoritative *Handbook for Travellers in Spain*, the third edition of which, and the last in his lifetime, was also published by Murray that same year.

Life was not always easy in the cocooned society of British Oporto. It could not expect always to remain isolated from events such as the radical revolt of 1820, and the far more serious situation which arose there a dozen years later, when the city was blockaded for eighteen months by Miguelite troops.

In March 1832 Dom Pedro, the ex-Emperor of Brazil, sailing from the Azores, landed some 7,500 men, in the face of which the Miguelites retired briefly, only to return and shell the place in a desultory fashion from batteries they had set up, as Wellington had done, near the Serra Convent.

Most of the citizens, as well as the British community, were intensely relieved by Dom Pedro's timely invasion, for ever since his brother Dom Miguel had seized power in 1828, the country had been oppressed by his absolutist regime. Whether Dom Pedro could win back the crown for Maria da Gloria, his daughter, was not such an easy matter, although later in the year Oporto was able to put up a more stubborn defence against the usurper's spasmodic attacks.

The garrison had been stiffened meanwhile by a motley 'International Brigade', consisting partly of contingents of out-of-work Glaswegians and Cockneys under the command of Charles Shaw, plus a sprinkling of Peninsular War veterans. The opposing forces were eventually increased: some 17,800 Liberals closely invested by 24,000 Miguelites. Shaw, incensed on hearing that one of his officers who had died of wounds had been refused burial in the English Cemetery by Consul Crispin, a reactionary civilian who he suspected of Miguelite sympathies, was naturally delighted to learn later that the British government had shown their disapproval likewise by transfering Crispin to La Coruña and replacing him by Colonel Sorrell.

Captain Nugent Glascock RN, with a small flotilla, patrolled the river mouth, keeping a weather eye on British interests, and Colonel Lovell Badcock remained in the city as the British Government observer. Cholera raged. A soup kitchen was set up by the Factory, but cats and dogs, including Colonel Shaw's pets, became the common ingredient of stews.

Unfortunately, the wine lodges at transpontine Vila Nova de Gaia stood in Miguelite territory, who, as a parting shot, contrived to blow up and set fire to the warehouses of the Old Wine Company. It was only due to the resolute action of the spirited Captain Glascock and a party of marines that the blaze did not spread to other lodges. Nevertheless, some 27,000 pipes of boiling wine gushed into the swirling Douro, turning it a muddy red.

The environs were devastated likewise, for during the siege thousands of trees had been cut down for stockades and other purposes, and Whiteley refers in particular to the area around the Serra Convent as being shorn of its original beauty, with the felling of its splendid oaks, chestnuts and pines, which had covered Wellington's approach to the river in 1809 so well.

By 1834 life had resumed its complacent course, at least for the British community, if we are to judge from young Joseph James Forrester's drawings. In one he depicts the high-hatted merchants on their daily stamping-ground in the Rua Nova, many of them among the Factory members he was to accuse of encouraging the adulteration of port wine. It is not my intention to describe this complex controversy, which is well explained in more than one study.

In 1871, nine years after Forrester's tragic death (cf. Cachão de

Valeira), it was confirmed that the port wine vineyards had been attacked by Phylloxera. It took decades to uproot them, and to replant with immune American stocks grafted with native vines. In one of the first *quintas* ravaged by the pest, their production of fifty-five pipes in 1865 was reduced to one only in 1872, which may give some indication of the seriousness of the scourge, in which hundreds of the smaller growers were ruined entirely. Furthermore, in 1909 many of the wine lodges at Vila Nova da Gaia were inundated by a devastating flood.

But, surviving these and several other disasters, the shippers flourished. And when not working, they were playing. A cricket pitch was laid out in a field near the Palácio dos Carrancas, which quite bewildered any *Portuense* curious enough to watch the game; while at the beach at neighbouring Foz, referred to as 'the Brighton of Oporto', it was noted that 'The English ladies have a bathing-place to themselves at some distance from the rest'.

Oporto continued to weather the several political storms of the nineteenth century, and the expanding second city of Portugal continued to be a base of opposition to reactionary regimes, in 1878 electing the first Republican deputy. It was now the hub of the largest industrial and commercial conurbation in the country, providing some sixty per cent of its revenue.

Most of Oporto's monuments may be reached with ease by the energetic, map in hand, once warned that 'To walk about this city is, I assure you, rather a violent exercise, not one street in it being on a level excepting that where the most part of the English inhabit', in the veracious words of 'Arthur Costigan'. The contours of Oporto have not changed.

And part of its population still seethes in squalid *ilhas*, badly ventilated alleys leading off the main streets; and well may one wonder what conditions must have been like earlier this century, before it had been stated that 'great progress has recently been made in the cleanliness of the place'. A well-conceived project is under way to restore and rehabilitate a number of old buildings flanking the narrow lanes near the riverside Praça da Ribeira and Largo do Terreiro, which should provide its citizens with some incentive to keep the area less sordid.

The northern extremity of the Ponte de Dom Luís I, thrown across the chasm of the Douro in 1886, its vertiginous upper span some sixty metres above water level, is no bad place from which to start the exploration. The bridge itself commands several impressive views: of

the stretch of medieval town wall known as the Muralha Ferdi-
nandina; of Gustave Eiffel's railway bridge of 1877, his first important commission; and of the new bridge spanning the river further
east.

Behind these relics of earlier fortifications shelters the church of
Santa Clara, the gold leaf of its lavishly carved woodwork dimmed
by dust. To the west rises the granite cathedral, drastically and ineptly
'modernized' in the eighteenth century, when Nicolau Nasoni
added a porch to the north portal. He designed also the grand stair-
case off the main cloister, the organ-cases, probably the railings and
gates of the chancel arch, and completed the silver altarpiece in the
north transept, said to have been saved from Soult's rapacious hand
by masking it with a plaster wall. Nasoni was responsible also for the
façade of the former archbishop's palace, flanking the cathedral
terrace.

This commands a good view over the medieval *enceinte*, and
towards the serried ranks of the port wine warehouses or *armazéns* at
transpontine **Vila Nova de Gaia**, their large-lettered roofs advertising
their owners. Among the better-known shippers are Cockburn,
Croft, Delaforce, Harvey, Osborne, Taylor, Graham, Warre and
Sandeman. I will leave it to professional oenologists to detail the
intricacies of actual ownership and which family, distiller or
international conglomerate of vintners may now have the controlling
interest.

Steps descend steeply past a fourteenth-century tower towards the
former Jesuit church of São Lourenço, better known as 'Dos Grilos',
to approach the Feitoria Ingleza, the British Factory House. The so-
called 'House of Henry the Navigator', once used as a Customs House
and heavily restored over the centuries when not rebuilt, stands in the
neighbouring Rua da Alfândega Velha and now houses the city
archives.

Further west rises São Francisco, its interior festooned profusely
with late Baroque and Rococo carving, hardly an inch of which has
escaped the gilders' leaf, which gave it, in the eyes of Richard Twiss, 'a
very disgusting effect'; but also noteworthy are the Tree of Jesse,
organ-case, and a Renaissance tomb.

Further uphill, opposite a restored Market-hall, is the Balsa or
Stock Exchange, erected soon after the Miguelite siege on the site of
conventual dependencies. It contains a particularly hideous ballroom decorated in a pseudo-Moresque style, of which, as it cost a great
deal, the commercial hierarchy are inordinately proud. Adjacent are

the city offices of the Port Wine Institute (cf. Peso da Régua).

Nearby is São João Novo, completed in the mid-seventeenth century, from which a lane descends precipitously to São Pedro da Miragaia, said to contain yet another elaborately carved and gilded chancel. Facing the former church is the imposing façade of Nasoni's Palácio de São João Novo, with its characteristic granite-framed mezzanine windows. It now houses the city's Historical and Ethno-graphical Museum, in which a section describing the variety of vessels peculiar to the Douro is of particular interest; the archaeological collections also deserve attention.

In the ancient Rua das Flores, flanked by silversmiths, stands the Misericórdia, in the council-chamber of which is an anonymous early-sixteenth-century Flemish painting of *The Fountain of Mercy*. It is certainly one of the finest of its type to be seen in Portugal. The central subject is Christ crucified between the Virgin and St John, while kneeling below it are depicted the founders of the Miseri-córdia, Dom Manuel and his wife, together with members of their family, nobles and ecclesiastics.

Lanes ascend towards the Jardim de João Chagas, overlooked by the late-eighteenth-century façade of the former Law Courts. To the east rises the lofty Torre dos Clérigos and the abutting oval-shaped church, both the work of Nasoni.

Close by are the twin churches of the Terceiras do Carmo and the Carmelitas, and the only completed wing of John Carr's Hospital.

Further west, installed in the former royal palace 'das Carrancas', is the Soares dos Reis museum, containing representative paintings by Frei Carlos, Cristovão de Figueiredo, Gaspar Vaz and 'Grão Vasco'; and from a later period, Sequeira's canvas of Junot 'protecting' the city of Lisbon, Ströberle's portrait of José Moreira da Cruz[7], and works by Jean Pillement. The collections of ceramics, costumes, sil-ver, glass and furniture, are of exceptional quality, and not unnatur-ally, several pieces show English influence.

Beyond gardens, in the Quinta da Macieirinha, is the charming 'Romantic' museum, displaying portraits of Baron Forrester, and of Sir Charles Napier, Dom Pedro's naval commander who captured Dom Miguel's fleet at Cape St Vincent, among others. The *quinta* has an unexpected association with Charles Albert, the former king of Sardinia, who died here in July 1849, shortly after his defeat by the Austrians under Radetzky at Novara.

Not far north of the gardens is the Cemitério Inglês, in which lies Consul Whitehead, responsible for its inception; while some dis-tance beyond lies tenth-century São Martinho da Cedofeito, much

altered since it replaced a mid-sixth-century church said to have been
run up in a hurry – thus its name – to mark the place where
Theodomir, king of the Suevi, had been converted from Arianism to
Orthodoxy.

NOTES

1. Nasoni, born in Tuscany in 1692, studied painting in Siena with
   Giuseppe Nasini, before establishing himself as a decorative artist at
   Malta, and becoming an architect after his arrival in Portugal *circa* 1725.
   He married a local girl, and died at Oporto in 1773.
2. Eight-hundred-and-forty-eight men and fifty-four women were con-
   victed, twenty-one of whom were condemned to death, although several
   made their escape.
3. Sadly diminished a decade ago, when some 2,300 volumes of nineteenth-century fiction, many of them rare three-decker novels, were sold
   via a London dealer to an American university.
4. The firm was one of the first to have been founded at Oporto, in 1670.
   Another William Warre (born 1706) in 1745 married Elizabeth Whitehead, the future consul's sister. It was their grandson, yet another
   William (1784–1853), who, dismissed from the firm for playing a boyish
   prank, at the age of nineteen was commissioned in the 52nd Light Infantry, survived the retreat to La Coruña, and was later aide-de-camp to
   Beresford, ending his days as a Lieutenant-General. He also took part in
   'The Passage of the Douro' in May 1809, and his intimate knowledge of
   the city must have been invaluable to Wellington.
5. Murray had published two impressions of 250 copies each of Whiteley's
   ninety-two-page booklet, and eventually returned 171 unsold copies to
   its author, although it would appear that the publisher still held stocks in
   1861, the year in which Whiteley, in a letter to the Bishop of London,
   mentions that he had asked Murray to send him an example of his *Hints
   to travellers*, 'put together a few years ago to induce Men of Taste to visit
   this singularly picturesque Country'. The worthy chaplain later retired
   to Sutton Montis in Somerset.
6. For a more detailed history of the publication of Neale's *Handbook*, the
   reader is referred to *Murray's Portugal*, by John Gretton and William
   Lister, published in the *Antiquarian Book Monthly Review* of April
   1989. Their comprehensive bibliographical guide to Murray's *Hand-
   books* for travellers are in the press.
7. João Glama Ströberle, whose father was German, was born in Lisbon in
   1708, and after some twenty years in Rome, returned to Portugal, spending much of his time in Oporto, where he died in 1792.

27

Barcelos – Braga – Guimarães

A roundabout route has been described to take in as many as possible of the more memorable things to be seen when driving north from central Oporto, among them several important Romanesque churches. Almost two-thirds of the Romanesque churches surviving in Portugal are to be found in the old province of the Minho.

Following the N13 towards Póvoa de Varzim, we pass **Leça do Bailio**, once the headquarters of the Knights Templar in Portugal, and where in 1372 Dom Fernando announced his marriage to Leonor Teles. The severe granite building, heavily restored, dates from 1336, but the cloister is part of an earlier edifice. Among its more obvious features are the crenellated parapet and tower corbelled at each corner, its rose-window, and the interior capitals; while it contains two well-preserved tombs: of João Coelho by Diogo Pires the younger; and of Cristóvão de Cernache, dating from half a century later, which shows the influence of Philippe Houdart.

Vila do Conde, a fishing port at the mouth of the Ave, defended by a seventeenth-century fort, is next entered. It is dominated by the huge eighteenth-century convent of Santa Clara designed by Henriques Ventura, but founded in 1318 by Afonso Sanches, a natural son of Dom Dinis. His elaborate tomb, with that of his wife, and of Brites Pereira, daughter of Nun 'Alvares and wife of the first Duke of Braganza, may be seen in the adjoining church. The abutting aqueduct is now partly in ruins. Down in the town is São João, displaying a Plateresque portal by João de Castilho.

Adjacent **Póvoa de Varzim**, of slight interest, was the birthplace of Eça de Queiroz (1845–1900), author of *The Maias* and other novels, who was for many years Portuguese Consul in Newcastle-on-Tyne, Bristol, and then Paris, where he died.

Turning inland between the two towns we reach **Rio Mau**, where mid-twelfth-century São Cristóvao contains well-carved capitals and sculpture, as does São Pedro at neighbouring **Rates**. The latter is said to have been built by Count Henry of Burgundy on the site of the martyrdom of Pedro de Rates, a native of the village and convert from Judaism, who became the first bishop of Braga.

A byroad leads north across country to **Barcelos**, an attractive old town on the north bank of the lamprey-laden Cávado, spanned here by a fifteenth-century bridge abutted by a pyramid-capped chapel. It is overlooked by remains of the palace of Dom Afonso, natural son of Dom João I by a certain Dona Inês. (She also provided Dom João with a daughter, Beatriz, who was married off by Philippa of Lancaster in 1405 to Thomas Fitzalan, Earl of Arundel.[1]) Dom Afonso received the county of Barcelos on his marriage in 1401 to Brites Pereira, referred to above, for the last count of the old line, a member of the Meneses family, had been killed at Aljubarrota.

Pride of place in the museum here is given to the Cross associated with the 'Cock of Barcelos'. Legend relates that in the distant past a roasting rooster miraculously crowed in protestation at an innocent Galician being sent to the gallows; and this gaily painted bird, long under the wing of folk art, has even been pressed into service as a national symbol.

Nearby are a church preserving a thirteenth-century door; the fifteenth-century Solar dos Pinheiros, with its twin towers; and an eighteenth-century palace, now the Town Hall. The main street leads to the Torre Nova, a relic of the fortifications of Barcelos, housing a regional handicraft centre. Adjacent Bom Jesus, attributed to João Antunes, with its granite cupola, has an unusual octagonal ground plan in which a Greek cross has been combined with a cylinder.

Close by are gardens embellished by Baroque statuary and fountains, and the extensive Campo da República, where the Thursday Market takes place, still one of the more animated and interesting to survive in Portugal, selling everything from its characteristic pottery to lowing, lyre-horned cattle, not forgetting the ubiquitous cocks. Regrettably, little of the ceramic ware is of the imaginative quality of the productions of the late Rosa Ramalho.

To the north is Nossa Senhora do Terço, the ceiling panels of which describe the life of St Benedict, as do the early-eighteenth-century *azulejos* surrounding the gilded pulpit with its double-headed eagle, which remained a popular decorative element long after the Spanish Habsburg domination of Portugal.

On re-crossing the river, bear east through **Vilar de Frades**, with a

Baroque church retaining both Manueline and Romanesque portals; and at Martim, turn for **Tibães**, where the huge and long-ruined monastery of São Martinho is undergoing restoration. The main features of the church of 1624–61, by Manuel Alvares, are its contemporary stalls, mid-eighteenth-century woodcarving by the *entalhador* André Soares, and Baroque organ. Its formal gardens, which are said to have inspired the stair of Bom Jesus, and described by Lord Porchester in 1827 as enchanting when its roses were in full bloom, are also being rehabilitated.

On reaching the main Braga-Ponte de Lima road, turn right and then left to approach the church of São Francisco. Abutting it is the tiny Visigothic chapel of **São Frutuoso de Montélios**, dating from the second half of the seventh century. Its plan is that of a Greek cross, with a (reconstructed) central dome and barrel-vaulted apsidal arms; while the vaulting in each bay is supported by marble columns. An ornamental frieze is preserved also, but the whole was remodelled in the eleventh century, and has received the attention of restorers more recently. Note on the exterior wall the Lombardic blind arcading terminating in alternate pointed and semicircular sections, surrounded by decorative bands of marble.

Braga, a rapidly growing industrial and agricultural centre, claims to have been founded in 296 BC, but there is only slight and inconclusive evidence of a pre-Roman settlement of any importance. Regrettably, the once extensive *oppidum* of Bracara Augusta, until the 1950s largely a wasteland, was allowed by the municipality to be built over, and systematic archaeological excavation did not get under way until 1976.

In AD 411, having flourished as the main Roman station in northern Lusitania, Braga became the capital of the Suevian kingdom of Gallaecia. Forty-five years later, it fell to Theodoric II. The conversion of the Arian Visigoths to orthodox Catholicism at the two synods held here in 563 and 572 marked the beginning of its ecclesiastical hegemony; and it long disputed with Tarragona and Toledo the primacy of the Peninsula. From *circa* 730 until reconquered definitively by Fernando I of Castile in 1040, it was under Moorish occupation when not virtually abandoned; and the see was only restored in 1070.

Some thirty years later, Diego Gelmirez, the ambitious bishop of Santiago de Compostela, determined not to be dependent on Braga, descended on the place and forcibly carried off the relics of saints Victor and Fructuosus. Deprived of these shrines, Gerald, a

Cluniac monk from Moissac, who was then metropolitan, had to recourse to Rome for confirmation of his supremacy over all sees in the west of the Peninsula as far south as Coimbra.

Some stability was provided by João Peculiar, archbishop for several decades in the mid-twelfth century. But pontifical wrangling persisted, even after 1716, when the creation of the Lisbon patriarchate reduced its pre-eminence; and Braga still retains some of the bigotry of an episcopal city, as reflected in the local proverb: 'Every good house has its cattle and its tonsure'.

Significantly, it was from reactionary Braga that in 1926 General Gomes da Costa addressed his successful appeal to all citizens 'of dignity and honour' to overthrow the Democratic regime, and thus precipitated the quasi-hierocratic dictatorship which lasted for the next half century. And it was here, during the recent revolutionary period, that the archbishop is said to have instigated a mob attack on the local Communist headquarters.

Braga does not appear to have been much damaged during the Peninsular War, although Sergeant Cooper vividly recalled an incident, which certainly was not isolated. In May 1809, when in pursuit of the French, the 7th Fusiliers found a church in the vicinity in which to doss down.

> In a minute or two the band had possession of the altar, and the big drummer of the pulpit. All were cold, hungry, tired, and ill-humoured. Fires were wanted, and fires were made. Smash went the forms, down came the priest's stalls. The crashing of wood, the bawling and swearing of hundreds in the blinding, choking smoke that completely filled the edifice, were awful; and when darkness set in the place was a perfect pandemonium. During the uproar, a box of large wax candles used at the altar was found. Many of these were distributed and lighted in different parts of the church, and the scene was complete and fit for Hogarth's pencil.

From the west, the medieval *enceinte* of Braga may be entered at the Arco dos Porta Nova. Little remains of the Romanesque cathedral except the south portal and part of the west doors, now sheltered by a late-Gothic porch added in 1532. Above rise two incongruously pinnacled belfries. The chapel adjacent to the chancel is not too spoilt by later 'improvements'; but perhaps the most impressive features of the interior are the magnificently carved and gilt organ-cases of 1738. According to Sacheverell Sitwell, the original organs were played upon by Carlos de Seixas, a pupil and colleague of Domenico Scarlatti in the 1720s, and the composer of several hundred keyboard sonatas. The organs themselves were restored not long ago, and this was doubtless necessary.

When conducting me round the chestnut-floored cathedral treasury (a chaotic collection of cult objects, in which a Hispano-arabic ivory casket was remarkable), the sacristan, just to prove to me that it still 'worked', took it into his head to kick into action a japanned portative organ, which naturally emitted a pained groan. This gentle character, having given proof of his musical prowess, then proudly escorted me to the King's Chapel, 'dos Reis', where lie the tombs of Count Henry of Burgundy, its founder, and of his wife Teresa, the illegitimate daughter of Alfonso VI of Léon. Count Henry must have been taller than his peers, for to allow his remains to be fitted into a comparatively constricted space, the Chapter truncated his legs, which saved them a deal of bother. Also preserved here is the mummified body of Archbishop Lourenço, who after confessing Dom João before the battle of Aljubarrota, took a prominent place in the mêlée, being seriously wounded on the cheek, and – as your *cicerone* will not fail to point out – the scar was very properly carved on his effigy.

The Chapel of São Geraldo shelters the tomb of the first archbishop of Braga; and the adjacent Capela da Glória, with its *Mudéjar* decoration, that of Archbishop Gonçalo Pereira.

From the cathedral apse, we may make our way east to the chapel of Nossa Senhora da Conceição of 1525, with a well-carved Entombment and quaint statues of Anthony of Padua and Paul the Hermit. Close by is Santa Cruz (1624), and the eighteenth-century façade of the Hospital de São Marcos, while an adjacent street is dominated by the too brilliant blue *azulejo* façade of the Palácio do Raio. In the lane opposite is the Fonte do Idolo, a fountain of Roman date or earlier, with a female bust carved into the rock, together with a figure swathed in a toga.

A few steps from Santa Cruz is the so-called Casa dos Crivos, a sixteenth-century dwelling retaining latticed shutters to its windows, a rare survival in Portugal of Moorish *mushrabiyas*. Just beyond it rises the *torre de menagem*, part of a late-fourteenth-century fortress-palace guarding this corner of the *enceinte*.

Nearby is the Museu Nogueiro da Silva, named after a Maecenas of the Salazar era, the contents of which were left to the municipality and, as I was informed with a cynical glance, had been preserved as a 'sociological warning', and well can I believe it. But prelates too had more money than taste, and the interiors of comparatively few of Braga's churches, meretriciously embellished during the eighteenth century, merit our attention. Few travellers were impressed at the time, among them Dalrymple, who commented on 'some gaudy churches . . . loaded with superabundent ornaments', which gave them 'a most Gothic appearance'.

Traversing the main street of the old town, we pass the archbishop's palace, which since ravaged by fire in 1866 has been put to a variety of secular uses, and now contains an important library formed from the spoils of twenty convents and those archiepiscopal collections which survived the conflagration. Among the 10,000 manuscripts is one dated 1128 confirming Afonso Henriques as king of Portugal, the Testament of Dom Afonso II, and the Codicil of Dom Dinis; but more interesting is the mid-eighteenth-century topographical study of the city entitled *Mappa das Ruas de Braga*.

Further west is the Town Hall and neighbouring Nossa Senhora do Pópulo, rebuilt in the last quarter of the eighteenth century by Carlos da Cruz Amarante. Nearby is the charming Casa dos Biscainos, housing the main museum of Braga, the entrance-hall alone, with its granite statues in contemporary costume, meriting a visit. The collections are largely devoted to the decorative arts, but with ethnographical and archaeological sections on the ground floor, where a passage skirting the stables leads into its formal gardens.

The main sights of interest in the environs are Bom Jesus, and the Citânia de Briteiros, both of which are described in the latter part of Chapter 25, and São Frutuoso, referred to above.

While the main road leads directly south-east, travellers preferring byroads may climb a spur of the Serra de Falperra, on which stands **Santa Maria Magdalena**, by André Soares da Silva, later passing near the *castro* of **Sabrosa**, smaller but similar to that of Briteiros and surrounded by a single more massive wall, and probably abandoned at an earlier date.

Guimarães contends with Braga the distinction of being the cradle of the Portuguese monarchy. It was here in AD 840 that Alfonso II of León convened a council of counts and bishops with a view to the restoration of Braga once recovered from the Moors, which in the event did not occur for another two centuries. In 860 or so a certain Vimara Peres established it as a burgh in the Germanic tradition in what was former Suevic territory, calling it Vimaranes or Guimarais. Its burghers were subsequently granted a charter of privileges by Count Henry of Burgundy, who made his court there in the last decade of the eleventh century, and reconstructed its castle. It is probable that his son Afonso Henriques, who is first referred to as king of Portucale in a document of 1127, was born there. But in order to maintain his inheritance he had to contend with his mother and a faction supporting Alfonso VII, whom he defeated on the nearby field of São Mamede.

It was at Guimarães, in July 1372, that a provisional alliance with England was signed, confirmed by the Treaty of Windsor fourteen years later.

In the broad Alameda da Liberdade stands São Francisco, with a thirteenth-century west portal and Renaissance cloister. Within the wide, barrel-vaulted nave is a fine Tree of Jesse, while among other features are the *azulejos* of St Francis preaching to the Fishes, and the elaborate carving of the *capela-mór*. From the *alameda* extends the leafy Largo da República do Brazil, attractively terminated by André Soares da Silva's Igreja dos Santos Passos, its bowed façade framed by twin belfries surmounted by obelisks.

The Largo da Oliveira, within the medieval *enceinte*, is flanked by the Colegiada, which, together with the square, takes its name from the olive tree which once burgeoned there. According to legend, when chosen to be king in AD 672, Wamba the Visigoth demurred, vowing not to accept that august office until the staff he drove into the ground took root. Providentially, it did so immediately, branches shooting out in all directions. When all attempts on his part to uproot the potent staff proved fruitless, Wamba fell on his knees and prayed for strength to govern, at least.

Nossa Senhora de Oliveira was founded in the tenth century, but little of the earlier Romanesque edifice survives. The west portal is surmounted by a door-like window, now blind, both dating from a rebuilding by Dom João I. The Manueline tower was reconstructed after 1515 by Pedro Cogominho, whose tomb with that of his wife, with its curious headstone, lies within. The Classical organ over the entrance, and the fluted pilasters at the crossing are also of some interest.

Adjacent, installed in the conventual dependencies surrounding the restored Romanesque cloister, is the Museu Alberto Sampaio. The slightly horseshoe-shaped arches flanking the entrance to the chapter-house in its east walk, will be noticed; while at its south-west corner is a Gothic chapel. Remarkable in the treasury is the silver-gilt triptych of Juan I of Castile, said to have been seized at Aljubarrota together with that king's travelling chapel, and given to Dom João, but it may well have been executed for him at a later date for presentation to this church in thanksgiving for the victory. Also displayed is the tattered '*loudel*' or tunic, said to have been worn by Dom João under his armour during that battle. A charming sculpted group representing the *Flight into Egypt*, the ceramic collection and, among paintings, works by Frei Carlos and António Vaz are memorable.

On the north side of the square stands the agreeable *pousada* of Nossa Senhora da Oliveira, and in the neighbouring Paço do Concelho, a battlemented edifice over massive arcades.

Continuing uphill, the former Convento de Santa Clara and the Carmo are passed to approach the fake Paço dos Duques, a relic of a fortified Braganza palace built *circa* 1420 by Dom Afonso (cf. Barcelos) for Constança de Noronha, his second wife, but abandoned *circa* 1660. It was almost entirely reconstructed after 1930 as an official residence of the Head of State, Dr Salazar, and other dignitaries when visiting the Minho. It was here, when first entering what was only too obviously a bogus building, and which would have been better left as a 'Romantick' ruin, that I had my only experience in Portugal of impudent discourtesy. The letter of introduction provided by the cultural authorities was brusquely waved aside as of no account, as the Ministry of Finance laid claim to the structure, and anyone wishing to enter had naturally to pay for the privilege; there was no discussion. On another occasion, learning that this particular ministry was no longer in residence, and as it was raining in torrents at the time, I steeled myself to gain entry, and my reception was hospitable. But in spite of the display of several individual pieces of furniture and porcelain of value, and copies of late-fifteenth-century tapestries depicting the *Taking of Arzila* by the Portuguese in 1472,[2] it was not too difficult to persuade myself that my time in Guimarães would have been more profitably spent elsewhere.

On the summit of a grassy knoll, beyond the Romanesque chapel of São Miguel, rises the massive keep of the over-restored castle, its granite towers topped by pointed monolithic battlements.

However, the hill provides a good view of the former monastery of Santa Marinha da Costa extending along the lower slope of the Penha ridge to the south-east. This had been founded in 1154, probably on the site of a fourth-century sanctuary, but the whole was rebuilt in the eighteenth century together with a new church. It has been reconstructed recently to accommodate the luxurious Pousada de Santa Marinha.

To the west of the castle is the Misericórdia, the chapel containing a fine stucco ceiling of 1775 apparently executed under the direction of a local goldsmith. From here, descending the hill by a street parallel to that by which we climbed, the Rua da Rainha is reached, with its medieval tower and the imposing Casa do Lobos Machados.

A short walk brings you to the Museu Martins Sarmento, named after the archaeologist responsible for the excavations of the *citânias* of Briteiros and Sabroso. Naturally, its collections are devoted mainly to the artefacts found at those sites, the larger objects being displayed in the cloisters of secularized São Domingos, adjoining. Of particular interest is the 'Pedra Formoso', a carved slab which served as the decorative front to a mausoleum, the form of which is curiously similar to the traditional design of the *cangas* or ornamented wooden yokes of the lyre-horned Minho oxen. Also important are the statues of Lusitanian warriors, although decapitated, who clasp their circular shields before them protectively; and also the roughly hewn *Colossus of Pedralva*, together with a number of geometrically carved door-jambs and lintels. Smaller objects found on local sites include a bronze votive coach and a hermaphrodite figure holding a bunch of grapes. Several other collections may be seen, together with an eighteenth-century litter, and portraits by August Roquemont (1704–52), an artist of Swiss origin who died at Oporto.

NOTES

1. Thomas Fitzalan died in 1415, and Beatriz (1392–1439) later married John Holand, Earl of Huntingdon, who was royal lieutenant at Bordeaux, where she died. However, Beatriz chose to be buried with her first husband at Arundel, where their tombs lie in the Fitzalan Chapel.
2. I was curious to inspect them, having seen the originals at Pastrana, Spain, which had been trimmed at one time to fit round ecclesiastical wardrobes; not that I was surprised at such treatment, for in the cathedral at Zamora too, I had admired its famous 'Black Tapestries' when displayed in conditions which should have made any bishop blush.

28

From the Lima to the Minho

An attractive tour of the Minho may be made with ease from either Guimarães or Braga, or by making your base at Ponte de Lima, at the centre of an area in which the splendid institution of 'Turismo de Habitaçao' first took root (see Appendix III).

Other than São Fructuoso and Tibães, referred to in the previous chapter, there is not much in the way of monuments to be seen *en route*, but the road passes through some charming country as it winds over the hills to enter the valley of the Lima. It is a district which has enchanted many travellers, among them Major Dalrymple some two centuries ago, fascinated by its vines 'twining round the oaks, and other trees in the hedges' and forming 'most beautiful festoons', as they still do. He observed that although the females were neatly dressed, and wearing English baize petticoats and cloaks, they rarely wore shoes or stockings. Dalrymple goes on to describe

> a kind of carriage, like the Irish car, drawn by oxen yoked by the neck; the wheels are never greased, on purpose, as they told me, that they should give notice to each other in the narrow roads . . . a most barbarous custom, as it encreases the draught considerably: and they make a most disagreeable screetching.

They do so still.

Ponte de Lima is named after its ancient bridge of thirty-one arches, five of which survive of the Roman original, the rest being rebuilt in 1360 and restored in the fifteenth century. The story is told that Decimus Junius Brutus, on reaching this sequestered spot after having traversed the greater part of Iberia, had difficulty in persuading his troops to cross the stream, which they imagined to be the river Lethe, its beauty having the effect of the lotus in making the traveller forget his own country and home. It was only by seizing a standard, once more exhorting the remnant of his legion, and wading deep into the river himself, that he induced them, lemming-like, to follow.[1] The place became known as 'Forum Limicorum', and later, as Lemici. It was probably the birthplace in AD 394 of the Suevic annalist Hydatius, who became Bishop of Chaves.

One can but agree with Sacheverell Sitwell, who remarked that this delightful town 'is pleasant to walk about in, but there is little to see'; that is, in the way of important buildings, although several mansions have been restored since his visit, not only in the central nucleus of Ponte de Lima, but also in its vicinity.

Near the southern bridgehead extends the riverside *alameda*, sheltered by huge plane trees, and where the Monday market still takes place, having been established by charter in 1125, the oldest recorded in Portugal. Adjacent to mid-fourteenth-century Santa Maria dos Anjos are relics of fortifications, taken by Dom João I in 1385 with the assistance of a contingent of English archers, no doubt those who served him so well at Aljubarrota.

At the far end of the leafy promenade are Renaissance São António dos Frades, part of a late-fifteenth-century convent, and neighbouring São Francisco.

On crossing to the north bank, the road west passes the imposing **Solar de Bertiandos**, largely eighteenth century, but retaining the tower of an earlier building, to approach the mouth of the Lima at **Viana do Castelo**. Viana is overlooked by the hill of Santa Luzia, on which is a Celtic *citânia* with its defensive wall, circular stone huts and paved alleys. Nearby rears an ugly neo-Byzantine basilica. No Roman remains are recorded at Viana by Jorge de Alação, but a fishing port appears to have flourished there later, trading in *bacalhau*.

By the sixteenth century a small British community had established itself, engaged in exporting the wines of the region, but in 1580 they were expelled by the Spanish. John Page, who was signatory to a document in 1664 as representing the Lisbon Factory, was building a house here in 1703, but the family business, which had connections with Monção and Melgaço on the Minho, later moved to Oporto. This was partly due to the harbour silting up, although the firm of Hunt Roope & Co., also trading in dried cod, retained their offices here. Apparently coopers had been sent out from England to supervise the manufacture of casks, but they were a pretty drunken lot, so Thomas Woodmass reported with regret.

When making his exploration of the Minho in search of wines,

Woodmass was entertained here by Job Bearsley and the vice-consul, Christopher Battersby, and records that after dinner 'some Portugal cockerels did engage in battle. Ye Minister directing', which would confirm that the community here had a sporting chaplain, who believed in enjoying himself on his diocesan rounds.

The hub of the old town is the triangular Praça da República, flanked by the late-sixteenth-century Misericórdia, with its façade of three superimposed loggias, the upper storeys supported by caryatids of original design by João Lopes the younger. Adjacent, built over arcades, is the Town Hall of 1502 and, a few steps to the south, the Igreja Matriz, with a Gothic door and Romanesque towers bearing unusual sculptures, while several characteristic façades may be seen in neighbouring streets.

A short walk west brings one to the former Barbosa Macieis palace, attributed to Manuel Pinto de Vilalobos, a local architect. It is now the municipal museum, with notable collections of ceramics and furniture (including a superb japanned sideboard), *azulejos* by Policarpo de Oliveira Bernardes, and paintings by both Vieira Lusitano and Vieira Portuense.

Adjacent is São Domingos, a large Classical church built for Archbishop Bartolomeu dos Mártires of Braga, buried there in 1590. Apart from attending the Council of Trent, he was an indefatigable visitor of his diocese, penetrating into its wildest recesses, where certainly no bishop before him had ever ventured. It is recorded that he once met a procession of villagers chanting 'Blessed be the most holy Trinity, and her sister the most pure Virgin', to his certain consternation.

Not far beyond the church is the Castelo de Santiago da Barra, originally constructed during the Spanish domination to guard the mouth of the Lima, in which a collection of Minho folk art and a maritime museum may be installed.

The coastal road skirts **Camina**, preserving its fortifications and several seventeenth-century houses, while the central square is overlooked by a sixteenth-century clock-tower on an eleventh-century base, and a Misericórdia with a good portal. The late-fifteenth-century Igreja Matriz, the finest in the district, retains several interesting features, among them its gargoyle-crowned apse, a Tree of Jesse, *azulejos*, *artesonado* ceiling, and a carved granite pulpit.

We now bear inland along the southern shore of the Minho, here forming the frontier and providing several picturesque views across the wide estuary towards Monte Santa Tecla rising beyond the

Spanish bank. **Vila Nova de Cerveira** is traversed, where an early castle has been converted to house the luxurious Pousada Dom Dinis.

There is another (São Teotónia) within the fortified *enceinte* of neighbouring **Valença do Minho**, whose seventeenth-century ramparts, in a perfect state of preservation, sustained two minor sieges in the nineteenth century. Eiffel's bridge of 1885 spans the river here to **Tui**, with its fortified cathedral, and there is another under construction, which will cross the Minho further west, bringing the district into closer communication with Galicia, although some have wondered to whose benefit.

From a junction south of Valença, an attractive road climbs over the hills direct to Ponte de Lima, passing the fine Romanesque church of **Rubiaes**; but unless pressed for time, continue to skirt the wooded left bank of the Minho near the Romanesque churches of **Ganfei** and **São Fins** to approach **Monção**. Although it is now better known for its *vinho verde* and *bagaceira* or *eau-de-vie de marc* than for its red wines, it was the latter which were exported formerly by English factors who had settled at 'Monson', as they chose to call it. The place was founded by Dom Afonso III and fortified in the seventeenth century. Its local hero, Deuladeu Martins, buried in the Romanesque church, had defended the town successfully in 1368 by the expedient of throwing loaves at the besieging Spaniards to fool them into thinking that they were still well supplied; but in 1658 its starving inhabitants, although holding out for four months against the Marquis de Viana, were forced to capitulate, admittedly on advantageous terms.

It was at the neighbouring hamlet of **Ponte de Mouro** that Dom João I met John of Gaunt in November 1386 to discuss his future marriage with Philippa of Lancaster and their projected joint invasion and dismemberment of Castile.

From Monção the main road climbs inland past the early-nineteenth-century mansion of **Brejoeira** and up a boulder-strewn valley to the Portela do Extremo, commanding a wide view over the vale of the Lima, before descending to **Arcos de Valdevez**. Here in about 1140 took place an inconclusive tourney between the knights of Afonso Henriques and those of Alfonso VII, which was a presage of later claims to the independence of Portugal. There are several attractive *quintas* some distance above the north bank of this stretch of the Lima, crossed at **Ponte de Barca** by its mid-sixteenth-century ten-arched bridge. A short distance west of the town is the Romanesque church of **Bravães**, the finest of several in the district.

A slow but beautiful road leading east skirts and later ascends high above the south bank of the Lima to the frontier village of **Lindoso**, with its castle. Nearby is an unusual concentration of *espigueiros*: small, granite-built granaries raised on mushroom-shaped pillars to keep vermin from entering. They are seen perhaps more frequently in continguous Galicia, where they are known as *hórreos*.

Crossing a range of hills south of Ponte de Barca, the valley of the Homem is reached, near the entrance of which is **Caldelas** and the Benedictine monastery of **Rendufe**, largely rebuilt in the eighteenth century and retaining elaborate rococo decoration. Numerous columns may be seen along the south side of this valley, marking what was a highway leading from Bracara to the Portela do Homem and eventually to Astorga, Roman Asturica Augusta.

Another road ascends the parallel valley of the Cávado, traversing several old villages preserving ancient mansions, to approach **Bouro**, with a ruined Cistercian monastery, already in existence in 1148, but transformed in the seventeenth century. When Professor Link visited Bouro in 1798, he found that the 'feeble old abbé suffered all the young monks to run wild, which rendered them as ungovernable as they were ignorant; and a young lay brother, the apothecary, was the only one who shewed any desire of knowledge'. Link was astonished by the amount the acolytes were able to eat, for they always had four courses at dinner, even if their dishes, which consisted largely of joints of meat of various kinds, were dressed without art. To his intense irritation, some of the monks had shown sufficient curiosity – in his absence, naturally – to handle and break both his barometer and his thermometer. Although the curious statues on the monastery's façade and the *azulejos* in the sacristy were still in place when I was there, quite recently the building was despoiled of its lead and ironwork and the fabric left to deteriorate.

Regaining the main road, on approaching Braga the hamlet of **Dume** is passed, where in the mid-sixth-century the Suevic king Carriaric, converted to Catholicism during the illness of his son Theodomir, founded a church. Its priest was to become St Martin of Dume, who in AD 572 directed the activities of the Second Council of Braga. Some shafts and capitals of Roman columns may be noticed embedded in farm buildings near the present church.

For neighbouring São Frutuoso, Tibães, and Braga itself, see Chapter 27.

NOTES

1. In 1875 Oswald Crawfurd, consul at Oporto from 1867 to 1891, in
   attempting to split this mythological hair, suggested seriously that the
   Romans, who are supposed to have made this crossing *circa* 133 BC,
   may have confused the Lethe, later described as the 'flumen oblivionis'
   by Livy, with the Leça, a narrower stream much closer to Porto.

APPENDICES

I

Approaches to Portugal

Much is being done to improve the roads leading south from the Channel ports, and now that so many towns in France have been provided with bypasses, it is pleasanter and cheaper to follow some of the less obvious routes south rather than scorching along *autoroutes*. However, it is often wise to turn on to the latter to cover certain stretches, such as when circumventing Bordeaux and bypassing both Bayonne and San Sebastian when crossing the Spanish frontier.

Travellers preferring a shorter drive may take the Plymouth-Santander ferry, and join the main road at Burgos, although the much slower but very beautiful road from Santander, which skirts the Asturian coast to enter Galicia, should be considered by those in no hurry.

The Spanish *autopista* may be followed from the border to just beyond Burgos. I will not attempt to describe here the various points of interest on or near the main routes, on the assumption that the reader will be intent on reaching Portugal as quickly as possible. I have listed below some of the main alternatives only:

a. From beyond Burgos, one may bear west across country via Palencia and Benavente to approach Chaves from Verín; or continue on via Xinxo de Limia to enter the Minho at either Lindoso, Melgaço, or Valença.
b. Turn west at Tordesillas for Zamora, from there entering either at Miranda do Douro or Braganza.
c. Continue south-west past Salamanca and Ciudad Rodrigo to cross the frontier at Vila Formoso.
d. Continue south at Salamanca for Cáceres, there turning west to enter below Marvão; or bear south-west from Cáceres (or south via Mérida) for Badajoz and Elvas.
e. If approaching Portugal from Madrid, one would normally follow the main road bypassing Talavera to Trujillo, there bearing west to Cáceres or continuing south-west via Mérida to Badajoz.
f. The two main entrances from Seville are to the north-west via Rosal de la Frontera for Serpa; and due west to cross the Guadiana, now spanned by an international bridge just north of Ayamonte, to enter the Algarve.

It cannot be sufficiently emphasized that a great deal of Portugal is remarkably hilly, and although there are several good and comparatively fast roads in some areas – such as in parts of the Alentejo – plenty of time must be allowed for, particularly when off the beaten track, where the narrow roads are tortuous if not purgatorial.

Do not expect an easy ride east from Oporto to Entre-os-Rios, there crossing to and following the high south bank of the Douro to Lamego, and, via Pinhão, climbing to Alijó; and from there continuing the switchback course east across country via Carrazedo de Ansiães to Torre de Moncorvo. I have driven it; but not all in one day. One is surprised no longer that William Lithgow, that great Elizabethan traveller, complained of having done 'twenty dayes fastidious climbing' in Portugal in the summer of 1620.

When one has driven along the road from Santa Clara-a-Velha to Monchique, or north from São Bras de Alportel to Almodôvar, it is not difficult to understand why the Algarve was for so long isolated from the rest of the country.

Note also that petrol stations are comparatively few in many areas, and it is wise to keep the tank topped up.

A word of caution. The road accident rate in Portugal is high, largely due to inexperienced drivers in fast cars.

II

Cartography

Travellers approaching Portugal via France and Spain would be well advised to acquire the latest Michelin general maps for both countries (numbers 989 and 990 respectively), both at 1: 1,000,000. Those approaching from the north or north-east may find number 441, at 1: 400,000, helpful; numbers 444 and 446 cover approaches from central Spain and from Andalucía.

For Portugal itself, Michelin number 437, also at 1: 400,000, is usually reliable, perhaps supplemented by the Instituto Geográfico e Cadastral *Carta de Portugal* at 1: 500,000 (two sheets), which give a better idea of contours, and the Automóvel Club de Portugal *Mapa do Estado das Estradas* at 1: 550,000. The Robertson McCarta map of Portugal at 1: 500,000 is reasonably clear, but does not show contours.

For additional detail, maps published by the Instituto Geográfico e Cadastral (Praça da Estrela, Lisbon) at 1: 200,000 (eight sheets) are good, and there are several other series, at different scales.

III

Practical information

CLIMATE

The climate is much milder than in neighbouring Spain in general and, except in the Trás-os-Montes, the high-lying frontier area near Guarda, and on such ranges as the Serra da Estrela, it is rarely very cold. The Minho is inclined to be damp in winter, with heavy rainfall. In Lisbon this averages sixty-nine centimetres annually, mostly falling between October and March. The Alentejo and Algarve can be very hot during the summer, particularly inland, untempered by sea breezes, and are perhaps best avoided in high summer, except by salamanders.

The preferable season in which to visit the south is perhaps the early spring, when the almond blossom is out; areas to the north of the Tagus are at their best between May and November.

FORMALITIES AND TRANSPORT

National or EC passports are required for travellers visiting Portugal. The British Embassy and Consulate is at Rua São Domingos à Lapa 35–37, 1296 Lisbon, with a Consulate at Avenida da Boavista 3072, Oporto. The Portuguese Embassy in London is at 11 Belgrave Square, SW1X 8PP, with the Consulate at 62 Brompton Road, SW3 1BJ.

The Portuguese National Tourist Office in London is now at 22–25A Sackville Street, W1X 1DE. It can provide much up-to-date practical information on a variety of subjects, such as hotels and *pousadas* and their facilities, and the *turismo de habitação* scheme (see below). ᴼ ᐟ ᐟ ⁄ ᐟ 4 9 4 1 4 4 1

Any reliable travel agent can give the latest information concerning ferries to the Continent, and can supply tickets, etc., and details of rail services through France and Spain to Portugal, fly/drive facilities, etc.

Regular air services are provided by British Airways and Air Portugal (TAP, Transportes Aéreos Portugueses), in London at 75 Regent Street and 19 Lower Regent Street respectively.

Most towns of any size and the more important frontier posts and airports have a tourist office (the main one in Lisbon being at the Palácio Foz, on the west side of the Praça dos Restauradores), which can advise on rail and bus services. The latter (*autocarros*) are maintained by the

210

Rodoviária Nacional; a bus-stop is a *paragem*.

There is an underground railway or *metropolitano* serving parts of Lisbon, and a cheap *passe turístico* may be bought at ticket offices marked CARRIS.

Comparatively inexpensive taxis, distinguished by their green roofs, can be invaluable when getting about Lisbon or Oporto, rather than attempting to negotiate in one's own car the steep and narrow warrens of one-way streets.

CURRENCY

The monetary unit is the *escudo*, written 1$, subdivided into *centavos*. The Banco de Portugal issue coins of 1, 2$50, 5, 10, 20, 50, 100 and 200 escudos, and notes of 500, 1,000 (also known as a *conto*), 2,000, 5,000 and 10,000 escudos.

ACCOMMODATION

Some hotels are known as *estalagems* or *albergarias*; pensions are known as *pensãos*. Lists of these may be requested from local or national tourist offices.

Pousadas in mainland Portugal are listed below in five areas, reading from north to south. Accommodation may be booked in advance via ENATUR, Avenida Santa Joana a Princesa 10A, 1700 Lisboa (Telephone 01 848 1221 or 848 9078/9/0; Fax 80 58 46). Those which have been installed in buildings of architectural or historical interest, tend to provide luxurious accommodation and are priced accordingly. They are marked with an asterisk.[1]

North of the Douro:
  São Teotónia, in the fortress of Valença do Minho
  *Dom Dinis, within the ramparts of Vila Nova de Cerveira, south-west of the former
  *Nossa Senhora da Oliveira, Guimarães, near the Colegiada
  *Santa Marinha da Costa, overlooking the town from the south
  São Bento, Caniçada (thirty kilometres (eighteen miles) north-east of Braga), with a view towards the National Park
  São Gonçalo, twenty-seven kilometres (seventeen miles) east of Amarante
  Barão Forrester, Alijó, sixteen kilometres (ten miles) north-east of Pinhão
  São Bartolomeu, Braganza, with a view of the walled upper town
  Santa Catarina, Miranda do Douro, with a plunging view of the river

Between Oporto and Coimbra:
  Da Ria, Murtosa, approximately forty-five kilometres (twenty-eight

miles) by road north-west of Aveiro, and overlooking the lagoon
Santo António, Serém, on the N1 east of Aveiro
São Jerónimo, Caramulo, south-west of Viseu
Santa Bárbara, Póvoa das Quartas, on the N17 east of Oliveira do
    Hospital, with a fine view across a wooded valley
São Lourenço, Mantiegas, in the Serra da Estrela
*Senhora Neves, within the walls of Almeida, fifteen kilometres (nine
    miles) north-west of Vilar Formoso

Between Coimbra and the Tagus:
    Mestre Afonso Domingues, Batalha
    *Do Castelo, Obidos
    São Pedro, Castelo do Bode, overlooking the reservoir thirteen kilo-
        metres (eight miles) south-east of Tomar

Between the Tagus and Evora:
    Santa Maria, in the hilltop village of Marvão
    Santa Luzia, Elvas
    *Santa Isabel, in the castle at Estremoz
    *Dos Lóios, in the monastery at Evora
    *São Filipe, within the castle at Setúbal
    *De Palmela, in the restored castle

In the South:
    De Val do Gaio, overlooking the reservoir near Torrão, off the N2
    São Tiago, Santiago do Cacém
    São Gens, on the outskirts of Serpa, and with an extensive view
    Santa Clara, overlooking the reservoir at Santa Clara a Velha, approxi-
        mately thirty-five kilometres (twenty-two miles) south-east of
        Odimira, on the N120.
    São Brás, at São Brás de Alportel, approximately twenty kilometres
        (thirteen miles) north of Faro
    *Do Infante, Sagres, thirty-three kilometres (twenty-one miles) west of
        Lagos

Turismo de Habitação. A very laudable scheme has been initiated,
notably in the Minho, but also in other parts of the country, whereby
owners of private houses, *quintas, paços*, and *solares*, have been encouraged to accommodate guests, which would at the same time enable them
to defray the cost of the upkeep of their properties. Some are simple,
others are more palatial; and charges vary accordingly. All offer comfortable accommodation in attractive surroundings where one may meet the
Portuguese in their own homes.

    For fuller information, and a prospectus, apply to the more reliable of
the associations formed to ensure the upkeep of standards and to advertise

more effectively, known as TURIHAB, Praça da República, 4990 Ponte de Lima (Telephone 058 942729; Fax 058 941864).

FOOD AND WINE

Restaurants of all categories are to be found in Portugal, but they may be thinly distributed in some areas. The traveller should not hesitate to try the numerous local dishes, emulating Joseph Baretti, who remarked: 'Let it be dinner-time, and I care not a fig for the difference between macaroni and roast-beef, herring and frogs, the olla and the sourcrout; a very cosmopolite in the article of filling one's belly'.

Note that helpings are often generous, and that a half portion, *um meia dose*, is often enough, or one *dose* for two, the differing prices being shown on the menu (*lista* or *ementa*). SP indicates that the food (usually seafood) is charged by weight (*segundo o peso*). Service is now included on the bill or *conto*.

Breakfast or *pequeno almoço*, lunch (*almorço*), tea (*chá*) – both the beverage and the meal – and dinner or *jantar* are served at 'English' rather than 'Spanish' hours. Coffee (*café*) may be ordered *simples*, black; or with milk, *com leite*.

Tap water (*água da torneira*) is usually quite safe; those who prefer bottled water, which is not as expensive as in some countries, may order it with (*com*), or without (*sem*, pronounced 'sin'), gas. Portuguese beer or *cerveja* is good. *Gelo* is ice.

The range of wines is extensive. The *vinhos da casa* are often surprisingly good, and the prices of the *vinhos de marca* are not prohibitive. Local wines are known as *vinhos da reiao*, and may be red (*tinto*), white (*branco*), sweet (*doce*) or dry (*seco*).

LANGUAGE

Although the visitor with a pocket dictionary or phrase-book to hand should not find too much difficulty in making himself understood, learning a few everyday words and expressions is of course useful: *sim*, yes and *não*, no; *bom dia*, good morning, *boa tarde* and *boa noite*, good afternoon and good evening or goodnight; also *por favor*, please and *obrigado*, thank you, noting that the latter, if spoken by a female, is *obrigada*.

Among language peculiarities which may take a little getting used to are the days of the week, apart from Saturday (*Sábado*) and Sunday (*Domingo*): *Segunda-feira* for Monday; *Terça-feira*, Tuesday; *Quarta-feira*, Wednesday; *Quinta-feira*, Thursday; and *Sexta-feira*, Friday. This system, different from other European countries, is probably Suevic in origin: a tombstone in the Minho is carved with the date 28 April, AD 616, SECUNDA FERIA.

OPENING TIMES

Most museums are open daily from ten until five *except Mondays and public holidays*; most churches are open earlier but are often closed between one and four. When churches and other monuments appear to be closed, it is usually possible to find the guardian and his key, although in remoter districts it is wise to enquire first at a tourist office in the nearest town; and there are several monuments which are still not adequately signposted.

SECURITY

Obviously, one should take all the normal precautions to protect one's personal property, particularly in the larger cities, although pickpocketing and handbag-snatching have not yet become as widespread as in some Peninsular cities, such as Barcelona or Seville.

NOTES

1. *Pousadas* are also projected at Queluz, Beja, Alvito (between Evora and Beja), Sousel (north-west of Estremoz), and Piedao (near Arganil, between Oliveira do Hospital and Coimbra).

Chronology

Kings are usually referred to by the title of Dom. Dates within brackets after the name refer to the year of their marriage.

c.1100 BC	Phoenicians active in southern Portugal.
c.700–600 BC	Northern Portugal invaded by Celtic tribes.
c.600 BC	Greek traders reach Portugal.
c.535 BC	Carthaginians in control.
218–202 BC	The Second Punic War, after which Iberia is dominated by the Romans, and Portugal forms part of the province of Hispania Ulterior.
154 BC	The Lusitani revolt, and their leader Viriatus is assassinated in 139 BC.
138–6 BC	Expedition into Gallaecia under Decimus Junius Brutus, who then established his capital at Olisipo (Lisbon), likewise that of Julius Caesar in 60 BC.
19 BC	The territory which now constitutes Portugal is pacified by the Romans.
AD 409	Northern Gallaecia and Baetica invaded by the Vandals, and Lusitania occupied by the Alans (in *circa* 429 crossing to Africa).
c.411	The Suevi settle between the Minho and Douro. Their king, Rechiarus (448–57), is killed by the Visigoths.
c.415	The Visigoths enter the Peninsula.
585	Leovigild suppresses the Suevic kingdom; and Recared, his successor, is converted to Catholicism (589).
711	Muslims led by Tariq ibn Ziyad invade the Peninsula from Africa, and Portugal south of the Mondego occupied by *circa* 716.
868	Oporto reconquered by the Christians; the area between the Minho and Douro referred to as 'Portucale' in 883.
1073	Alfonso VI king of Castile, Galicia and Portugal. His daughter Urraca marries Raymond of Burgundy, who by 1095 is also lord of Galicia and count of Coimbra.
1097	Raymond's cousin, Henry, given the County of Portucale and Coimbra. On his death (c.1112) his wife Teresa (an illegitimate daughter of Alfonso VI)

becomes regent for their son, Afonso Henriques.

c.1099   The Almoravids settle in the Algarve (al-Gharbh al-Andalus), followed by the Almohads in 1146.

1128   Battle of São Mamede (Guimarães) won by Afonso Henriques.

1139   The Moors decisively defeated at Ourique.

1143   By the Treaty of Zamora, Afonso (Henriques) I is recognized as king of Portugal by Alfonso VII, and formally by Pope Alexander III in 1179.

1146   Afonso Henriques marries Mafalda of Maurienne and Savoy. Lisbon falls to him in 1147.

1153   The Cistercians given land at Alcobaça, in construction between 1178 and 1223.

1158   Alcácer do Sal taken; and Beja and Evora in 1162 and 1165.

1171   The Christians pushed back to Santarém by the Almohads.

1185–1211   Sancho I, second ruler of the House of Burgundy or Afonsin dynasty – Dulce d'Aragón. He captures Silves in 1189, but territory south of the Tagus lost to al-Mansur the following year.

1211–23   Afonso II – Urraca (1208), daughter of Alfonso VIII of Castile and Eleanor Plantagenet. The first *cortes* held at Coimbra in 1211. The battle of Las Navas de Tolosa in Spain (1212), a watershed in the Reconquest of the Peninsula as a whole.

1223–48   Sancho II – Mécia López de Haro.

1248–79   Afonso III – Matilde, Countess of Boulogne; then Beatriz de Guillén (1253), daughter of Alfonso X of Castile.

1279–1325   Dinis, 'O Lavrador' (the husbandman) – Isabel of Aragón (1282).

1297   Frontier with Castile endorsed by the Treaty of Alcañices.

1319   The Order of Christ founded.

1325–57   Afonso IV – Beatriz of Castile (1309), daughter of Sancho IV of Castile. Afonso allied with Alfonso XI of Castile in defeating the Moors at the battle of Salado (1340).

1357–67   Pedro I, the Justicier – Blanca of Castile (1328); then Constanza of Castile (1340); then Inês de Castro (?1354), murdered in 1355.

1367–83   Fernando – Leonor Teles de Meneses (1372). Lisbon sacked in 1373, in which year an Anglo-Portuguese alliance is signed.

1381	Edmund of Cambridge's troops land at Lisbon.
1383–5	Interregnum of Leonor Teles.
1385	Battle of Aljubarrota (14 August). João of Avis proclaimed king, and reigns until 1433.
1386	The Treaty of Windsor signed.
1387	João I – Philippa of Lancaster, daughter of John of Gaunt, married at Oporto.
1388	Construction of Batalha commences.
1415	Ceuta captured.
1419 and 1427	Madeira and the Azores discovered or rediscovered.
1437	Tangier expedition fails.
1433–38	Duarte (Edward) – Leonor of Aragón (1428).
1438–81	Afonso V, 'the African' – Isabel of Portugal (1441).
1449	Battle of Alfarrobeira, in which the Duke of Coimbra is killed.
c.1457	Cape Verde Islands discovered.
1460	Death of Prince Henry the Navigator, who instigated much maritime exploration.
1471	Tangier eventually taken.
1476	Indecisive Battle of Toro against the Castilians.
1481–95	João II – Leonor of Portugal (1471).
1487	The Cape of Good Hope rounded by Bartolomeu Dias.
1492	Approximately 60,000 Jews expelled from Spain take refuge in Portugal.
1494	The Treaty of Tordesillas divides the new discoveries between Spain and Portugal.
1495–1521	Manuel I, 'the Fortunate' – Isabel of Castile (1497); then Maria of Castile (1500); then Leonor of Spain (1518).
1497–8	Vasco da Gama discovers the searoute to India.
1500	Brazil discovered by Pedro Álvares Cabral.
1510–15	Goa, Malacca and Ormuz occupied.
1519–22	The surviving ship of Magellan's expedition, commanded by Elcano, circumnavigates the globe.
1521–57	João III – Catarina of Spain (1525).
1531	The Inquisition introduced into Portugal.
1557	Trading post established at Macão.
1557–78	Sebastião, 'the Regretted'; killed at the disaster of Alcácer-Quibir.
1572	Camoens' Os Lusíadas published; the author died in 1580.
1578–80	Henrique, the Cardinal-king.
1580	António, Prior of Crato, proclaims himself king, but is defeated by the Duke of Alba at Alcântara.

1580–1640	Castilian usurpation – the 'Sixty Years Captivity'.
1581	The Cortes at Tomar proclaim Felipe II of Spain king as Felipe I of Portugal.
1588	A large part of the Spanish 'Armada' sails from Lisbon.
1598–1621	Felipe II (III of Spain).
1621–40	Felipe III (IV of Spain).
1637	Revolt at Evora.
1640	The Spanish governor overthrown at Lisbon and the Duke of Braganza (who had married Luisa de Guzmán in 1633) ascends the throne as João IV.
1656–83	Afonso VI – Mlle d'Aumale, Marie-Françoise-Isabelle of Savoy (1666), but the marriage is unconsummated.
1663	Spanish defeated at Battle of Ameixial (May).
1662	Catherine of Braganza sails to England to marry Charles II.
1663–5	Portugal defeated Spanish forces at the battles of Ameixial, Castelo Rodrigo and Montes Claros.
1668	Afonso's brother Pedro marries his former sister-in-law (in Portugal known as Maria-Francesca-Isabel) and becomes prince regent.
1683–1706	Pedro II – Maria-Sofia-Isabel of Neuberg (1687).
1703	The Methuen Treaties signed.
1703–13	Portugal sides with Britain during the War of the Spanish Succession.
1704	The Archduke Charles reaches Lisbon (March). Spain declares war on Portugal (April). Berwick advances into Portugal, but retires that July.
1705	The widowed Catherine of Braganza regent for several months. Portuguese take Valencia d'Alcantara and Albuquerque (May).
1706–50	João V – Maria-Ana of Austria (1708).
1709	Portuguese defeated near Arronches (May).
1712	Suspension of arms in Portugal (November).
1715	Portugal concludes peace with Spain (February).
1717	Construction of Mafra commences.
1750–77	José – Mariana Victoria of Spain (1729); Pombal in office.
1755	The Great Lisbon Earthquake (1 November).
1761	Slavery abolished in mainland Portugal.
1777–1816	Maria (Francisca) I – Pedro III (her uncle; in 1760).
1792	Regency of the future João VI (1816–26) – Carlota-Joaquina of Spain (1784). João titled prince-regent in 1799.

1797	Battle of Cape St Vincent (14 February).
1801	'The War of the Oranges', in which Spain invades Portugal, and coerces her to cede Olivença.
1805	The Battle of Trafalgar (21 October).
1807	Portugal invaded by the French under Junot; the royal family embark for Brazil. Lisbon occupied from 30 November.
1808–14	The Peninsular War.
1808	The occupying French are defeated by Wellesley (later Wellington) at Roliça (17 August), and Vimeiro (21 August), and repatriated after the Convention of Cintra.
1809	Battle of Corunna (16 January). Soult driven from Oporto (12 May). Battle of Talavera (28 July).
1810	Masséna's advance into Portugal checked at the Battle of Busaco (12 September), and obstructed by the Lines of Torres Vedras.
1811	The French retreat to the Spanish frontier. Battles of Fuentes de Oñoro (3–5 May), and Albuera (16 May).
1812	Ciudad Rodrigo (19 January) and Badajoz (6 April) taken by Wellington. Battle of Salamanca (22 July).
1813	The French finally thrust out of Portugal in mid-May. Battle of Victoria (21 June).
1826	Pedro IV (who then abdicates, leaving the kingdom to his daughter, Maria) – Maria Leopoldina of Austria (1817); then Maria Amelia of Leuchtenberg (1829).
1828–34	The War of the Two Brothers. Miguel, appointed regent, and who proclaims himself king, is eventually forced to capitulate at Evora-Monte.
1834–53	Maria II, 'da Glória' – August of Leuchtenberg (1834), brother of her father's second wife, who died within days of reaching Portugal; then Ferdinand of Saxe-Coburg-Gotha (1836).
1834	The religious orders expelled from Portugal.
1853–61	Pedro V – Stéphanie of Hohenzollern-Sigmaringen (1858), who died of diphtheria two months after reaching Portugal.
1861–89	Luis – Maria-Pia of Savoy (1862).
1895	Mozambique occupied.
1889–1908	Carlos, (who was assassinated) – Marie-Amélie of Orléans (1886).
1905	Angola occupied.

1908–10	Manuel II, 'the Unfortunate' – Augusta-Victoria of Sigmaringen (1913).
1910	The Republic proclaimed.
1926	Military dictatorship of General Gomes da Costa, and from 1926 to 1951 General Fragoso Carmona President.
1932–68	António de Oliveira Salazar 'Prime Minister'.
1958–74	Admiral Américo Tomás President.
1974	Revolution (25 April).
1986	Portugal enters the European Community.

Glossary

The following glossary, of words not necessarily referred to in the book, may be of some help.

Abóbada, vault
Alfândega, customs
Ajimece, two-light window, divided by a slender column
Albufeira, reservoir
Aldeia, village
Alfarrobeira, carob tree
Almoço, lunch
Almofados, rusticated masonry; or large raised panels in furniture
Artesonado, coffered wooden ceiling
Azulejos, tiles, usually of painted and glazed panels, either of scenes, designs, or with floral patterns (*albarrada*)
Bairro, district or quarter of a town
Baixo, lower
Barragem, dam of a reservoir
Bêco, no through road
Bilros, elaborately turned finials
Cadeiral, choir-stalls
Câmara municipal, town hall
Capela-mór, chancel or sanctuary
Chafariz, public fountain, often monumental
Chave, key
Citânia, pre-historic hill settlement
Claustro, cloister
Coro, choir; the *coro alto* or upper gallery often containing the stalls
Correio, post office
Cortes, Parliament
Cruzeiro, the crossing of a church, or a cross
Direita, right
Entalhador, woodcarver; see *talha*. The carver of images is an *imaginário*
Ermida or *eremitério*, hermitage or chapel, often isolated
Espigueiros, equivalent to the *hórreos* of Galicia, and ubiquitous in the Minho, these granaries or store-houses are raised on mushroom-shaped pillars to obstruct the entrance of vermin
Esquerda, left
Estalagem, hotel or inn
Fado, see Chapter 8

221

Fechado, closed

Feira, fair; *férias*, a holiday

Foz, mouth of a river

Horta, a kitchen-garden

Igreja, church; a parish church being an *igreja matriz*

Ilha, island

Janela, window

Jantar, dinner

Jardim, garden

Joanino, late-Baroque style in fashion at the time of Dom João V

Judiaria, ghetto

Largo, small square or market-place

Manuelino, the characteristic late-Gothic style of architecture current during the reign of Dom Manuel I and later

Marfim, ivory

Mármore, marble

Marrano, former derogatory name for a Portuguese Jew, assumed to be converted only ostensibly to Catholicism

Mata, wood or forest

Miradouro, balcony or belvedere

Mosteiro, monastery

Moçárabe, or *Mozárab*, Christian subject to the Moors; a term extended to their architecture

Mudéjar, a Muslim subject to the Christians; and a term extended to their architecture and decoration

Muralha, walls

Nora, water-wheel

Paço, country house, or palace (usually *palácio*)

Paragem, halt

Pau preto or *Jacarandá*, Brazilian rosewood; *Pau santo* is lignum vitae. Among other woods (*madeira*) are *mogno* or mahogany

Pedra lioz, calcareous white stone, resembling marble

Pelourinho, stone column, sometimes ornamented, and ubiquitous in the towns and villages of northern Portugal, but seen less south of the Tagus. They were the emblem of feudal or municipal jurisdiction and were also used as pillories or gibbets

Planicie, plain

Poço, well

Pombalino, the architectural style employed in the rebuilding of Lisbon after the earthquake of 1755, and named after the Marquês de Pombal

Portagem, toll

Pousada, see Appendix III.

Povoação, market-town

Praça, place or square

Prado, field or meadow

Praia, beach or shore
Quadro or *pintura*, painting
Quartel, barracks
Quartelões, bracketed pilasters
Quarto, room
Quinta, country estate, or the main residence on such
Rés do chão, ground floor
Retábulo, reredos or high altar, often highly decorated
Retrato, portrait
Saída, exit
Sé, cathedral
Século, century
Sobreiro, cork oak
Solar, manor house, or the seat of an armigerous family
Talha, carved work, usually of wood, and frequently *dourada* or gilded
Tecto, ceiling
Torre de menagem, castle keep
Tremido, parallel grooving in furniture
Zimbório, a cupola or dome

Bibliography

The list of books printed below is selective and idiosyncratic. With a few exceptions they are in English, and have been read – if not always entirely digested – by the author. They are concerned basically with mainland Portugal (although some may stray across the frontier) and those fields touched on in this guide. Unless stated otherwise, they were published in the United Kingdom. Several titles will describe in detail a subject on which I have hardly digressed, not being sufficiently well-informed to write on them, such as the intricacies of the port wine trade.

I have chosen to divide the Bibliography into sections, some of which overlap. Appended to each is a further list of some of the more interesting earlier descriptions or histories, increasingly hard to acquire and correspondingly expensive, but which may be found in the London Library and elsewhere.

TRAVEL, TOPOGRAPHY, AND GENERAL DESCRIPTION

Ann Bridge (Lady O'Malley) and Susan Belloc Lowndes Marques, *The Selective Traveller in Portugal* (1949; revised 1967), referred to as being 'thuriferous', is now dated.

Rose Macaulay, *They Went to Portugal* (1946; reprinted 1986); and
—— *They Went to Portugal Too* (1990) containing material not included in the former volume, are both essential and inimitable reading.

The *Naval Intelligence Division Geographical Handbook*, Vol. 2, *Portugal* (1942) contains much information, even if some is dated and quaint.

Ian Robertson, *Portugal* (Blue Guide, 1982; third edition 1988), describes monuments and museums in detail.

Sacheverell Sitwell, *Portugal and Madeira* (1954), urbane if uneven, but provides some insights.

Among the numerous, if unequal, earlier descriptions of Portugal, are:

Anon. [A.P.D.'G.'], *Sketches of Portuguese Life, Manners, Costume, and Character* (1826).

Marianne Baillie, *Lisbon in the years 1821, 1822, and 1823* (1825).

Joseph Baretti, *A Journey from London to Genoa* (1770; reprinted 1970, with an Introduction by Ian Robertson); earlier chapters only.

Huldine V. Beamish, *The Hills of Alentejo* (1958).

William Beckford, *The Journal of William Beckford in Portugal and Spain 1787–1788*, ed. Boyd Alexander (1954).

—— *Italy, with Sketches of Spain and Portugal* (1834).

—— *Recollections of an Excursion to the Monasteries of Alcobaça and Batalha* (1835; reprinted 1972, with an Introduction by Boyd Alexander).

Jean François Bourgoing, *Travels of the Duke de Chatelet in Portugal* (1809).

George Borrow, *The Bible in Spain* (1843); earlier chapters only, supplemented by *Letters to the British and Foreign Bible Society*, ed. T.H. Darlow (1911).

William Bromley, *Travels through Portugal, Spain, etc.* (1702).

Anon. [J.B.F. Carrère], *A Picture of Lisbon taken on the spot* (1809), being a translation of his *Voyage au Portugal et particulièrement à Lisbonne* (Paris, 1798).

'Arthur Costigan' [Major James Ferrier], *Sketches of Society and Manners in Portugal* (1787).

Oswald Crawfurd, *Travels in Portugal* (1875), and *Portugal Old and New* (1880), the former written under the pseudonym of 'John Latouche'.

William Dalrymple, *Travels through Spain and Portugal in 1774* (1777).

General Dumouriez, *An Account of Portugal as it appeared in 1766* (1797).

William Henry Harrison, *Jenning's Landscape Annual, or, Tourist in Portugal* (1839), illustrated with steel engravings by James Holland.

Henry John George Herbert, Viscount Porchester, later third Earl Carnarvon, *Portugal and Galicia* (1836).

Elizabeth, Lady Holland, *The Spanish Journal*, ed. the Earl of Ilchester (1910).

William Henry Giles Kingston, *Lusitanian Sketches* (1845).

William Morgan Kinsey, *Portugal Illustrated* (1828), a pretentious account, and of slight value.

Henry Frederick Link, *Travels in Portugal* (1801).

Richard Muller, *Memoirs of the Right Hon. Lord Viscount Cherington* (1782).

James Murphy, *Travels in Portugal . . . in 1789 and 1790* (1795).

—— *A general view of the state of Portugal* (1798).

—— *Plans, elevations, etc . . . of Batalha* (1795).

John Mason Neale, *Handbook for Travellers in Portugal* (1855). Crawfurd (see above) refers to it as being 'not only the worst handbook in that eminent publisher's series – for that might still be high praise – but probably the very worst handbook that ever was printed'; nevertheless, it is a curiosity of its period.

Dorothy Quillinan (née Wordsworth), *Journal of a few months' Residence in Portugal* (1847).

Robert Southey, *Letters from Spain and Portugal* (1797).

—— *Journal of a Residence in Portugal 1800–1801*, ed. Adolfo Cabral (1960).

Richard Twiss, *Travels through Spain and Portugal in 1772 and 1773* (1775).

HISTORY

Jorge de Alarção, *Roman Portugal* (1988; four volumes, including a comprehensive gazetteer).

Charles R. Boxer, *The Portuguese Seaborne Empire, 1415-1825* (1969; reprinted 1991).

C.R. Boxer and J.C. Aldridge (eds.), *Descriptive List of the State Papers Portugal 1661-1788 in the Public Record Office, London* (three volumes, Lisbon 1979-83).

Sarah Bradford, *Portugal* (1973).

John Brande Trend, *Portugal* (1957).

Marcus Cheke, *Dictator of Portugal* (1938); a biography of Pombal.

—— *Carlota Joaquina, Queen of Portugal* (1947).

Harold E.S. Fisher, *The Portugal Trade. A Study of Anglo-Portuguese Commerce, 1700-1770* (1971).

David Francis, *The Methuens and Portugal, 1691-1708* (1966).

—— *Portugal 1715-1808, Joanine, Pombaline and Rococo Portugal as seen by British diplomats and traders* (1985; regrettably published without an index).

Peter Fryer and Patricia McG. Pinheiro, *Oldest Ally: Portrait of Salazar's Portugal* (1961).

Tom Gallagher, *Portugal: a Twentieth Century Interpretation* (1983).

Michael Glover, *Britannia sickens: Sir Arthur Wellesley and the Convention of Cintra* (1970).

Henry Kamen, *The War of Succession in Spain 1700-15* (1969), largely concerned with the economic issues.

Sir Benjamin Keene, *The Private Correspondence*, ed. Sir Richard Lodge (1933).

Thomas D. Kendrick, *The Lisbon Earthquake* (1956), will disappoint those expecting to find much of a description of the disaster itself in its pages.

Harold V. Livermore, *A History of Portugal* (1947).

—— *New History of Portugal* (1966; revised edition 1976, more compact than above.

—— *Portugal: a Short History* (1973).

—— *The Origins of Spain and Portugal* (1971).

Fernão Lopes, *The English in Portugal 1367-87* (1988), extracts from the Chronicles of Dom Fernando and Dom João, eds. Dereck W. Lomax and R.J. Oakley.

D.L. Raby, *Fascism and resistance in Portugal* (1988).

Richard A.H. Robinson, *Contemporary Portugal: a History* (1979).

Cecil Roth, *A History of the Marranos* (1933; 4th edition, 1974), dated in part.

Peter Edward Russell, *The English Intervention in Spain and Portugal in the time of Edward III and Richard II* (1955).

L.M.E. Shaw, *Trade, Inquisition and the English Nation in Portugal, 1650-1690* (1989).

Violet M. Shillington and Annie B.W. Chapman, *The commercial relations of England and Portugal* (1907).

A.R. Walford, *The British Factory in Lisbon* (Lisbon 1940).

Douglas L. Wheeler, *Republican Portugal: a political history, 1910–1926* (1978).

George Young, *Portugal, old and young; an historical study* (1917).

Among earlier works of some interest are:

Anon. [John Murray Browne], *An Historical View of the Revolutions in Portugal, since the close of the Peninsular War* (1827).

John Colbatch, *An account of the Court under Pedro II* (1700).

Baron Nicolas Fagel, *Account of the Campaign in Portugal, 1705* (1708).

Sir Robert Southwell, *Letters* (1740).

William Young, *Portugal in 1828* (1828).

MILITARY

Anthony Brett-James, *Life in Wellington's Army* (1972), a fascinating compilation.

Thomas Henry Browne, *The Napoleonic Journal of Captain Thomas Henry Browne* (1987), ed. R.N. Buckley.

David Francis, *The First Peninsular War, 1702–1713* (1975).

David Gates, *The Spanish Ulcer: a history of the Peninsular War* (1986).

Richard Glover, *Peninsular Preparation: the Reform of the British Army, 1795–1809* (1963, reprinted 1988).

Donald D. Horward, *Napoleon and Iberia – The Twin Sieges of Ciudad Rodrigo and Almeida, 1810* (1948); and

—— *The Battle of Bussaco: Masséna versus Wellington* (1965).

J.A.C. Hugill, *No Peace without Spain* (1991), also describing the War of the Spanish Succession.

George Lawson Chambers, *Bussaco* (1910).

Charles W.C. Oman, *Wellington's Army* (1913; since reprinted).

—— *History of the Peninsular War* (seven volumes, 1902–30), not easy to find complete, for owing to the decimation of subscribers during 1914–18 the later volumes were published in much smaller editions.

Edgar Prestage, *Portugal and the War of the Spanish Succession* (1938).

August Ludolf Friedrich Schaumann, *On the Road with Wellington* (1924), ed. Anthony M. Ludovici, a particularly racy narrative.

Stephen G.P. Ward, *Wellington's Headquarters* (1957).

Jac Weller, *Wellington in the Peninsula* (1962; reprinted 1991).

Peter Young and J.P. Lawford, *Wellington's Masterpiece* (1973), the background to the Salamanca campaign.

Earlier or contemporary works are legion. They include the general histories of Southey, Napier, et al. (including the latter's very readable *English Battles and Sieges in the Peninsula*, reprinted 1990), Wellington's own *Dispatches*, and – apart from the reminiscences of those who reached the theatre of operations late in the war – most of the narratives describe events in Portugal or near its frontier. One may list at random: Blakeney, Bragge, D'Urban, Frazer, Grattan, Harris, Hennell, Kinkaid, Larpent, Leach, Ormsby, Sherer, Simmons, Stothert, Surtees, Tomkinson, Warre, and Wheeler; but there were many more, nearly all of whom have something of interest to say.

Among those of particular relevance are:

William Granville Eliot, *A Treatise on the Defence of Portugal* (third edition, 1811).

Andrew Halliday, *The Present State of Portugal and of the Portuguese Army* (1812).

John Thomas Jones, *Memoranda Relative to the Lines thrown up to cover Lisbon in 1810* (1829), included in his *Journal of the Sieges in Spain* (3rd edition, 1846).

Adam Neale, *Letters from Portugal and Spain* (1809).

The following are of interest for their illustrations:

William Bradford, *Sketches of the Country, Character and Costume in Portugal and Spain* (1809).

Henry L'Evêque, *Portuguese Costumes* (1812–14).

—— *Campaigns of the British Army in Portugal (1813).*

George Thomas Landmann, *Historical, Military, and Picturesque Observations in Portugal* (1818).

Thomas Staunton St Clair, *A Series of Views . . . taken during the Peninsular War* (1815).

George Vivian, *Scenery of Portugal & Spain* (1839).

Little has been written in English since the 1830s concerning the 'War of the Two Brothers', or Miguelite War, during which years appeared:

James Edward Alexander, *Sketches in Portugal during the Civil War of 1834* (1835).

Lovell Badcock, *Rough Leaves from a Journal kept in Spain and Portugal* (1835).

William Bollaert, *The War of the Succession in Portugal and Spain* (1870).

W. Nugent Glascock, *Naval Sketch Book* (1834).

Charles P. Hawkes and Marion Smithes (eds.), *Siege Lady: the Adventures of Mrs Dorothy Procter of Entre Quintas* (1938).

Thomas Knight, *The British Battalion at Oporto* (1834).

G. Lloyd Hodge, *Narrative of an Expedition to Portugal* (1833).

Charles Napier, *Account of the War of Succession in Portugal* (1836).

Hugh Owen, *The Civil War in Portugal, and the Siege of Oporto* (1835).

Charles Shaw, *Personal Memoirs and Correspondence* (1837).

ART AND ARCHITECTURE

Associação dos Arquitectos Portugueses, *Arquitectura Popular em Portugal* (Lisbon 1980), containing several hundred photographs and some English text.

Carlos de Azevedo, *Baroque organ-cases of Portugal* (? Lisbon 1972).
Robert Chester Smith, *A Talha em Portugal* (Lisbon 1962), a study of gilded wood-carving.
—— *The Arts of Portugal, 1500–1800* (1968).
—— *Nicolau Nasoni, 1691–1773* (Lisbon 1973).
Walter Crum Watson, *Portuguese Architecture* (1908).
José-Augusto França et al. (eds.), *Arte Portugués* (Madrid 1986; volume XXX in the 'Summa Artis' series).
Julio Gil, *The Finest Castles of Portugal* (Lisbon 1986).
George Kubler, *Portuguese Plain Architecture, 1521–1706* (Middletown, Connecticut 1972), to be used with caution.
George Kubler and Martin Soria, *Art and Architecture of Spain and Portugal etc., 1500–1800* (1959).
James Lees-Milne, *Baroque in Spain and Portugal* (1960).
Anne de Stoop, *Quintas e Palácios nos arredores de Lisboa* (Lisbon 1986).

OTHER SUBJECTS

Aubrey F. Bell, *Portuguese Literature* (1922; reprinted 1970, with an up-dated Bibliography).
Patrick Bowe, *Gardens of Portugal* (1989).
Sarah Bradford, *The Englishman's Wine* (1969), revised under the title *The Story of Port* (1978).
Manuel Carlos de Brito, *Opera in Portugal in the Eighteenth Century* (1989).
Helder Carita and Homem Cardosa, *Portuguese Gardens* (1991).
Gerald Cobb, *Oporto Older and Newer* (1966).
John Delaforce, *The Factory House at Oporto* (1979; revised edition 1990).
David Francis, *The Wine Trade* (1972).
Joseph James Forrester, *A Word or Two on Port Wine* (1844).
Rodney Gallop, *Portugal: a Book of Folk-ways* (1936; reprinted 1961).
Alex Liddell, *Port Wine Quintas of the Douro* (1992).
Harold V. Livermore and William J. Entwistle (eds.), *Portugal and Brazil: an Introduction* (1953), with essays covering a variety of topics.
Jan Read, *Wines of Portugal* (revised edition 1987).
George Robertson, *Port* (1978).
Charles Sellars, *Oporto Old and New* (1899).

LOCAL GUIDES

I have been impressed by the quality of production of local guides produced in Portugal with an English text, among them, at random:

Teresa de Almeida d'Eça, *Guide to the Biscainhos Museum, Braga* (1990).
Museu Nacional de Arqueologia e Etnologia, *Portugal from its Origins through the Roman era* (1989).
Cláudio Torres and Luís Alves da Silva, *Mértola: a museum town* (1989).

Index

Topographical names are printed in roman type; persons in *italic*; and subjects in **bold**.